RULERS
OF
ANCIENT
EUROPE

Herodotus reads his History to Hellenic men of letters of Pericles' entourage.
Illustration by Emilian Stankev

RULERS
OF
ANCIENT EUROPE

*The Great Statesmen
of Ancient Greece, Macedonia
and Thrace*

TEXT
Konstantin Boshnakov

ILLUSTRATIONS
Hristo Hadjitanev, Emilian Starkev, Atanas Atanasov, Rosen Toshev,
Plamen Vulchev, Marin Marinov, Maya Buyukliiska

HISTORICAL MAPS
eng. Krasimir Andreev

DESIGN
Krassimira Despotova

KIBEA

We are most grateful to our consultant
Professor Alexander Fol, Ph. D.

FROM THE PUBLISHER

© 2003, Konstantin Boshnakov, text

© 2003, Hristo Hadjitanev, all portrait illustrations
subject illustrations
on pages: 46-47, 50-51, 66-67, 98-99
replicas after original images
on pages: 13, 15, 21, 25, 27, 31, 45, 93, 115

© 2003, Emilian Stankev, subject illustrations
on pages: 12, 13, 18, 22-23, 27, 28, 34, 40-41, 49, 52-53, 60-61, 70, 73, 94, 96-97, 108

© 2003, Atanas Atanasov, subject illustrations
on pages: 11, 32, 36, 54-55, 64, 84, 86-87, 90-91, 100-101
replicas after original images
on pages: 17, 20, 57, 74

© 2003, Rossen Toshev, subject illustrations
on pages: 42-43, 59, 112-113

© 2003, Plamen Vulchev, subject illustrations
on pages: 82, 85

© 2003, Marin Marinov, subject illustrations
on pages: 79, 104, 116

© 2003, Maya, Buyukliiska, replicas after original images
on pages: 25, 65

© 2003, Krassimira Despotova, design

© 2003, Krassimir Andreev, historical maps

© 2003, KIBEA PUBLISHING COMPANY

ISBN 954-474-342-1

RULERS OF ANCIENT EUROPE

First edition

Text Konstantin Boshnakov
Portait illustrations Hristo Hadjitanev
Subject illustrations and replicas after original images Hristo Hadjitanev, Emilian Stankev, Atanas Atanasov,
Rossen Toshev, Plamen Vulchev, Marin Marinov, Maya Buyukliiska
Historical maps Krassimir Andreev
Design Krassimira Despotova
Editor Aneta Mecheva
Controlling editor Ivanka Nikolova
English translation Janeta Shinkova
Editor of the English translation Danielle Troussoni
Computer processing Krassimir Lyudov

Printed in Slovakia

KIBEA PUBLISHING HOUSE
Sofia 1336, P.O. Box 70
Tel.: 359 2 24-10-20; Fax: 359 2 925 07 48
E-mail: office@kibea.net, Internet: www.kibea.net

SALES DEPARTMENT
Poligraphicheski kombinat „D. Blagoev", 2 Rakitin Str., Sofia 1000, tel.: 359 2 943 49 33

KIBEA'S BOOKS & HEALTH CENTRE
Sofia 1000, Dr G. Valkovich Street 2A (close to Angel Kanchev and Solunska streets),
tel.: 359 2 988 0193

About the book

RULERS OF ANCIENT EUROPE
is a glimpse at the roots of European civilization. For the first time, a single volume presents the biographies of twenty-four eminent statesmen who ruled over the lands of the ancient Hellenes, Macedonians, and Thracians, and who left a lasting mark upon world history.
These were rulers with strong personalities, political ambitions, and remarkable abilities as diplomats and commanders, each with his own personal relations and dramatic destiny, who founded the state structures that are still in place today.
You will find vivid descriptions of the militant Agamemnon, the wise Spartan lawgiver Lycurgus, the Athenians Solon and Pericles, the powerful Thracian kings Sitalces and Cotys, the Macedonian rulers Philip II and Alexander III and their political heirs who fought to the last against the Roman invasion, paving the way for a new epoch.
In this region of Europe, monarchy, democracy, oligarchy, tyranny, and anarchy appeared for the first time in world history, revealing their potential in public life and becoming established for centuries to come.
In the narrative of events from the Trojan War in the 13th century B.C. to the Roman conquest of the Balkans by Emperor Trajan in 106 A.D., a colorful, ethnic world comes alive, one whose diverse cultural traditions have determined the course of our civilization.

About the authors

Konstantin Boshnakov
For many years, Konstantin Boshnakov has taught the history of Ancient Greece, Thrace, Rome, and the Mediterranean as a Professor in the Department of History at the St. Kliment Ohridski University of Sofia, Bulgaria. He obtained his Doctoral Degree in 1992, and in 2001 became an Associate Professor of Ancient History. The scope of his research includes comparative studies of the political, military, and social history of ancient cultures, the historical geography of ancient states, the analysis and interpretation of written sources and archaeological finds, and the study of cults and religious practices. His monographs and articles have been published in Bulgaria, Germany, and France. In 2002-2003 he was awarded a fellowship by the Alexander von Humboldt Foundation and was invited as a visiting lecturer by the Martin Luther University at Halle-Wittenberg, Germany.

Hristo Hadjitanev
Hristo Hadjitanev graduated from the Academy of Fine Arts in 1987 with a specialization in mural painting. Since 1986, he has taken part in the exhibitions and autumn salons of the Union of Bulgarian Artists. In addition to murals, his works include applied graphics, posters, and illustrations.

Emilian Stankev
Emilian Stankev graduated from the National Academy of Fine Arts, working under Professor Hristo Neikov, and specializing in illustration and book design. He has worked for Bulgarian and foreign publishing houses, illustrating more than 300 books, and designing over 150 postage stamps. He is the winner of prestigious international awards for graphic art, and has had many exhibitions in Bulgaria and abroad.

Atanas Atanasov
Atanas Atanasov graduated from the National Academy of Fine Arts in 1991. He specialized in painting with Professor Svetlin Rousev. His works include paintings, illustrations, and murals. Since 1983, he has taken part in many exhibitions in Bulgaria and abroad. Since 1993, he has worked for the Italian publishing company Lo Scarabeo.

Rossen Toshev
Rossen Toshev graduated from the National Academy of Fine Arts in 1994, with a specialization in painting with Professor D. Dobrev. He teaches painting at the Professor N. Rainov Secondary School of Fine Arts, and Non-Conventional Forms of Fine Art at the Academy of Fine Arts. He is the winner of many awards from prestigious festivals.

Plamen Vulchev
Plamen Vulchev graduated from the National Academy of Fine Arts in 1977, where he studied with Prof. Petar Mihailov. He became an Assistant Professor in 1981, and has, since 1990, been an Associate Professor at the Academy. His works are included in the collections of the National Art Gallery, the Sofia City Gallery and the regional galleries in Kazanluk, Dobrich, Vidin, Turnovo, etc. He has also had exhibitions in Greece, Turkey, Sweden, Norway, and Germany.

Marin Marinov
Graduate of the Secondary School of Fine Arts (1975) and the National Academy of Fine Arts (1983), he specializes in monumental decorative art. His works include murals, glass paintings, mosaics, paintings, and portraits. He is the author of monumental decorative murals in public buildings, restaurants and offices.

Maya Buyukliiska
Maya Buyukliiska graduated from the Academy of Fine Arts in 1975 with a specialization in applied graphic art. Her works include applied graphics, packaging, postal stamps and book designs. She takes part in national and international exhibitions and poster biennials. She is the winner of awards from exhibitions and international contests in Bulgaria and Italy.

Eng. Krassimir Andreev
Krasimir Andreev graduated from the Construction, Architecture, and urban Planning Institute in Sofia with a specialization in cartography and photogrammetry. Since 1966, he has worked as a designer-cartographer at Cartography Ltd. He is an expert on historical and urban cartography, and has designed atlases and wall maps for Bulgarian schools, as well as maps for a variety of publications.

Krassimira Despotova
Krassimira Despotova graduated from the National Academy of Fine Arts in 1975, where she studied with Professor Petar Chouklev, with a specialization in illustration and book design. Since 1974, she has taken part in many exhibitions in Bulgaria and abroad. She is the winner of awards for book and stamp design. Her works include illustrations, book designs, and postage stamps.

HERITAGE SERIES

RULERS
OF ANCIENT EUROPE

RULERS
OF ANCIENT ROME

RULERS
OF THE BYZANTIME EMPIRE

RULERS
OF THE OTTOMAN EMPIRE

RULERS
OF THE RUSSIAN EMPIRE

RULERS
OF THE AUSTRO-HUNGARIAN
EMPIRE

RULERS
OF THE WORLD

Agamemnon

INTRODUCTION 9

AGAMEMNON 10
13th c. B.C.

RHESUS 14
13th c. B.C.

LYCURGUS 16
10th/9th c. B.C.

SOLON 20
c. 640 – 560 B.C.

MILTIADES THE ELDER 24
c. 590 – c. 520 B.C.

Peisistratus

PEISISTRATUS 26
c. 600 – 527 B.C.

CLEISTHENES 30
second half of the 6th c. B.C.

Contents

Alexander III the Great

Alexander I the Philhellene 34
494 – 454 B.C.

Themistocles 38
524 – 459 B.C.

Pausanias 44
the second half of the 6th c. – 467 B.C.

Pericles 48
c. 490 – 429 B.C.

Sitalces 56
c. 445 – 424 B.C.

Archelaus 60
413 – 399 B.C.

Alcibiades 63
c. 450 – 404 B.C.

Seuthes II 68
c. 407 – c. 386 B.C.

Cotys I 71
384/83 – 360/59 B.C.

Epaminondas 76
late 5th c. – 362 B.C.

Philip II of Macedonia 80
359 – 336 B.C.

Syrmus 89
4th c. B.C.

Alexander III the Great 92
336 – 323 B.C.

Lysimachus 102
305 – 281 B.C.

Pyrrhus 106
306 – 302; 297 – 272 B.C.

Philip V of Macedonia 110
221 – 179 B.C.

Decebalus 114
c. 86 – 106 A.D.

Philip II of Macedonia

Glossary 120

Chariot race at Olympia

Introduction

History was generated by the human desire for knowledge, for keeping an accurate record of the past, and for the appreciation of unchanging wisdom. This book will take you through the layers of time to distant antiquity – illuminated by the first inscriptions on stone, metal, and parchment – when the foundations of fateful processes were laid, and the early Europeans' consciousness developed.

Historical reality is a global, comprehensive process, and this was equally true at the time of the myth of Europa, the Phoenician king's daughter who was carried off by Zeus, disguised as a bull, to the island of Crete – the land where Minos, the first European ruler with a divine origin, was born. It is interesting to note that from this ancient time to the very end of antiquity, no one was able to draw conclusively the borders of the continent named Europe, named thus after an Asian princess.

This book is about her first sons who, driven by their destiny, through years of friendship and bitter enmity, remained anchored to their common origin. The political actions and the bold plans of the rulers of Hellas, Thrace, and Macedonia reshaped their worlds and personified their ages, transcending the limits and the thinking of their time.

We shall fly on the wings of history over the events of fourteen centuries, from the heroic battles of the Trojan war in the 13th century B.C. to the rumble of the Roman Emperor Trajan's Thracian wars with King Decebalus in 106 A.D.

Our narrative starts with Agamemnon, the mighty king of Mycenae and leader of the Achaean forces against Troy. It follows the complex winding road walked by Athenians and Spartans toward the wise laws of Solon and Lycurgus. The age of the great Hellenic colonization comes alive, exemplified by Peisistratus. Due attention has been given to the Athenian democratic reformer Cleisthenes; to the talented strategist Themistocles who made Athens a leading naval power and checked, albeit temporarily, the Persian invasion; and to Pausanias, who humiliated the arrogant Persians at Plataea.

We have followed the creation of the Macedonian Kingdom, and its consolidation under Alexander I, the Philhellene and Archelaus. The portrait of the famous statesman Pericles embodies the triumph of democracy in Athens, accompanied by a continuous cultural upsurge and followed by the backbreaking Peloponnesian War.

An integral part of the events in South-Eastern Europe at that time were glorious Thracian rulers such as Rhesus, Sitalces, Seuthes II, Cotys I, and Syrmus. The life of Alcibiades of Athens demonstrates the fate of the cosmopolitan person – a recurring character-type throughout human history. It is hardly a coincidence that the victories and the death of Epaminondas of Thebes swept away the ideals and the authorities of the past.

A new age set in with the arrival of the Macedonian rulers Philip II (359-336 B.C.) and Alexander III the Great (336-323 B.C.). United against the common enemy, the Persians of Asia, numerous Hellenes, Macedonians, and Thracians advanced together by land and by sea into Asia Minor, Egypt, Babylonia, Persia, and India. However, instead of the much desired unification, that expedition amounted to an irreparable dispersal of precious human resources. The ensuing large-scale wars for Alexander's heritage had their roots in the fact that few of Alexander's closest associates understood his ideas as a statesman. Rulers such as Lysimachus and Pyrrhus in the 3rd c. B.C. successfully imitated the great commander, but finally became known only for their human drama. Of Alexander's vast state which, during his lifetime, spanned three continents, only Macedonia in Europe remained, and its size was not much different from the state of Philip II prior to his son's grandiose expedition to the East. The Macedonian state, and the world in general, now had to live with the consequences of Alexander the Great's fame, and with the ostentation of the ensuing epoch.

The Macedonian king Philip V (221-179 B.C.) was the first to face the Romans, who were to remain undefeated for centuries to come. King Decebalus of Dacia was the last defender of the centuries-old Thracian state and spiritual tradition. In 106 A. D., he could no longer fend off the invasion of the Roman legions that crushed natural and human obstacles alike.

Throughout these fourteen centuries, history has always awarded the privilege of choice to those who ruled over lands and human destinies. It gave generously and took away mercilessly. Not everything given was acceptable; not every defeat was inevitable. It has been so from times immemorial to the present. Although many people are now skeptical about the statement "history is the teacher of nations," it is undoubtedly a clarion call to the muse of memory in the face of pending tumultuous events. Indeed, history can be a teacher, but only for those with a sincere desire to draw a lesson from it, for progress lies in the aspiration to strive for higher virtues.

While we live for the future, we should never forget that we owe our life and our identity to the past. Somewhere in the distant past lies our own beginning, archetype, and meaning.

KONSTANTIN BOSHNAKOV

Portrait illustration by Hristo Hadjitanev

AGAMEMNON
13th c. B.C.

MANY FAMOUS HEROES were associated with Mycenae's power and fate. Throughout antiquity, the remains of its impressive citadel commanded the admiration of the Hellenes and fuelled their historical awareness. The ancients knew well that Mycenae was the place where the palace of Agamemnon, son of Atreus, once stood. The legend went that in the citadel, in underground chambers, the local rulers kept their untold wealth. It was no coincidence that the ancient poet Homer, in his account of the ten-year war of the Achaeans led by Agamemnon against Troy in Asia Minor, praised Mycenae as "golden." Unique in antiquity, the citadel's walls were built of huge stones, and were some 900 m long. Ancient sources refer to the legend that the walls had been erected by the mythical Cyclopes. According to the traveller Pausanias who saw the ruins of Mycenae in the 2nd c. A.D., even the smallest of the stones could not be moved by two mules. However, in later antiquity, much larger and better organised fortifications were built. Mycenae inspired awe not with its size but rather becouse of its role as unifier of the Achaeans – a group of related tribes inhabiting a large part of ancient Greece.

Mycenae's rising power won it numerous enemies. For ten years, the king was the head of the Achaean warriors who came from all over Greece, besieging the strongly fortified city of Troy on the gate between Europe and Asia, the strait of Hellespont (today's Dardanelles). In the 4th c. B.C., the ancient philosopher Plato pointed out that Agamemnon's persistence and ambition for leadership had been coded into his name from his birth.

According to the legend, Mycenae was founded, at the will of the gods, by the hero Perseus. His grandfather Acrisius had once been told a prophecy that he would die at the hand of his daughter's son. This is why Acrisius, king of Argos, built an underground chamber for his daughter Danae and doomed her to eternal imprisonment. However, the god Zeus visited Danae and had intercourse with her in the shape of a stream of gold which poured through the roof into Danae's lap. This is how the demigod Perseus was born. After many adventures and heroic deeds, the glorious hero fulfilled his destiny and inadvertently killed his grandfather in a tournament. Ashamed, he did not dare claim his kingdom of Argos but instead founded a city and a kingdom on the hill where the cap *(myces)* fell from his scabbard, and the town was called Mycenae. It so happened that Perseus had many sons, and some of them married daughters of the wealthy Pelops. Later, the brothers fought bitterly for their father's throne. Those who survived settled in the neighbouring lands and islands. Atreus, son of Pelops, became the king of Mycenae, and the throne was then inherited by his son Agamemnon.

The rocky hill of Mycenae had been inhabited for centuries but the construction of the stronghold began in the 16th c. B.C. The rich funeral gifts in the tombs of the local rulers indicate that as early as in the 16th c. B.C. Mycenae had diplomatic and trade contacts with the rich kingdom of Minos of Crete as well as with Egypt, Cyprus and Asia Minor. Over the years, Mycenae expanded and grew stronger in the Peloponnesus, and representatives of the dynasty ruled over island territories. A volcano eruption on the island of Thera and the subsequent earthquakes destroyed the civilization on the island of Crete.

In the 14th c. B.C., the Achaeans conquered the island, mastered to perfection the seafaring skills of the Cretans and the inhabitants of the Aegean islands, and brought to their palaces Cretan scribes, mural- and vase-painters, jewellers and obedient servants. The Achaean warriors and princes came to rule over vast lands and the seas from Cyprus and Asia Minor in the east to Sicily and Southern Italy in the west. Although they fought continually among themselves, they guarded jealously their royal acquisitions and their common interests against the outside world. At the peak of their might, everyone was aware that Mycenae was ruled by the descendants of Perseus, son of Zeus. Great was their justice, and devastating their wrath.

Like many other heroes, descendants of divine fathers or mothers, Agamemnon referred to himself as *vanax* – as Zeus was called, for he was the most eminent among gods and men. He owned a vast and fruitful sacred land or *temenos* (the same term was later used to describe the land dedicated to the

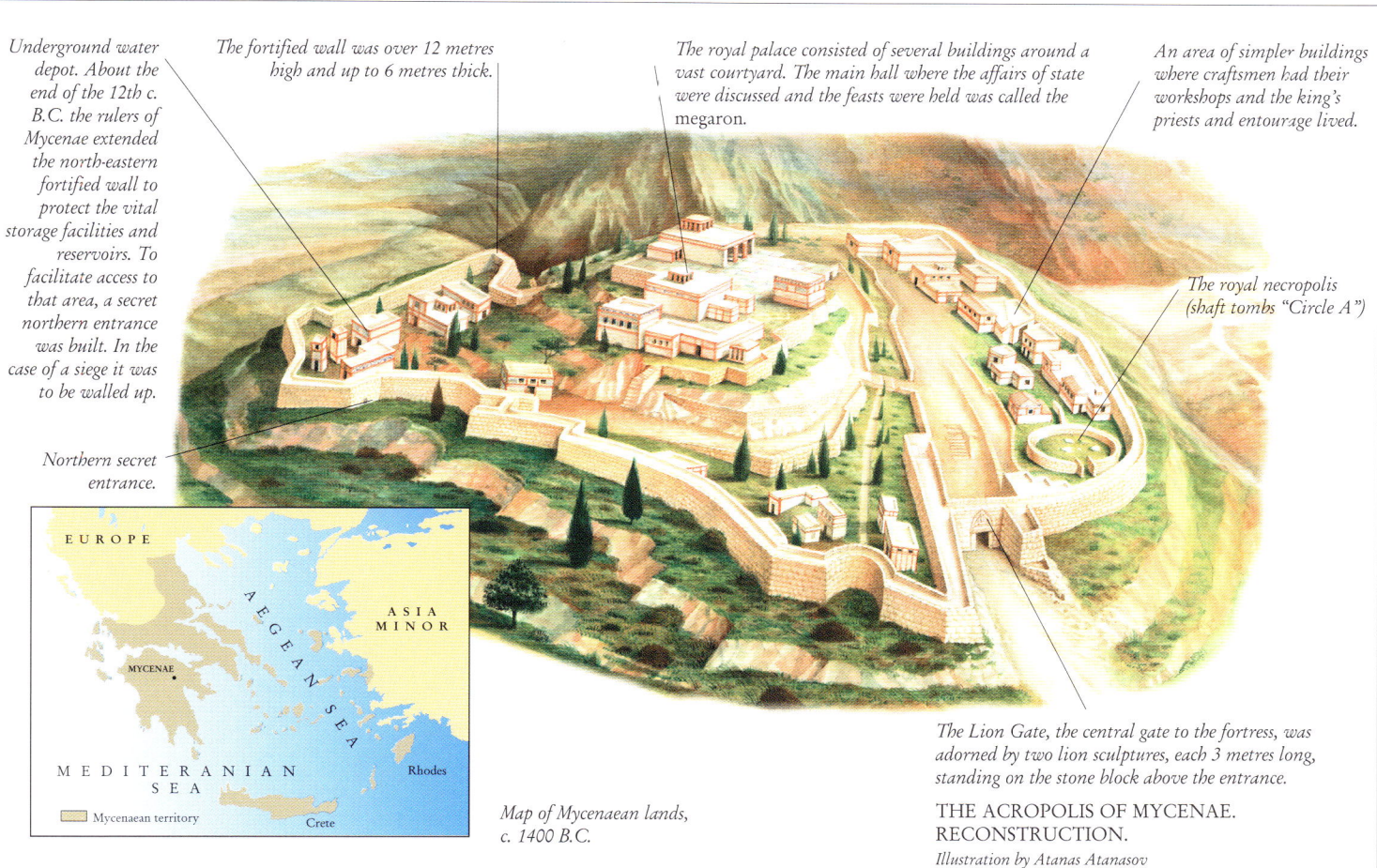

Underground water depot. About the end of the 12th c. B.C. the rulers of Mycenae extended the north-eastern fortified wall to protect the vital storage facilities and reservoirs. To facilitate access to that area, a secret northern entrance was built. In the case of a siege it was to be walled up.

Northern secret entrance.

The fortified wall was over 12 metres high and up to 6 metres thick.

The royal palace consisted of several buildings around a vast courtyard. The main hall where the affairs of state were discussed and the feasts were held was called the megaron.

An area of simpler buildings where craftsmen had their workshops and the king's priests and entourage lived.

The royal necropolis (shaft tombs "Circle A")

The Lion Gate, the central gate to the fortress, was adorned by two lion sculptures, each 3 metres long, standing on the stone block above the entrance.

THE ACROPOLIS OF MYCENAE.
RECONSTRUCTION.
Illustration by Atanas Atanasov

Map of Mycenaean lands, c. 1400 B.C.

A narrow, winding stony road crossed the plain of Argolis between Argos and Corinth. Having crossed the Isthmus, the traveller entered the land of Pelops (named Peloponnesus after him), and following that road, reached the hill where the glorious Mycenae rose. About the middle of the 13th c. B.C., he would first see the Lion Gate, erected of three monolithic stone blocks. It was adorned by the sculptures of two lions, the symbol of the Mycenaen king's might and valiance. They not only guarded the entrance to the citadel but also showed clearly that no aggression against Mycenae would remain unpunished. The imposing buildings, supposedly erected by the Cyclopes, seemed to rise from the rocks themselves. Inside the citadel, immediately to the right, was a stone circle where the traveller could see the tombstones of Mycenae's founders. They had been buried with their gilded bronze arms, with gold masks on their faces, and a wealth of finery: gold and silver jewellery, crystal, amber and ivory objects. To the left were fortified rock terraces where the Mycenaean nobles had their homes. The winding road climbed between them, taking the visitor to the gates of the royal palace. The guards were clad in armour made of large bronze plates and helmets of wild boars' tusks, the usual outfit of Achaean soldiers. They were armed with spears and figure-eight-shaped shields of nearly human size. Inside the palace were the apartments of the royal family and the courtiers' rooms, but those were not accessible to visitors. The king's reception hall where the meetings were held and the religious rituals were performed was called *the megaron*. A large hearth on a circular platform occupied the center of the hall. Smoke escaped from an opening on the ceiling, supported by four tall columns. The walls were painted with elaborate hunting, battle and religious scenes. The expensive jewellery, the fabrics from faraway lands, the gold, silver and bronze vessels, the ornamental clay pots, the furniture made of exotic wood and ivory created an atmosphere of unparalleled splendour.

immortal gods in temples). However, Agamemnon was destined to shed blood for his royal power and for his land. While his kingdom was growing stronger, Priam's kingdom of Troy was also gaining strength and wealth to the north-east. Goods from faraway lands were pouring into Agamemnon's palace. The metals were particularly valuable, for they were used for the make of Achaean weapons. The copper came from Cyprus, the lead and the tin were brought by land and by sea from the faraway Carpathians to the north; the gold, the silver, the amber and the timber for building ships were also brought from distant places. With the expansion and consolidation of the strongly fortified Troy and Priam's military alliance with the Thracian rulers from the northern Aegean and western Asia Minor, Mycenae's communications with the outside world were disrupted and the regular inflow of raw materials was disturbed. As the Achaean princes could not give up their luxurious life-style, nor Agamemnon lock himself up in his citadel – a sign of weakness in the eyes of his subjects – the historic war that shook the foundations of statehood in the entire Aegean world began. To Mycenae and its world, the Trojan War was to be a life-and-death fight. As it is commonly known, when there is a cause, an occasion for battle is easy to find. The Trojans grew so self-confident that the young prince Paris carried off Helen, the beautiful wife of Menelaus, king of Achaean Sparta and Agamemnon's brother.

For his march on Asia, Agamemnon summoned dozens of Achaean princes, from Thessaly in the north to the island of Crete in the south. Even the brave mountain warriors of Arcadia who had no traditions as seafarers went on his ships. Thus, with an army of elite warriors, impressive in size for those times, Agamemnon besieged the city of Troy. The war was long and hard. Each of the warriors boasted his semi-divine origin and fought bravely for his name and fame. Dozens of duels took place between heroes in full armour, riding wildly in their chariots. The discord between the Achaean princes themselves also brought a lot of trouble; the most disastrous being the conflict between Agamemnon and Achilles. The poet Homer praised the heroes' exploits at Troy in his famous epic poems. In them, an important role was attributed to the gods as well, for like the warriors, they fought among themselves. According to Homer, Troy finally fell as a result of the stratagem of the wooden horse, a gift from the Achaeans that the Trojans accepted. The horse was hollow and full of warriors who attacked the city and the palace of the old king Priam at night. Whatever the stories told in myths and epic poems, today's researchers are confident that Priam's Troy was destroyed by a disastrous

Map of the territories that sent armies to take part in the siege of Troy.

After the ten-year siege, the fall of Troy brought to some death, to others exile in faraway lands, and to still others slavery in the distant palaces of the victorious Achaeans.
Illustration by Emilian Stankev

Black–figure vase depicting Achaean and Trojan heroes, 6 th c. B.C.
Illustration by Hristo Hadjitanev

The epic poet Hesiod who lived in the 7th c. B.C. was admired by the ancient Greeks for his wisdom, for he described in elegant verse both the creation of the world of the gods and the human plight in the world of men who had to work hard to earn their living. It is to Hesiod that we owe the ancient legend of those distant times when gods and men had the same descent and lived in harmony and happiness. The immortal dwellers on Olympus where the god Cronos reigned supreme created for the mortals the first Golden Age. Life was carefree, a never-ending enjoyment, unthreatened by the misery of old age. Death was like sleep. Then the silver age followed. It took children a hundred years to grow up, tended by their mothers, but once they reached maturity, their life was short, for they did not praise the gods for their generous gifts to humanity, and they perished through the thunderbolts of Zeus, son of Cronos. They paid their penalty in the Underworld of the shadows. Then the third age, the age of bronze followed. Infatuated with the deplorable, bloody affairs of Ares, men's hearts became cruel, as if made of metal, and their strong bodies were clad in bronze armour. The bronze generation died at their own hands, and although powerful and fearful, they remained nameless. After them, Zeus created a stronger and more honorable generation of heroes. Hesiod praised that generation which inhabited the vast earth as demi-gods, for they partly descended from the gods themselves. When the darkness of death fell upon the heroes, they went far both from the mortal men and the immortal gods, to the Islands of Blest by deep-swirling Oceanus. There, their hearts knew no grief, and their fields bore fruit three times a year. They were ruled by the divine ancestor, Cronos.
Unlike their predecessors, the heroes left their mark on the following generations with their heroic exploits.

earthquake. Maybe Homer suggested that the celebrated Achaean warriors won an inglorious victory against Troy with the help of the god of earthquakes Poseidon whose sacred animal was believed to be the horse.

As so often happens in the history of mankind, the war was so prolonged and exhausting, and the opponents were so equal in strength that the fall of Troy marked the beginning of Mycenae's decline as well. Heroes such as Menelaus and Odysseus were to wander for many years; other Achaeans were to face coups in their own palaces; still others were driven into exile, to look for new kingdoms in faraway lands. Some paid a heavy price for the time when they were away at war, as bold ambitions for power and countless administrators who had seen little of the burden of war had drained the last resources of the small kingdoms. The population was heavily indebted and got no return for the goods it produced. King Agamemnon's fate was the most dramatic of all. He had ignored the sages' advice not to leave his throne unattended for a long time. During his absence, his wife Clytemnestra had organised a conspiracy with her lover Aegisthus. Agamemnon was brutally murdered in his palace, and his son Orestes was driven into exile. Eight years later, he returned, god-like, to avenge the death of his father. However, that was not the end of the tragic events in the house of the Atreids. Soon the seas and the lands were invaded by new warriors and settlers, bringing new potential and ideas for the future. They started giving new names to these lands. History repeated itself, as human nature invariably does.

From antiquity to the present, there have been people who believe the Trojan War never took place, and Agamemnon's might was entirely due to the talent of the poet Homer. Indeed, it is hard to produce incontestable evidence in support of the poet's inspired epic. One thing, however, seems certain. The devastating Trojan War marked the end of the glorious generation of the heroes.

Clytemnestra, the wife and murderer of Agamemnon. Clytemnestra was the sister of Helen who according to the legend was the cause for the Trojan war.
Illustration by Emilian Stankev

Rhesus
13th c. B.C.

Portrait illustration by Hristo Hadjitanev

O**N A DARK NIGHT** in the tenth year of the siege of Troy, a horrible piece of news spread in the camp of the Trojans and their allies. Before dawn, dread seized the defenders of the fortress. The Achaean heroes Odysseus and Diomedes, men of courage and perfidy, had slaughtered the recently arrived Thracians, and their king, in their camp while sleeping. The king was Rhesus, son of Eïoneus, after whom the village of Eïon on the estuary of the river Strymon (Struma) was named. Another legend goes that he was the son of the river god Strymon and the Muse Euterpe, the patron of flute playing. Believed to be god-like, he had been given a prophecy that if he and his horses drank from the local river Scamander, he would become immortal. Neither the armour of Ajax, nor the divine Achilles would be able to resist his spear. He was credited with having inflicted in a single battle heavier losses on the Achaeans than they had suffered during the ten years of the siege of Troy. The Trojans placed much hope on the

Location of the military powers in the siege of Troy.

Thracian king Rhesus. Homer described his horses as "the finest I ever saw and the biggest, they are whiter than snow, and their speed of foot is the winds' speed." His chariot was "fairly ornate with gold and with silver" from the rich deposits in the Pangaeum mountain in his native land. His weapons were gilded, huge, and filled enemies with fear. In his magnificence, Rhesus looked more like an immortal god than like a human.

Odysseus and Diomedes sneaked into the Thracian camp between the sleeping guards, and slaughtered twelve Thracian nobles; Diomedes then killed king Rhesus. Only Hippocoon, Rhesus' cousin and military advisor, survived the massacre and called his king's name desperately in the night. In the meantime, the sly Odysseus untied the fabled Thracian horses, took the Thracians' beautiful weapons, and headed for the Achaean camp with his spoils. According to Homer, the gods were also involved in this event, for the most disastrous fate for a hero was to die in such an unfortunate way, not on the battlefield. Apollo was on the Thracians' side but he was helpless at night and was overpowered by Athena who filled the militant Achaeans with courage.

The Thracian king's dramatic fate inspired Greek poets for centuries after the Trojan War. The playwright Euripides described Rhesus as a kinsman of Orpheus. The famous singer was also believed to be the son of a Muse – Calliope, the patron of poetry and kithara playing. Indeed, Thrace was famous not only as the homeland of valorous warriors, horses as white as snow, and abundant herds. It was also the land of music and musical instruments where royal priests cured illnesses and ailments with incantations addressed to the soul so that the body might heal as well. In the Thracian lands the noble rulers were initiated into the secret teaching of immortality. Euripides, who was well acquainted with Thracian cults, conveyed the words of the mourning Muse Euterpe. She believed that her son Rhesus "will lurk hidden in a cavern of the land with veins of silver," like a prophet of Dionysos in the mountain Pangaeum. There, he would be worshipped as god by the initiates.

Today, very few researchers specializing in ancient history believe that a Thracian king of the name of Rhesus actually existed to come to the Trojans' help in their war

Diomedes and Odysseus capture a Trojan spy. Replica of a red-figure vase. Illustration by Hristo Hadjitanev

with Agamemnon. This part of Homer's epic is considered to be a later addition. In any case, both the Thracians and the Hellenes who later settled in the lower valley of the Struma river believed in the divinity of King Rhesus. Once, to win his benevolence, they had to move his remains from Troy to his native land. With time, history and archaeology will shed more light on the significance of these lines from Homer's epic. It will likely become increasingly clear that the image of Rhesus was in line with the realities of that distant epoch.

The Achaean lands boasted fortresses and castles but Thrace also had impregnable strongholds. The local rulers were familiar with the technology of producing bronze, silver and gold objects. The Thracian lands were an indelible part of the world of Mycenae and Troy, and their rulers shared visible and invisible treasures. Here we should probably mention the words of the ancient historian Thucydides who wrote that the measure of power was not the size of material acquisitions but the excellence of the spirit and the firmness of traditions. After the decline of the Achaean world and Mycenae, the Thracian north and the Hellenic south went their own ways. The epoch of the heroes marked the destiny of the Thracian state all the way to the Roman conquest.

Diomedes and Odysseus kill Rhesus and take away his horses. Replica of a red-figure vase. Illustration by Hristo Hadjitanev

LYCURGUS
10th/9th c. B.C.

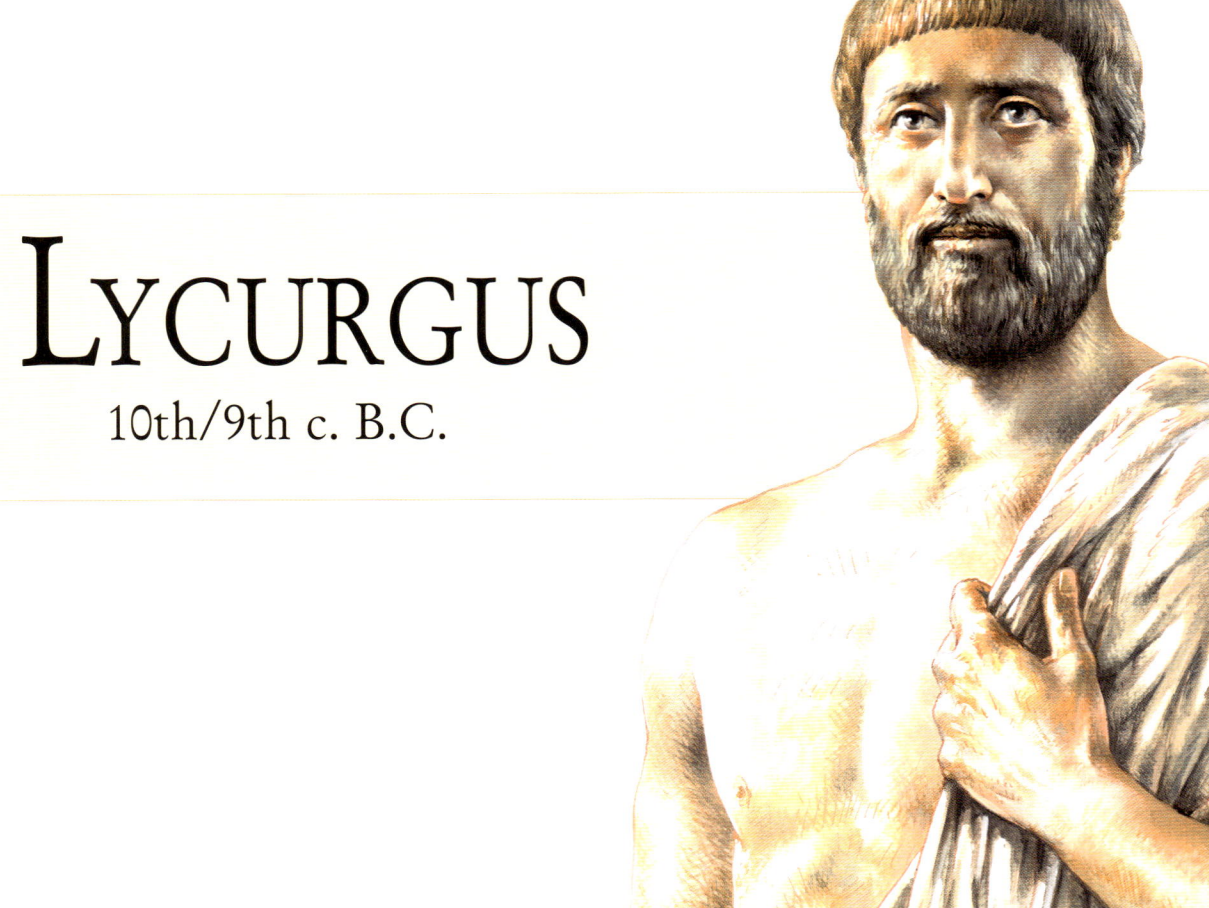

Portrait illustration by Hristo Hadjitanev

More than ever before, the land of Hellas was inhabited by a multitude of related and unrelated tribes. The consequences of the Doric invasion in the crucial years of the 12th/11th c. B.C. were fading away slowly. The Dorians believed themselves to be the descendants of the hero Heracles, and with the unyielding persistence of god-appointed avengers, took citadel after citadel, setting fire to the Achaean kings' rich palaces. On their victorious march, they conquered the few fertile valleys of Hellas, all the way to southern Peloponnesus. Before long, they crossed the sea, and settled on the island of Crete, the Dodecanese and the shore of Asia Minor. Long afterwards, one could see on the crumbling walls of Achaean palaces battle scenes from the times when Achaean warriors could still drive back the attacking invaders. The skillful painters depicted them with long dishevelled black hair, dressed in furs. But the Dorians were not all-out destroyers and sacrilegious grave-desecrators. They came to stay in the conquered fertile land, and took its defence as their duty. To the right of the Lion Gate of the strongly built but by that time deserted Mycenae, the graves of the ancestors of Atreus and Agamemon, full of rich funeral gifts, stayed intact throughout antiquity. In fact, the Dorians were not complete strangers in the Achaean world, their language was very similar to the Achaean and they worshipped the same gods as their enemies from the "golden" palaces, although their ways and customs were different. With time, the wave of migration and the need to adjust to the new circumstances changed them considerably.

The Doric invasion gave many Balkan neighbours the courage to plunder and ravage Hellenic lands. The roads were suddenly full of bandits, and the seas of pirates. The busy trade from the time of Mycenae's flourishing went into a decline. The magnificent Achaean citadels, purportedly built by the mythical Cyclopes, a symbol of hope and fear, were the only remnants of the bustle and splendour of court life, of the exploits of the glorious heroes, of the plots and the bloody conflicts between dynasties. The new kings – the *basileis*, – the descendants of mortals, did not settle in the ruined citadels, neither did they erect palaces of their own. Dusty village squares and the roads on which the armies marched became the site of politics. The armed people – the *demos* – honoured the basileis, the wartime leaders who made sacrifices to the gods before and after battle, praised the brave and punished the cowards, but regarded them more and more as state officials rather than kings. In times of peace, the basileis worked for their living. Life was uneventful in the small communities, absorbed by the monotonous rhythm of country life, and in the family estates where the elders had the first and the last word. The monotony was broken only by passing craftsmen and merchants, offering objects made of the new and rare metal, iron as well as salt and other goods from distant lands. Scattered among mountains and hills, in small valleys, indented coasts and islands, the land of Hellas remained for centuries hardly known to settlers old and new.

THE HARVEST-TIME was just over in the plain of Laconia, where the river Eurotas made its way and ancient Sparta spread. Everywhere around, all the way to the slopes of the mountains Parnon and Taiyetos, the fields were covered with rows of barley sheaves, all of equal size. At the sight of these fields, Lycurgus once exclaimed that his native land was like a vast heritage distributed equally among many brothers. It was Lycurgus, one of the most remarkable lawgivers of antiquity, who brought justice and harmony to Sparta. The ancient Hellenes compared the remarkably stable social order in Sparta to the Cosmos which the divine will brought about from the Chaos.

Having made a sacrifice in Delphi and asked the all-seeing god Apollo whether he would send good laws to the Spartans, Lycurgus was called by the oracle "loved by the gods" and "more divine than human." Once uttered, these prophetic words were preserved for centuries in the Hellenes' memory, until the time came for historians and biographers to put them in writing on papyrus.

The Spartans who were of Doric origin needed a wise lawgiver more than any other Hellenes. The victors were to keep in subjection the much more numerous conquered Achaean population. United by their tribal memory, these slaves or *helots* were a constant threat to their free masters, the *Spartiates*.

According to local chronicles, Lycurgus descended from Heracles through eleven generations. His father was Eunomes, and his mother Dionasa. His family was one of the many to fall victim to the lawlessness in Sparta. His father, at that time a Spartan basileus, died in a street fight while attempting to reconcile the adversaries. Lycurgus ascended the throne in 880 B.C. but only reigned for eight months. According to the legend, during this brief period he won the deep respect of his compatriots with his admirable spirit and power of reasoning. Lycurgus was not tempted by the well-being or the adulation that went with power, nor was he attracted by the glory of separate military or political victories. His sober sense of reality and his genuine, sincere patriotism brought him to the conviction that triumph had a flip side, too, and sooner or later one had to shoulder its burden. With the coming of peace the victor inevitably inherited the troubles of the conquered enemy. The Spartans were doomed to take root in that land and to be constantly at war with the helots, even when there was no visible threat.

Lycurgus also realized that neither the vain resolution of one individual nor the crowd's uncontrollable "justice" could tune the lyre of social life the way harmonic education *(paideia)* and the divine moral law could. Thus, with the will of a divinely inspired lawgiver, he set about erecting an eternal monument, drawing his contemporaries into this grand undertaking.

As soon as he was told that his recently deceased older brother Polydectes' wife had given birth to a son, Lycurgus put the baby on the throne, declared him the lawful basileus of Sparta and gave him the name of Charilaus, meaning "joy of the people." He became the child's guardian. His conduct was so honest and unusual that it stirred up envy among his adversaries. They spread the rumour that Lycurgus was plotting against the newborn king and the Spartiate state. Again, Lycurgus acted wisely. He left his country to avoid fuelling the disastrous partisan conflicts, and decided to travel until Charilaus grew up.

On the island of Crete, Lycurgus met with the talented lyrical poet Thales, who was also a remarkably wise law-maker. The ancient biographer Plutarch, like many philosophers, was convinced that the poet was practically pursuing the same objectives as the best lawgivers. With his poems, he was seeking to inspire by love of order and harmony. Those touched by their music suddenly relented, and their hearts were filled with a thirst for the noble, ignoring the universal discord around them.

Thales told Lycurgus the secret of the ancient Cretan laws' origin, and how the mighty king Minos got them in the cave of Zeus. He thus indicated the way to educate the Spartans.

From Crete, Lycurgus travelled to the coast of Asia Minor, inhabited for centuries by Achaean and Ionian exiles. There, he got acquainted with the carefully preserved Homeric epics in which he found invaluable political and ethical guidelines. He was purportedly one of the first to be acquainted with Homer's heritage and to take it to continental Hellas.

The Egyptians claimed that Lycurgus had spent some time in Egypt, too. There, he got to know the long-established social divisions, and admitted that it was reasonable to have separate social classes such as soldiers, craftsmen and merchants.

Thus, during his prolonged travels the future lawgiver accumulated experience and drew from the wisdom of many statesmen. He realized that even the best law could not save a vice-ridden state from perishing. Such a state, like a sick person suffering from many and different ailments, needed a fundamental change in its way of life.

Years later, Lycurgus returned to his homeland where he was awaited eagerly, as meanwhile the situation in Sparta had become deplorable.

Having consulted the oracle in Delphi and having received a favourable response, Lycurgus brought to Sparta his oral laws knows as the Rhetra. He convinced the Spartans that he had received them as a manifestation of the divine will, and they were to be passed on from generation to generation as sacred answers. This is why these laws were never put down, and we know about them only owing to the efforts of diligent ancient writers who shared the universal interest the

An idealized image of a young Spartan warrior.
The wreaths and the wading birds suggest a forthcoming maturation
ceremony in the sanctuary of Artemis in Sparta.
Illustration by Atanas Atanasov

Hellenes took in the Spartan past. Lycurgus believed that written laws were subject to perishability, oblivion and greed, while unwritten ones, like the music of Homer's poems, were preserved in the minds of many. But that would not be sufficient, either, if the observance of the laws did not become a way of life, a need for every new generation.

Like many prominent statesmen in human history, Lycurgus did not break with traditions but drew on and developed further the best of them. He preserved the institution of the two kings, as well as the assembly of the warrior Spartiates, but his reforms were based on the council of the *Gerontes* (elders) known as *Gerusia*. It consisted of twenty-eight prominent Spartiates over the age of sixty, and they were Lycurgus' faithful supporters. The Gerusia was intended to pacify the population's political passions and to curb the unscrupulous aspirations for autocratic power. The power of the Gerontes was central because it brought balance, order and stability to the government. The Gerusia was in charge of preserving the historical memory and the rulers' wisdom. It assured the continuity between generations. The population in turn had the right to accept or reject the motions laid before them by the Gerontes and the basileis, but not to discuss them. The assembly decided on matters such as war and peace, praise and censure. At Lycurgus' order, the assembly held its meetings by the bridge over the river Knakion, a barren place with nothing to distract the attention: no statues, no paintings, no colonnades, no decorations, not even a building. Thus, putting an end to rulers' arbitrariness and the population's insubordination, he determined the authorities' prerogatives. The Spartans soon appreciated the wisdom of their lawgiver when social unrest and bloody feuds set in in the neighbouring Doric regions of Argos and Messenia.

The Spartiates, i.e. those warriors enjoying full privileges, were obliged to exercise and harden their bodies every day, as well as to keep their morale high. They were also responsible for their armor as foot soldiers, *hoplites*, that built the famous *Spartan phalanx*. In case of threat, younger soldiers left Laconia, but seldom went more than two days away. The older Spartiates were the ones to defend the town. In his special Rhetra, Lycurgus described the tactics, the camping, the armament, the colour of the battle outfit and even the young soldiers' haircut. For centuries, the Spartan phalanx would be famous for its invincibility. The free people who did not enjoy full rights – the *perioikoi* who inhabited the border regions of Laconia – were engaged in crafts and trade. The slaves – the helots, who had no rights – cultivated the land of the Spartiates. It was impossible to pass from one social division into another. Lycurgus divided the Spartan land equally among the warriors. In the community

Death in the Taiyetos Mountain: cruel was the fate of the feeble and the frail Spartan children, cruel as the war-ridden age of Lycurgus and his successors.
Illustration by Emilian Stankev

of equals each got from his allotted land an equal share of barley, wine and olive oil, without regarding this land as a potential source of wealth; the helots that cultivated it also remained community property.

Lycurgus encouraged the Spartans to lead a simple and open life, with no indulgence or luxury to soften the warriors. Fortifications were erected in a matter of days but those who had once conquered the impregnable Achaean citadels had learned their lesson: the stone walls would serve equally impersonally their old and new defenders. Lycurgus taught that there was no better wall than the one made of the bodies of the brave Spartan hoplites. The houses in Sparta were built of rough wood, using only a saw and a rasp. The lawgiver banned all crafts related to gold and silver, and drove away sculptors, artists, dancers, orators and brothel-keepers. Foreign ships seldom cast anchor in Spartan ports. Travellers, diplomats and merchants were detained at Laconia's border until their mission was clarified. Wealth gradually ceased to be an advantage in Sparta. Exhibiting it publicly became disreputable. However, the Spartiates' ways and the simplicity of their relationships were best revealed during the daily *syssitia* or common meals. The attendance was obligatory to all except those involved in making sacrifices to the gods or those late from hunting. The food and the vessels in which it was served were as simple as possible. Children were often taken to the syssitia to learn good manners, listen to the conversations about politics, and admire the adults' moderation in drinking and their good humour in accepting crude jokes. After the syssitia, the participants went home without torches, for they were not afraid of walking in the dark.

Wishing to consolidate his reforms, Lycurgus paid particular attention to marriage, the birth of children and their upbringing. The Spartiates' mothers enjoyed great respect. 'To produce healthy children, girls similarly to boys were expected to exercise daily, run, wrestle, and throw the discus and the javelin. Lycurgus introduced stern rules of education. Immediately after birth, the babies were submitted to the elders for evaluation of their health and potential to withstand future hardships. The frail and the sickly were left to die in a chasm in the Taiyetos mountain. Lycurgus banned the upbringing and education of Spartan children by slaves or hired tutors, as was the practice among other Hellenes. As soon as they turned seven, the children left their homes to join "flocks" where, overseen by respected Spartans, they were to learn blind obedience, endurance and courage. In summer, their life was particularly hard. They cut their hair to the skin and made them walk barefoot and play naked. Their skin became tanned and rough. They slept on reeds they plucked with bare hands at the river Eurotas. In winter, they wove thorns into the mats to keep them warmer. Boys were necessarily taught to read and write. Their education in music went no further than singing the blood-freezing *paeans*, hymns to the god Apollo with which the Spartan hoplites walked into battle to the sound of flutes. From an early age, Spartan children were taught to speak shortly, clearly and meaningfully, i.e. *laconically*. The children's units had a strong hierarchy. They were headed by the strongest, the bravest, the most skillful and enduring among the boys. Decades after Lycurgus' rule, some of them would bring home Olympic victories and be admitted to the basileis' closest circle. All Spartiates, however, were expected to be victorious in battle and to regard death with contempt.

Map of the Peloponnesus featuring the region of Laconia and the polis of Sparta.

Having taken the difficult road of radical reforms, Lycurgus was bound to face strong opposition. He lost an eye in a street fight but did not despond. Instead, he took the attacker to his house, so that he had a chance to see what a hardworking and gentle husband and father Lycurgus was; from being an enemy, the attacker became an admirer and a friend. After Lycurgus' death, the Spartans worshipped him as a god, built him a temple and made annual sacrifices to him.

However, the fate of Lycurgus' laws was not to be an easy one. Once installed, the Rhetra were not always observed strictly. Sparta's political elite and the prominent warriors who were the first to shed their blood for their land naturally aspired after wealth and privileges. To curb the pernicious plans of the few notables, a hundred and thirty years after Lycurgus' death King Theopompos appointed five *Ephors* or "overseers." The situation became even worse in the temptation-full 6th c. B.C., the time of the Hellenic colonization of the coasts of Southern Europe. The wealth of goods that poured into Hellas offered wide opportunities for making money. The Spartans faced a fateful choice: to throw their families' lives at the mercy of the helots while they travelled foreign lands and seas, or to go back humbly to the stern conservatism of the Rhetra. Having chosen wisely, they won eternal glory.

The public order installed by Lycurgus was appropriate only for Sparta. To Sparta, it was vital and life-saving, although in many ways it was contrary to human nature, isolated from the outside world and nearly Utopian. It is no coincidence that it captured the Hellenes' attention every time they faced a turning point in their history.

They once asked Lycurgus why he had not opted for democracy. "Let the one who wants a democracy first introduce it in his own family," Lycurgus answered.

20 RULERS OF ANCIENT EUROPE

An ancient myth claims that the time came when each god was to choose a polis where they would be held in high honour. Poseidon, the god of earthquakes, and the wise virgin goddess Athena contested the sovereignty over Attica. Poseidon hit the rocks of the Acropolis, the hill on which the celebrated polis was to grow, with his trident, and a spring gushed forth from it. Athena's gift to the locals was an olive tree. The two gods argued bitterly who was to become the patron of Attica. The argument was finally decided by the twelve Olympian gods. The skillful and virtuous Athena became the patron of the land that was to bear her name, for King Cecrops bore witness that she had been faster than Poseidon in planting the olive tree.

Sometime in the 8th c. B. C., while the kings were still in power, Attica acquired a fortified political and administrative centre where the richest and the noblest built their homes around a central square known as the *Agora*. They funded the construction of the first, fairly crude, public buildings and temples.

The nobles – the *eupatridae* – controlled most of the agricultural land and the politics, and lived in luxury. At first, that was accepted as just by the *demos* that honoured its leaders for their services to the homeland. In ancient times, the involvement in politics brought no material reward; it was a matter of courage and patriotism, and each warrior had to provide his own weapons. Only the very rich had the means to arm themselves as *hoplites* – with helmets, armour, greaves, shields, swords and spears. They were in the front line of the Athenian army, and the first to die in battle. This is why they were universally extolled as *aristoi*, a word meaning the best, the bravest, the most capable and the noblest, all in one. They embodied the militant spirit of the god Ares as well as moral values, for they guarded their name and reputation from fault. The polis could not develop and survive without their involvement. Their rule was known as *aristocracy*. This is why the struggle of the demos for more balanced rights of the different classes, equality before the law, participation in politics and redistribution of the land, against the increasing greed and arrogance of the eupatridae, was a difficult one and had been going on in Athens for decades.

The aspirations of the demos were not historically groundless. Those of non-noble descent who had accumulated some wealth were allowed to participate in politics and had an opportunity to consolidate their acquisitions. The poor needed a source of income, most often a small piece of land that they could cultivate themselves, without the help of still expensive slaves. They provided the mass of the Athenian army. In those times, the Athenians fought bitterly with their neighbours for control over new lands on the continent and nearby islands. The aristocrats started to fear a prolonged conflict with the demos. In other poleis, this conflict was increasingly taken advantage of by power-seekers who came to rule as tyrants. No one suspected the pending glory of Athens that was to make it famous from antiquity to date, its legendary naval might and the introduction for the first time in human history of constructive democracy.

Portrait illustration by Hristo Hadjitanev

Athena and Poseidon.
Illustration by Atanas Atanasov

FOR YEARS, THE ATHENIANS had been fighting with the neighbouring coastal polis of Megara for the nearby island of Salamis. The war was so exhausting that a law was passed that anyone who advocated a renewal of the hostilities should be sentenced to death. The land of Attica was pervaded by hope that after the long years of suffering, a new ruler would arrive: a man of courage, justness, wisdom and magnanimity. One day a man did appear in the town's square and at first everybody thought him insane. He recited verses about his homeland Salamis with inspiration. His poem spoke to the courageous hearts of the young, the law in question was revoked, and the war was resumed with the poet in command of the army. That poet was Solon, the future lawgiver. A talented strategist and a statesman of great erudition, he brought Athens to victory in the backbreaking war. He proceeded to release the captured Megarans, thus avoiding to gain another mortal enemy to his country.

On his father's side, Solon was a descendant of one of the noblest families in Athens. The great king Codrus was his ancestor. On his mother's side, he was related to the future tyrant Peisistratus. His father had spent much of the genos' wealth on charity, so at young age Solon went into trade and

Solon

c. 640 – 560 B.C.

Territories of Greece and its colonies in the mid-6th c. B.C.

became a ship owner. Thus, he was quick to combine the dignity of gentle birth with the daring and pride of a self-made man, all with his usual moderation, intelligence and objectivity. Having conquered Salamis with Solon's crucial help, the Athenians now turned their attention to the confusion in their political life and in their society. Instead of subsiding, the consequences of the sacrilegious murder of their distinguished leader Cylon got worse. Seeking the powers of a tyrant, Cylon had found himself besieged on the Acropolis and sought protection at the altar of the goddess Athena. Although he was promised to leave unharmed, at the orders of the rulers of Athens he and his followers were brutally murdered: some were stoned, others were slaughtered in the temple. Many Athenians were stained by this bloodshed, but most of all the Alcmaeonid genos that was to produce eminent statesmen in the future. In the polis, enmity set in for decades to come. In one of his poems, Solon wrote: "... and my soul aches to see the thousand-year-old Ionian land devastated".

In 591 B.C., the patriot Solon was elected an *archon* and was invested with extraordinary law-making and reforming powers to reconcile the Athenians. He became the first leader of the demos in history.

It was not without hesitation that Solon went into politics, for he was apprehensive of the greed of the nobles and of the excessive demands of those of lower birth. He explained his political intentions and actions in thousands of verses, giving expression to his spiritual harmony and taste for moderation. "I took my stand, covering both in the protection of my mighty shield, nor did I allow either side to win unjustly," he wrote about himself. In those troubled times, many urged Solon to usurp the whole power and become a tyrant. His flat refusal was met with ridicule and accusations of weakness and indecision. It was that approach, however, that made the great Solon diff0erent from the myriad of other obscure statesmen. He would not yield to others' expectations, nor give in before the rich and the influential, nor would he try to appease the electorate, for he had a more distinct vision of his country's future than all other Athenians together.

Solon thoroughly reformed the laws of Athens. From the cruel and largely inapplicable laws of his predecessor Draco he preserved only those that concerned the punishment of

A merchant ship carrying food, metals and luxury goods, chased by a pirate ship.
Illustration by Hristo Hadjitanev

murder. The first thing he did was to abolish the degrading practice of enslavement for debt. He cancelled all existing debts to both the state and private persons. He proceeded to pull up the boundary markers indicating obligations from the land of Attica. Thus, at one scoop, he restored the freedom of many Athenian slaves, the unity of the polis and the integrity of the Athenian army. The loan-givers who had suffered losses as a result of the new legislation were quick to accuse Solon of having thus decreed so that his friends might profit: being initiated into his intentions, they had quickly incurred huge debts that were promptly cancelled. To dispel the unjust suspicions, the law-giver was the first to unwrite his debtors' obligations. They amounted to a sum that would have sufficed for the construction of several ships.

Moderate in everything, Solon avoided over-turning the existing social order for fear of losing control. He made appropriate laws on a case by case basis rather than molding circumstances to fit the laws. He felt it was just not to discourage the aspirations of the rich for high positions, but he also gave equal rights to the rich of noble and non-noble descent, thus seeking to give a higher moral aspect to the desire for success. He banned the export of produce other than olive oil. He encouraged crafts and made it a law that a son was not bound to relieve his father's old age unless the father had set him up in some craft. He prosecuted the idle Athenians and granted citizen's rights to migrants from other poleis who demonstrated exquisite skills in their crafts. He changed the measurement system to expand and facilitate overseas trade. Solon was aware that with time, the leading political role of large land-owners – the Athenian aristocracy – would diminish. The grain they produced was much more expensive than imported wheat and barley. By that time, the Athenians were sailing extensively and had conquered vast markets.

True to his convictions, Solon decreed that Athenians declare their annual income in *medimnoi* – the Athenian measure for dry and liquid products. He divided them respectively into four income groups or *phylai*. The richest were the *pentakosiomedimnoi*, i.e. those who produced more than five hundred bushels of grain. Next came the *hippeis* or cavalry, for they were able to keep a horse. They were followed by the *zeugitai* who owned a team of oxen. The poorest class were the *thetes*. The representatives of each class had their place in the Athenian army, depending on their ability to arm themselves. Only the richest were entitled to be elected for a period of one year among the nine *archons* (ministers). Some of the very old were members of the influential *Areopagus* or council of the elders. From Solon onwards, the archons swore an oath to observe the laws; if they failed, they were to offer a gold statue to the god Apollo in Delphi. The thetes had the right to participate and vote in the general assembly or *Ecclesia*. It was mainly for them that Solon instituted the system of courts which quickly acquired great significance. Increasingly, these were addressed by Athenians who felt that injustice had been done to them, or by convicts who had the right to a last appeal. Solon did not rule out the passing from one class to another, thus encouraging talent, diligence and resourcefulness. Neither did he restrict marriages between members of different classes, for he believed the purpose of marriage was to give love and joy and carry offspring. Another famous law concerned inheritance. Solon gave priority to the testator's will. An Athenian who had no children was now allowed to leave his property to a non-relative.

Being aware that the demos was gaining political confidence with every passing day, Solon established *the Boule* or Council of the 400. The Boule was a permanent representative organ, much similar to modern parliaments. Each of the four *phylai* had 100 representatives in it. Thus, every respected adult Athenian had an opportunity to serve on the Boule at least once in his life. That council was in charge of topical political issues and of the strict observance of the laws.

Solon also realized that the political passivity of the empowered demos (busy with making its living) might bring to power unscrupulous and greedy individuals, or tyrants whom no one actually wanted. This is why he made it a law that was as just as it was harsh: anyone who refused to take sides in a revolution would lose all civil rights.

Solon believed in the spiritual potential of his people. He attempted to inspire into Athenians a feeling of historical destiny, pride with their equality before the law, and satisfaction with its just application. He gave his laws validity for 100 years and posted them on revolving wooden tablets in the centre of Athens. Of course, his laws met with opposition. Solon was once visited by the famous Scythian sage Anacharsis who came from a land far north, from the steppes of the Pontus (the Black Sea). He mocked his laws, comparing them to a spider's net that could only catch the poor and the weak, while the rich and the powerful tore right through it.

Those were times of fierce political struggles and Solon's contemporaries found it hard to accept their lawgiver's moderation. The rich accused him for the losses they had suffered; the poor were disappointed in their hopes of acquiring land. Solon's home was constantly besieged by Athenians who demanded interpretations of the laws. To avoid becoming the cause of violence, Solon decided to leave his country for ten years and engage in trade. Again he made a wise choice. With time, the Athenians would accept his laws and realize that he had been right. Solon's laws were the first major step in the development of Athenian democracy.

Solon lived to a very old age. As most merchants who lived a life of adversity and hardship, he is said to have been fond of the pleasures of life and fun. He travelled extensively and met with many wise statesmen. Along with Anacharsis, he was later styled as one of the Seven Wise Men of Greece. Asked if he had made the best laws he could for the Athenians, he answered: "The best they were able to take".

Solon's laws on wooden tablets were put at a central place in Athens.
Illustration by Emilian Stankev

MILTIADES THE ELDER
c. 590 – c. 520 B.C.

Portrait illustration by Hristo Hadjitanev

FACING THE THREAT of assimilation by their belligerent neighbours, some Thracian tribes sought allies to help them survive longer. One of these tribes were the Dolonci who inhabited the Thracian Chersonese (today Gallipoli Peninsula), a long narrow peninsula on the Aegean coast, by the Dardanelles. Although small in territory, this ancient strip of land was densely populated with dozens of villages, for its fertile soil bore a lot of fruit, and was the home of numerous herds and flocks. For centuries, it also served as a bridge to the Asian coast. Heavily loaded merchant ships passed by it on their way to the new colonies on the Propontis (Sea of Marmara) and the Blak Sea. For years, the Dolonci were waging a life-and-death war with the neighbouring Thracian tribe, the Apsinthians, and their situation was desperate, so they decided to send their notables to Delphi to ask the Pythia for advice. The Pythia told them to take back with them as a colonist the man who should first offer them shelter and food on their way back. They followed the Sacred Road through Phocis and Boeotia but no one offered them hospitality. Maybe because they knew that the Athenians were falling behind in the redistribution of overseas markets, or because they had heard that the Athenians were distantly related to the Thracians, or because they were about to pass through lands that were not interested in colonization, the envoys of the Dolonci turned aside and travelled to Athens.

It was evident that they were strangers in those lands. Although they were dressed in short chitons and belts like the Hellenes, their pointed hats with ear-laps and their tall fox-skin boots betrayed their origin. They also wore colourful cloaks and were armed with crescent-shaped shields and a pair of long spears, characteristic of their tribe. The day was wearing away as Miltiades, son of Cypselus, was sitting in front of his home. He came from a rich and honoured Athenian family, the Philaeas, who owned lands in the most fertile region of Attica. Philaides, descendant of the glorious Ajax, had turned over the island of Salamis to Athenian rule, and his family had been awarded great honours. Miltiades himself had recently achieved great glory at Olympia by winning the chariot race. As soon as he saw the strangers, he invited them for dinner. Seeing the prophecy come true, the Dolonci told him their story and asked him to follow the divine order. Miltiades agreed, for influentual as he was in Athens, he was starting to feel oppressed by Peisistratus' tyrannic rule (561-527 B.C.) The Dolonci arrived shortly after Peisistratus had usurped power in Athens, and just a few years before a disastrous fire reduced the oracle at Delphi to ashes (548 B.C.)

According to the tradition, Miltiades himself addressed the Pythia and having received a confirmation of the words of the Dolonci, he started looking for volunteers among the Athenians for the undertaking. He then sailed to the Thracian Chersonese and conquered it, and the notables of the Dolonci proclaimed him their tyrant, as was the Hellenic tradition. Miltiades was not related to the local kings, he had no children of his own, he was always surrounded by several hundreds of bodyguards, and was regarded with mixed feelings by some of the Dolonci.

Miltiades first erected a strong wall at the isthmus to prevent the Apsinthians from raiding and ravaging the country. Having removed this permanent threat, he proceeded to build a settlement that he named Agora where he moved his residence and the all-important hearth.

Soon Miltiades' increasing influence got him into a war with the newly-founded settlement of Lampsacus in Asia Minor, over the profitable control of the Dardanelles. Sometimes the sea currents took the merchant ships to the European coast, sometimes to the Asian coast. The two sides competed for the collection of the wharfage and the customs duties. It so happened that Miltiades ran into an ambush and was captured by the Lampsakians. The Lydian king Croesus, influential and honoured for his generous gifts to Delphi, interceded for his release. He threatened the Lampsakians that he would "destroy them like pines." After prolonged arguments, only an old man was able to explain the meaning of these words: of all trees, only the pines did not grow offshoots when they were cut down, and were thus destroyed forever. Much frightened, the Lampsakians released their noble prisoner.

Miltiades died childless, and he left his power and property to Stesagoras, son of his brother Cimon. After the death of Miltiades the Elder, the Dolonci revered him as a founder-hero and organised horse races in his honour, in which the

A Thracian peltast armed with a pair of spears and wearing a cloak, a pointed hat and boots. He holds a shield in his left hand. Red-figure vase, 4th c. B.C.
Illustration by Hristo Hadjitanev

The tholos at Delphi: a marble rotunda erected in the first half of the 4th c. B.C. It stood at the temple of Athena Pronaea, not far from the temple of Apollo. A masterpiece of the architect Theodore. Reconstruction.
Illustration by Maya Buyukliiska

In the heart of ancient Hellas, just below the southern slopes of the snow-covered Parnasus, lay a fascinating sacred gorge dedicated to the Pythian Apollo, the god with the silver bow. According to an ancient legend, it was the centre of the earth, for once the aegis-bearer Zeus sent two eagles flying, one from the east and one from the west, and they met in the sky above Delphi. For many years, the monster serpent Python, itself originating from the barren rocks, reigned in these lands. Phoebus Apollo travelled many lands and islands, looking for a place to erect a temple with an oracle where the mortals might know the will of Zeus. Finally, Phoebus "the light-bearer" reached the gorge of Delphi, killed Python with his gold arrows, founded a sanctuary, and ordered the countless surrounding tribes to erect it stone by stone, to the eternal glory of god. Soon, the shrine became universally honoured for its oracle. The revealing of fate prompted visitors to serenity and humility. To some petitioners, Phoebus prophesied by encouraging or prohibiting their intended actions; others were not even allowed into the shrine.

The road to the temple meandered up the rocky terraces of Delphi. The antechamber was inscribed with the prophecies of sages, inside the temple there was a relief image of the earth's centre and altars, and in the innermost cave, where visitors were not allowed to enter, was the famous Pythia. She sat on a high tripod over a fissure, breathing the fumes of the earth and conveying in her trance the prophecies of Apollo. These were usually in verse, more rarely in prose, and were invariably ambiguous. Overpowered by the prophetic words, the inquirers sought poets and priests to interpret their meaning. There were also scribes who put the prophecies down on wooden boards, parchment or papyrus, and these were kept in polis, royal and temple archives. From lands near and far – from all Europe, Asia, Africa and the countless islands – petitioners crowded in Delphi, bringing gifts of gold, silver and ivory, and sacrificial animals.

Lampsakians were not allowed to participate. Stesagoras continued the war with Lampsacus, and was killed insidiously with an axe.

In 516 B.C., the sons of Peisistratus sent Cimon's other son, Stesagoras' brother Miltiades the Younger to consolidate the power of Athens over the Thracian Chersonese. He married Hegesypele, daughter of the Thracian king Olorus, and there, at the crossroads between the ancient East and the West he became known as the victorious warrior who, in 490 B.C., defeated the Persians in the famous battle of Marathon.

This short episode had long-term consequences. Soon afterwards, the historians stopped mentioning the Dolonci. Facing the threat of physical destruction and complete economic ruin, the tribe had chosen obscurity and oblivion. With the approval of Delphi, the Thracian Chersonese became Athenian territory. Always a contested land, it would often be a battlefield in the wars of many tribes on the two sides of the wall erected my Miltiades the Elder. He was a sober and pragmatic ruler, prepared to accept political compromises in his own country but conservative where the foreign political interests of Athens were concerned.

PEISISTRATUS
c. 600 – 527 B.C

Portrait illustration by Hristo Hadjitanev

PEISISTRATUS' FATHER HIPPOCRATES once went to Olympia to watch the games. While he was making the customary sacrifice to Zeus, a most unusual thing happened. The cauldron with the sacrificial meat boiled up by itself, without fire, and the water spilled over. The Spartan sage and clairvoyant Chilon who happened to be present and saw the augury advised Hippocrates not to marry a woman who could bear children, or if he was already married, to send away his wife and the son she would bear him. Naturally, Hippocrates refused to follow the wise man's advice, and indeed, shortly afterwards, he had a son – the future tyrant of Athens. The boy was named Peisistratus, after the son of the famous king Nestor of the Achaean island of Pylos from where the clan of Hippocrates originated. On his mother's side, Peisistratus was also the descendent of a royal family – he was related to Codris, as his mother and the mother of Solon the lawgiver were cousins.

The legend of the miracle in Olympia is hardly credible but it did reflect the Hellenes' anxiety regarding royal descent, and their apprehension of losing their independence to the inflexible and unpredictable will of a single individual. The words of Chilon the Spartan were disturbing. Sparta had once been given an oracle that it was to liberate Athens from tyranny, and whatever was predicted at Delphi invariably came true.

Born around 600 B.C., Peisistratus grew up in the atmosphere of Solon's reforms. The legend goes that despite the difference in age, and later in political views, the two harboured feelings of respect and attachment towards each other. Indeed, Peisistratus was a good-looking young man, with pronounced talents, who commanded admiration. He sought to display justice and moderation of character, and enjoyed listening to wise people, particularly to Solon whose courage and valour he admired. In his adolescence, Peisistratus witnessed the unrest following Solon's departure. For several years, unable to understand fully and apply his wise laws, the Athenians could not reach unanimity in the election of archons, and they lived in a disastrous state of lawlessness that they called *anarchy*. Peisistratus gradually took a strong dislike to those politicians and rhetoricians who instigated continuous and reckless disturbances in the state. Meanwhile, Athens was crowded with meritless people who had profited from the unrest to acquire the rights of citizens, and got involved in the political struggles. The faction of the Plain – the large landowners – were headed by Lycurgus, son of Aristolaides. Megacles of the notorious Alcmaeonids led the faction of the Coast. Reaching adulthood, Peisistratus, who was believed to be faithful to democracy, led the discontented poorer population of the rocky regions of Attica, the Hillsmen. Solon went back to find the Athenians bristling against each other. Although he was welcomed with honours and deep respect, the elderly law-giver didn't have the energy nor the willingness to bring to reason his compatriots who were not mature enough to obey his laws.

Of all contemporary politicians, Solon was the only one who knew Peisistratus from childhood, and he was the only one to see through his dangerous intention to usurp power and become a tyrant. He often spoke to Peisistratus, telling him that if he shed his ambition for tyranny he would have no equal in excellence and merit. But no one and nothing could deter Peisistratus while everything in Athens fuelled his secret aspirations.

At that time, a man of the name of Thespis aroused universal interest and amazement in the polis by staging the first dramatic performance in Athens. Solon who, in his old age, indulged in entertainment, famously asked Thespis if he was not ashamed of lying so unscrupulously to the audience. It is only a joke, Thespis replied. "Indeed, we now enjoy and honour that but we shall soon find it in the treaties," prophesied Solon.

The beginning of red-figure vase painting in Athens.
Illustration by Emilian Stankev

Replica of a red-figure vase drawing featuring the revival of nature through Triptolemus who gave grain to humans, and the goddess Demeter with her daughter Persephone.
Illustration by Hristo Hadjitanev

Soon afterwards, Athens fought a series of battles with Megara. They brought glory to Peisistratus and an intensification of political struggles in the polis. One day Peisistratus slashed himself and, covered with blood, made a dramatic entrance into the Agora and, amidst the cries of indignation, claimed that his enemies had attempted to kill him for his political views. Solon immediately saw through this cunning act, approached Peisistratus and warned him that it was evil to play the role of the sly Odysseus and deceive the Athenians. But no one would listen to the feeble old man. The assembly which consisted mainly of poor citizens, supporters of Peisistratus, voted him the right to an armed bodyguard. Peisistratus enlisted some three hundred men armed with clubs instead of spears, and they followed him everywhere. Soon he seized the sacred Acropolis, built himself a home and started ruling over the deceived Athenians as a tyrant. Solon was the only one who dared speak up publicly, calling on the citizens not to give up their freedom. He pointed out that if several days earlier it would have been easy to nip tyranny in the bud, a veritable exploit now lay ahead: the need to eradicate and destroy it after its establishment. According to Solon's written laws, the submission to the tyrant's autocratic rule was a disgrace, for it reduced the Athenians to the Eastern monarchs' resigned and subservient subjects whom the Hellenes often described as barbarians. Left alone, Solon stood fully armed in front of his home and declared that he had done all he could. Panic-stricken Athenians passed by, leaving their homeland because they feared the revenge of Peisistratus. One of them asked Solon why he stayed in the polis and where he placed his hopes. "Old age," Solon replied.

Despite all apprehensions, ancient historians were unanimous that Peisistratus ruled in conformity with the law rather than unjustly. He not only invited Solon for an advisor in handling polis affairs but also preserved many of his laws as well, such as the archonship, and respected the authority of the Athenian courts. Moderate in everything, Peisistratus did not seek vengeance and, unlike most tyrants, did not lash out with wild and blind hatred against his political opponents. Soon even his enemies realized that he wanted power because he could no longer tolerate the disunity in Athens rather than for the benefits and honours involved. The number of his supporters grew day after day. His former enemies Megacles and Lycurgus united and managed to force him out but soon their lust for power destroyed their alliance. Megacles then sent a messenger to Peisistratus, offering him his daughter's hand as well as taking over the tyrant's power again. Peisistratus accepted and as his influence was not yet strong enough, he once more resorted to a clever stratagem. Taking advantage of an ancient custom and the rumours he had already spread, he entered the town in a chariot, with a beautiful florist slave of the name of Phia, dressed up as the goddess Athena, and used the universal elation to make himself a tyrant a second time. Seven years later, he once again left Athens because he did not want to live with the daughter of Megacles of the Alcmaeonids, or to produce offspring for her blood-stained clan. This time he spent eleven years in exile, during which he amassed considerable wealth from the silver and gold mines of Mt. Pangaeum, and gathered courageous mercenaries and political allies in Southern Thrace, Thebes, Eretria, the large island of Euboea, Thessaly, Argos, Naxos island where he installed the

Actors in the first dramatic performance in Athens rehearsing in front of Peisistratus.
Illustration by Emilian Stankev

tyrant Lygdamis, and Samos island under the tyrant Polycrates and his brothers. Having raised a mercenary army, Peisistratus landed in Attica near Marathon and triumphed in the battle against his opponents by the temple of Athena. He spared the enemy soldiers who ran away. He took those who fought him to the end as hostages to the island of Lesbos which he had already conquered, and entrusted them to the rule of his ally Lygdamus.

When Peisistratus entered Athens, the first thing he did was to disarm the people. He organised an inspection of the troops by the temple of Theseus but he deliberately spoke very quietly. Those present could not hear him well and he asked them to come closer. Meanwhile, his loyal soldiers gathered the weapons the troops had left on the ground and locked them in the nearby temple. Having completed this task, Peisistratus gave his orders: the citizens were to go back peacefully to their private affairs, and he was to take charge of public ones.

Even at that time, many years after Solon's death, Peisistratus ruled with moderation, humaneness and mercy. He was always friendly to peaceful citizens, and just and lenient to those who broke the law. He gave generous loans to the poor whose support had brought him to power, so that they might get a richer harvest from their lands. At the same time, his personal wealth grew as he collected ten per cent from the incomes of all farmers. In order to save his taxpayers' time, he instituted a system of travelling judges to provide trials of rural cases on the spot. He himself travelled around to make inspections and mete out justice. A legend goes that on one tour he met a farmer digging in a field of stones and asked what his income was. The man had never seen the tyrant and answered ingenuously and frankly: "Just so many aches and pains, and of these aches and pains Peisistratus ought to take his ten per cent". Peisistratus promptly remitted all taxes to the farmer.

The tyrant also respected the authority of the court, and often demonstrated that he was everyone else's equal in regard to the ancient laws. Once, accused unjustly of murder, he appeared before the court but his accuser dared not press the charge.

Peisistratus also took care of the disabled soldiers; he was the first one to provide them with a state allowance. He issued a law against idlers and, similar to Solon, encouraged crafts. It was under his rule that the red-figure pottery emerged; it was to become so famous that it would provide subsistence to Athenian potters for generations. Peisistratus used his influence and connections in continental Hellas and the islands, as well as along the Thracian coast, to promote Athenian export of olive oil and fine artisanal products. He introduced the uniform silver coin of the Athenian polis which became a symbol of its commercial might throughout the ancient world, with the goddess Athena stamped on the obverse and the sacred owl on the reverse.

Similar to other outstanding tyrants, Peisistratus undertook large-scale construction, giving a lesson in statesmanship to the future generations. The construction projects provided jobs to poorer Athenians for many years, and attracted foreign merchants, undertakers and artisans. Peisistratus was the first to erect a monumental temple of Athena in the Acropolis; that temple was later desecrated by the Persians. The tyrant also developed the agora where the Athenians gathered to participate in the polis institutions and discuss politics and trade. Later, his sons Hipparchus and Hippias continued the tradition, erected a temple of Zeus, and developed the central square, the port of Munychia and the nearby sanctuary of Eleusis dedicated to Demeter, Kore and Triptolemus – gods of fertility, honoured by Athenian farmers. For the first time under Peisistratus and his sons the Peisistratids, the cult processions – the Panathenaea and the Dionysia – acquired the grandeur that was to impress the Hellenes for centuries. Peisistratus introduced the practice of dramatic performances by travelling companies. Thus, the festivals dedicated to Dionysus in the surrounding agricultural lands were adopted in the fortified Athenian polis and presented to the citizens not only the ancient myths but their own history as well. Under Peisistratus, the poets Anacreon of Teos and Simonides of Ceos found hospitality in Athens. Another prominent figure of his time was Onomacritus who collected oracles and was credited with putting down in writing Homer's *Iliad* for the first time (until then, it was recited by rhapsodes).

Peisistratus ruled until old age and died of an illness in the year of the archon Philon (528/27 B.C.), exactly thirty-three years after his coming to power (he spent nineteen years as a tyrant and the rest in exile). His sons Hipparchus and Hippius were less talented and got involved in disgraceful acts. After the murder of Hipparchus, the tyranny in Athens became particularly intolerable and odious. The oracle of the Pythia was coming true. Seventeen years after the death of Peisistratus, the Spartans led by king Cleomenes defeated Hippias in battle and forced him out. Peisistratus and the Peisistratids ruled in Athens for a total of fifty years, half a century in which notables and ordinary Athenians alike lost interest in active participation in politics, and their differences were reconciled. Having established peace in the polis, Peisistratus largely used Solon's heritage and followed many of his wise instructions. His name remained in history as one of the first talented builders of the Athenian state who took control of the power-invested people and protected it from the bloody extremes of democracy, so that it might gradually develop into a conscious need and way of life. All of this he did at a time when a mortal new threat for the Hellenic world was approaching from the East with surprisingly quick strides: the newly established, powerful Persia.

For about a century and a half, the Athenians did not have a king. The aristocrats distributed the monarch's prerogatives as supreme priest, judge and commander among several archons whose powers were strictly defined and, above all, temporary. At first the archons were elected among the notables because of their merits, and held the posts for life; later, a term of ten years was established; finally, archonship was limited to one year and not a day more. The new archons took over from the old ones on the 1st of July, when the Athenian new year started, and this was written in the annals with the name of the first of the nine archons, the eponymous. A distant reflection of the royal authority was found only in the name of the second archon, the basileus who was in charge of the official sacrifices to the gods. Although the Hellenes were renowned for their love of freedom, although they were the first in human history to reject royal power in their tiny states, in times of violent turmoil and bloodshed they felt the need for a just and strong-willed ruler who might install better laws and restore harmony. Thus, in many places, for shorter of longer periods of time, the general insecurity and the endless hostility brought to power not the much-needed lawgivers but absolute rulers known as tyrants. According to the ancient philosopher Aristotle, tyranny was distorted monarchy.

CLEISTHENES
second half of the 6th c. B.C.

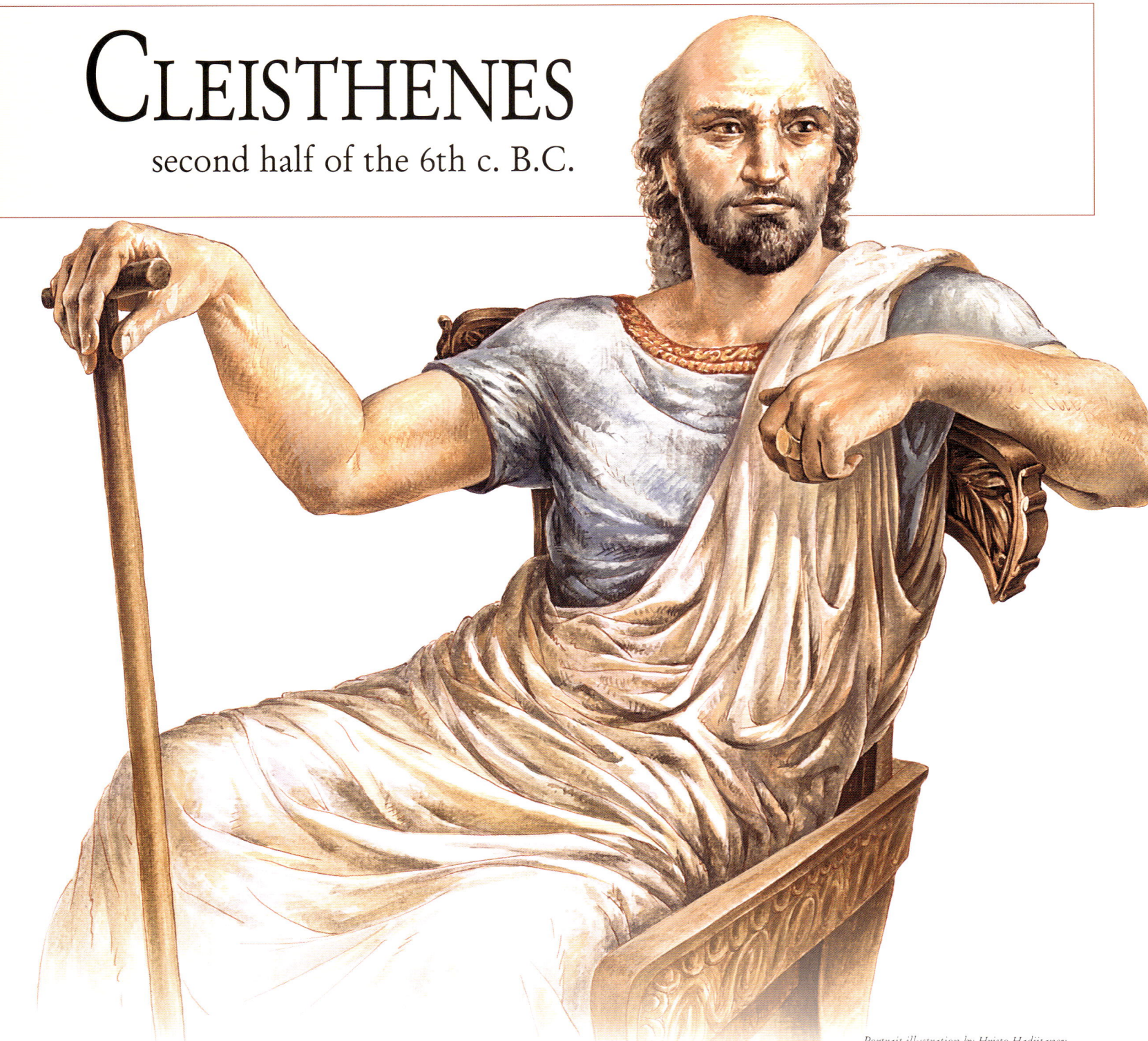

Portrait illustration by Hristo Hadjitanev

ON HIS FATHER'S SIDE, Cleisthenes was the grandson of the prominent Athenian Alcmaeon. His father was Megacles – the same Megacles who headed the struggle of the faction of the Coast against the notables of the Plain and the poor population or the Hillsmen before Peisistratus came to power. Later, Megacles offered his daughter in marriage to the tyrant but failed to achieve a lasting political unity because of the curse that had been pronounced on the Alcmaeonid clan. Although it was only a rumour that Megacles' grandfather of the same name had once participated as an archon in the bloody suppression of Cylon's attempt to seize power, that rumour was sufficient reason for most Athenians to reject the thought of having children from that clan. It was believed that the "cursed" clan was continually threatened by divine vengeance, and that was used at any occasion by political opponents of the otherwise talented statesmen of such descent. Probably this is why in 575 B.C. Megacles married Agariste of the Peloponnesian polis of Sicyon, daughter of the tyrant Cleisthenes. Their son was named Cleisthenes after his maternal grandfather of Sicyon. It is a shame that in the numerous sources from antiquity we find little information about the life of Cleisthenes, son of Megacles. We know neither when he was born, not his post, nor the date of his death. Not a famous quotation, not a single famous story, dream or oracle have been preserved. It is, indeed, a shame, for without Cleisthenes the flourishing Athens of the classical age would never have been what it was, and the Athenians would never have enjoyed the fruits of democracy under Cleisthenes' descendent Pericles. We can only judge his personality from his political acts that marked a new epoch in the Athenians' self-awareness and self-confidence, and outlined the inevitable development of the polis towards a democratic form of government. Initially, Cleisthenes followed the political views of his father who was prepared to make many compromises to avoid being forced out completely from Athenian political life. Thus, in 525 B.C. Cleisthenes accepted the archonship under the Peisistratid rule while the tyranny had not yet become so severe and onerous. At that time, every polis was like a packed boat in an infinitely rough sea that would easily overturn at any passenger's loud call for a swap of seats. No one could predict when and from where the changes would come, nor could anyone foresee their consequences. The all-out struggle for control over the polis life and politics was the only foolproof way to impose changes and get closer to the good, natural law – the one and only that was right for the Athenians. Any conscious and deliberate effort of the politicians towards democracy was out of the question, for during that age no one in Athens, Hellas or the world in general had any notion of democracy as a specific form of government. The Athenians started using the word democracy only decades later, under the democratic reformer Pericles, when the painful road of changes was a thing of the past and could be analyzed from the distance of time. Even in the context of their own struggle for power and survival, however the most talented Athenian politicians could sense that the new tendencies were better for their homeland. Only from our comfortable position far ahead in time can we describe them as democratic reformers.

It was as a leader of the demos in the last years of the Peisistratids' rule that Cleisthenes became a factor in political life. He continued the political heritage of Solon and, to a certain extent, of Peisistratus himself, as he had initially come to power with the decisive help of ordinary poor people. The three of them had a common goal: each attempted to curb the notables' privileges that generated inequality and injustice. At first, Solon's moderate laws, which held promise for the future, overestimated the power-invested but frustrated in its expectations Athenian demos. Peisistratus in his turn subjected all classes to his autocratic rule, winning peace at a moment when Solon's wise statesmanship was missing and there was no vision of the future. Only about 510 B.C., after a series of dramatic turns, did the demos reach political maturity and realize the need for a resolute leader. At that point, harmony was finally reached between the past and the future. That was when Cleisthenes came on the stage.

Cleisthenes was waiting for the right moment to come to power, and as it often happened, external influence was involved. At first Cleisthenes made an attempt to abolish tyranny and was forced to leave Athens. He then set about restoring the temple of Apollo in Delphi that had been destroyed by fire in 548 B.C. He got funding from the Spartans who, following an earlier oracle, sent an army headed by king Cleomenes to depose the tyrant in Athens. The Peisistratids had five days to pack, turn over the sacred Acropolis to the Athenians and leave the polis. The Spartans' involvement only contributed to the power of the prominent clans but their will for power was not as strong and persistent as before Peisistratus' rule. This time the notables were represented by one Isagoras, son of Tisandrus, who was believed to have been close to the tyrants, too. He was opposed by Cleisthenes, who had the demos on his side by promising it power. Isagoras was compelled to call the Spartan Cleomenes to help him drive away the "blasphemers." Cleisthenes yielded and left Athens again. Isagoras proceeded to send seven hundred families of his supporters into exile.

Counting the ostrakon votes.
Replica of a red-figure bowl, 470 B.C.
Illustration by Hristo Hadjitanev

32 RULERS OF ANCIENT EUROPE

*A chariot dedicated to the goddess Athena
for the deliverance of the polis from its numerous enemies.*
Illustration by Atanas Atanasov

Cleomenes supported the secret plan of Isagoras who proved to have no more vision that Peisistratus and was in fact far inferior to him in personal qualities. He enlisted three hundred supporters and attempted to become a tyrant. The armed Athenian people revolted and for two days besieged Isagoras and Cleomenes in the Acropolis. On the third day, Isagoras and Cleomenes retreated to Sparta, and Cleisthenes and the other exiles were called back. That was not the end of the unrest. Three new threats emerged. Attica was attacked simultaneously by the Spartans, the Euboeans and the Boeotians. All the enemies of Athens suffered defeat. The grateful Athenians dedicated a tenth of the spoils to their patron goddess, and placed a bronze chariot with four horses by the entrance to the Acropolis. Cleisthenes was given extraordinary prerogatives as a reformer and lawgiver. He was the person destined to become the true father of Athenian democracy.

The main political objective of Cleisthenes was to establish equality before the law, a principle that the Athenians called *isonomia*. Having suffered himself from the desperate disunity, he realized that most of the troubles were due to the unconsolidated nature of Attica. The hard-working farmers from the rocky hills had nothing in common with the rich landowners from the fertile plain or with the risky job of merchants, craftsmen and sailors of the coastal region. Initially, the population of Attica was divided into four phylai that were inevitably dominated by the influential nobles. Cleisthenes designed a fundamental reorganization. From the four *phylai*, he formed ten new tribes, mixing them skillfully to melt the distinctions, and allotted to each of them an equal share in the polis government. The three traditional regions he divided into thirty *demes*: ten for the fortified central part and the surrounding area, ten for the coastal region, and ten for the rocky inland. These he called *trittyes* (tribal thirds). Inland, coastal and city trittyes were appointed by lot to each tribe. The results of the lot were final and impartial, as the ancient people believed that like human fate, the lot was entirely in the hands of the gods. In order to assert the divine character of his reform, Cleisthenes addressed the Pythia, and among one hundred names of ancient heroes, she chose ten for the ten tribes. The new phylai comprised people of various backgrounds, territories and concerns. Through their participation in polis institutions, the Athenians for the first time came to think of the common good. Cleisthenes not only reorganized the population of Attica; he also transformed the awareness of the *politeia*, regardless of their self-confidence, regional, material or professional interests. Citizens were obliged to introduce themselves with the names of their demes along with their fathers' names, and that gave them a new sense of importance. The ten new phylai streamlined the entire organization of Athenian administration and political life. From the time of Cleisthenes onwards, each tribe supplied one of the ten *strategoi* who formed the general staff of the Athenian army. They were headed by the *polemarch*, an ancient post whose significance went on the decline. Each tribe also supplied ten inspectors in charge of keeping order in the city, ten market inspectors, and ten supervisors of weights and measures. Ten representatives of each tribe were in charge of the import and export of grain in Attica, and ten others controlled the regular payment of rents and the conformity of payments with the law.

Each year, the new ten phylai each appointed fifty representatives to the Council of the 500 *(Boule)*. The Boule was a standing organ that was in charge of the observance of the established laws and public norms. Its sessions were held daily except on holidays, and all topical issues were discussed there. The *bouletai* discussed the revenues and expenditures of the treasury, took care of public buildings, ports, ships and war horses, and summoned other institutions. They took turns in round-the-clock watches by phylai, each of them for 35 or 36 days (as the Athenians used the lunar calendar). The fifty representatives on duty were known as *prytanes* as they stood at the Prytaneum or the temple of the hearth. A chairman was appointed among them by lot for a single day, and no one had the right to hold that important post more than once in a year. That person held the keys to the temples where the treasures of the polis, the archives, and the state seal were kept. It is an indicative fact that Aeschylus compared the prerogatives of the chairman of the prytanes with the unconditional authority of a monarch. That was an excellent feature of the democracy introduced by Cleisthenes: instead of a single person invested with great power, he had almost every Athenian to face, at one point or another, the responsibilities of a statesman. This was an unprecedented way to keep Athenians' political awareness and public involvement alive.

Another resolute, although somewhat bizarre, initiative to assure the power of the demos is attributed to Cleisthenes: the so-called *ostracism*, a practice that seemed to be aimed at trimming the higher ears of wheat to keep level the large field of the state. The word *ostrakon* meant potsherd. At about the time of the rule of the sixth tribe, somewhere in January according to the modern calendar, proposals were made to the Boule for the banishment of those Athenians who had gained too much influence among the equal politeia and, because of their wealth or for any other reason, were perceived as a threat to the established order and as possible usurpers of power. The vote was held in the Assembly two months later. Each Athenian was to write on a potsherd the name of the person he believed ought to be ostracized. A majority of six thousand votes was required for the banishment. The ostracized had to leave Athens for ten years. Although that practice was initially introduced as a measure against would-be tyrants, it later affected many prominent Athenian statesmen whose merits aroused the suspicions of their political opponents.

This is all ancient sources say about the life and policies of Cleisthenes. Having resolutely put an end to the ancient tradition of the role of birth in politics, and having accomplished popular equality before the law through reasonable reforms, he seems to have chosen oblivion for himself. One thing is certain: as Herodotus pointed out, under and after Cleisthenes, Athens became more powerful than ever. While previously the Athenians would follow trustingly or without understanding the strong political will of lawgivers or tyrants, at the time of Cleisthenes each of them felt involved and responsible for the common good. The equality established by Cleisthenes did not deprive the Athenian politicians of their individuality but it did impose limits on their aspirations. Thanks to this, Athens avoided a lot of disastrous unrest. At that time, there was hardly a person in the Hellenic world who could foresee the impending years of disaster: the decades of wars with the Persian wave approaching from the East, the dramatic events from which Athens would rise as a phoenix from the ashes.

34 RULERS OF ANCIENT EUROPE

The Macedonians were among the younger tribes on the map of the ancient Balkans. They were not mentioned by Homer among the participants in the Trojan War (13th c. B.C.) There were many different legends about the origin of the Macedonian royal dynasty, which only increased with the kingdom's domination under Philip II and Alexander III of Macedonia. Today, very little is known about the time when the Macedonians settled between the lands of the Hellenes to the south, and the Illyrians, Paeonians and Thracians to the north. One of the legends (probably the most reliable) claims that three brothers, descendents of Temenus of Argos, fled from their country and went to Illyria. Their names were Gauanes, Aeropus and Perdiccas. As sons of Temenus, they were related to the Heracleides and to the glorious hero Heracles himself. From Illyria, they travelled to the mountainous part of the future Macedonia, and reached a village where they hired themselves out to serve the local king: one of them tended his horses, another his cows, and the youngest of the three, Perdiccas, was in charge of the king's smaller cattle. Every day, the king's wife herself baked their bread, and Perdiccas' bread always rose twice as much as the others'. Alarmed, the queen told her husband about it. He thought it was a bad omen and ordered the brothers to leave his land. They demanded their wages first. Outraged, the king pointed to a sunray that was shining through the chimney. "There are the wages you deserve," he said. The two older brothers were confused, but not Perdiccas. He kneeled, made a mark round the sunshine with his knife, and having thus "fenced" it, scooped up three handfuls and put the sunlight in his bosom. Only much later did the king realize what a precious gift he had made to Perdiccas. Before long, the exiled Temenids became masters of the Macedonian mountains, and their authority spread over the surrounding lands. Perdiccas thus became the founder of a new kingdom with a glorious future. Its first capital was in the mountains and was named Aegae because a goat showed the place where it was to be built. The ancient Macedonians' deity Karan was also depicted as a goat. Later, the Macedonian army always took with it a goat to bring them luck in battle, and the Macedonian kings traditionally wore goatskin cloaks from which gradually only the horned helmets were left. Perdiccas founded his state about 700 B.C. The first kings were good warriors who quickly subjected the royal houses of Orestis, Elimiotis, Eordaea and Lyncus.

Perdiccas scoops up the sun-lit ashes from the hearth, the symbol of the creation of the Macedonian kingdom.
Illustration by Emilian Stankev

Portrait illustration by Hristo Hadjitanev

ALEXANDER I THE PHILHELLENE

494 – 454 B.C.

IT IS A WELL-KNOWN fact that after the Trojan War many new peoples attempted to connect their origins with Heracles, the hero of heroes, the Lydians and the Moesians in Asia Minor and the Scythians from the faraway steppes north of the Black Sea among them. Similarly, the Macedonian rulers wished to boast of the fame of Heracles and his many sons. The ancient Hellenes did not acknowledge the Macedonians as related to them, nor did the Macedonians speak a language understandable to the Greeks. It contained elements of the Hellenic, the Illyrian and the Thracian languages, and reflected the country's position on a crossroads. Being neighbours to the Hellenic tribes on the north, the Macedonian rulers strongly desired to affiliate themselves with the Hellenic world, and to gain positions on the Aegean coast where all trade flowed. However, the Macedonian and the Hellenic worlds were so different that they could never merge. The Hellenes lived in poleis and enjoyed equality in political life, while the Macedonians would never think of giving up monarchy for democracy or oligarchy, not even in the hardest moments of their history. Yet, as their kingdom occupied the southernmost crossroads in the Balkans, it was to become involved in all dramatic events in Hellenic history. It was inevitable that the Hellenes and the Macedonians should draw closer with time.

The first major step in that direction were taken by Alexander, the son of Amyntas, who was descended in the seventh degree from Perdiccas the founder of Macedonia. It is no coincidence that he was named the Philhellene, i.e. "friend of the Greeks." His life and his rule embodied the fate of Macedonia, forever full of dramatic turns.

Alexander displayed the abilities and the resolve of a born statesman at an early age, while his father Amyntas was king of Macedonia. After an unsuccessful campaign against the Scythians, Darius I appointed Megabyzus as a governor of the empire's European territories. Megabyzus advanced successfully along the Aegean coast, reaching beyond the river Strymon and turning Thracians and Paeonians into obedient taxpayers to the Great King. Having thus reached the borders of Amyntas' state, Megabyzus demanded from the elderly king "land and water" for Darius. Being well aware of his helplessness against the Persian might, Amyntas complied and invited the seven noble Persian envoys to a feast. After quite some drinking, the envoys demanded Macedonian

Alexander I the Philhellene ordered the murder of the Persian envoys during a feast in their honour.
Illustration by Atanas Atanasov

women, as was the Persian custom during feasts. That was against the Macedonian ways but Amyntas again complied. He sent for female companions but the Persians started treating them in an unseemly way, as if they were masters of the Macedonian land. The young Alexander happened to be present, and he could hardly suppress his indignation and outrage. When he realized that his son had in mind something that Amyntas himself could not do without violating the rules of hospitality, the old king withdrew, leaving his guests to Alexander. Claiming that the women had to prepare for the night, he sent them out of the banquet hall and had them replaced by seven beardless young men in women's clothes, armed with swords. The heated Persian envoys were killed together with their retinue. When Megabyzus started looking for his envoys, Alexander bribed the new Persian envoy Bubares and gave him his own sister for a wife. Thus, gold drew a veil of silence over the violent death of the Persian envoys. The patriot Alexander achieved great glory from the very beginning of his political career. His deed was comparable only to the valour of the Spartans and the Athenians who, among all Hellenes, dared kill the Persian envoys who had come to demand "land and water." He reminds one of the king of the Thracian tribe Bisaltians who forbade his sons to join the campaign of Xerxes against Hellas. They disobeyed his will and he had them blinded. Alexander not only protected the interests of the Macedonian state, but he also applied for the first time the dual policy that would become characteristic of the dynasty. On the one hand, he established connections with the Persians; on the other hand, he declared himself a supporter of the Hellenic cause.

Soon Alexander succeeded his father Amyntas to the throne, just at the time when the Persians were busy suppressing the Ionian revolt in Asia Minor and their territories in Europe were out of control. The other son of Amyntas, Arrhidaeus, was installed as a ruler of the region of Elimiotis.

He submitted to the will of his brother. For the first time, Alexander had an opportunity to implement his ideas. He promptly established close connections with the Athenians who pronounced him their host and benefactor when Athenian envoys travelled to or through Macedonia. During the hard years of the Persian War when the army of Xerxes attacked the Hellenic lands, Alexander continued his dual policy. Although he paid tribute to the Persians, he followed closely the invaders' defeats on the east. Not far from the Macedonian lands, a large Persian fleet was destroyed in a violent storm off Mt. Athos. Many of the Persians were drowned in the raving sea or fell prey to predators. Still others met their death in fights with the local Thracians.

About a decade later (480 B.C.), according to his treaty with Persia, Alexander had to let the hordes of Xerxes pass through his country on their way to Hellas. Even then the Macedonian king took every opportunity to show his friendliness to the Hellenes. Once he warned his neighbours the Thessalians to abandon their weak defense positions, telling them of the impressive size of the Persian army. A year later, in 479 B.C., he was sent to Athens as an envoy for Persia to convince the Athenian population to surrender before the decisive battle at Plataea. Although in the battle itself the Macedonian army fought on the Persian side, the previous night Alexander sneaked out to the Athenian camp to encourage the Hellenes by telling them of the unfavorable omens the Persians had received at a sacrifice.

Seeking to gain as much as possible for his state from the dramatic events, the Macedonian king did not impede the withdrawal of the defeated Persians and their last military operations near the Macedonian borders. He did not impede the actions of the brilliant Athenian general Cimon, either, when he seized the Persian garrison of Aeion commanded by the adamant Persian noble Boges at the mouth of the river Strymon. When the fortress took fire, Boges threw his wife, his children, his slaves and all his gold and silver into the flames, and killed himself. The capture of that garrison was considered a great military success by the Athenians. They wanted to found a new settlement of strategic significance in the mouth of the Strymon river, but their plans met the violent opposition of the local Thracian population. Alexander watched the developments and the balance of forces with composure, and used the circumstances for the achievement of his own political ends. He interpreted the Persian withdrawal as final and took advantage of being their ally to considerably expand his territories, conquering the Thracian lands between the rivers Vardar and Strymon: Crestonia, Bisaltia and Mt. Dysorus, where the silver mines started bringing him a talent (26.5 kg) daily. For the first time in seven generations of Macedonian rulers, Alexander minted silver coins, with an image of himself on horseback, with a horned helmet and two spears, stamped on them. For the first time a Macedonian ruler claimed openly a portion of the Aegean trade, which caused his interests to conflict with the naval hegemony of Athens. The Athenians founded a powerful military and financial alliance including almost all seafaring poleis. All disobedience in that alliance was suppressed promptly by the experienced Athenian crews. Alexander witnessed the punishment of the rich island of Thassos that impeded Athens in its ambition to gain permanent positions on the Thracian coast with the rich gold and silver deposits of Mt. Pangaeum.

Alexander became a respected ruler of the subdued tribes. He even managed to temporarily suppress the continual conflicts between them. In order to preserve the fragile stability of his state and the strategic acquisitions that took his borders to the river Strymon and the ancient Royal Road on the north Aegean coast, the Macedonian king was very cautious in his foreign policy. He made a good impression on the Hellenes and quickly gained recognition. He decided to take part in the Olympic games but the organisers rejected him for not being of Hellenic origin (foreigners were not admitted to the games). The Macedonian king then claimed having his descent from Argos, took part in the games, and became a co-winner. After the end of the war with Persia, Alexander erected a golden statue to Apollo at Delphi, next to the statue the victorious Hellenes made from Persian spoils. Although it is believed that it was at the time of Alexander the Philhellene that the legend of the Temenid origin was first invented, his aspiration to share the Hellenic life and find allies and even friends among the freedom-loving Hellenes is indisputable. He gained the name of Philhellene by inviting talented Greek men of letters to his court. He entertained poets such as Pindar, Bacchylides and Simonides. As early as in the 5th century B.C., Alexander outlined the foreign policy of Macedonia from which great statesmen such as Philip II and his son Alexander would later draw inspiration.

According to some ancient sources, Alexander I died a violent death. The future held difficult years for Macedonia, years that would be marked by palace coups and rivalries.

Map of Macedonia under Alexander I the Philhellene.

THEMISTOCLES
524 – 459 B.C.

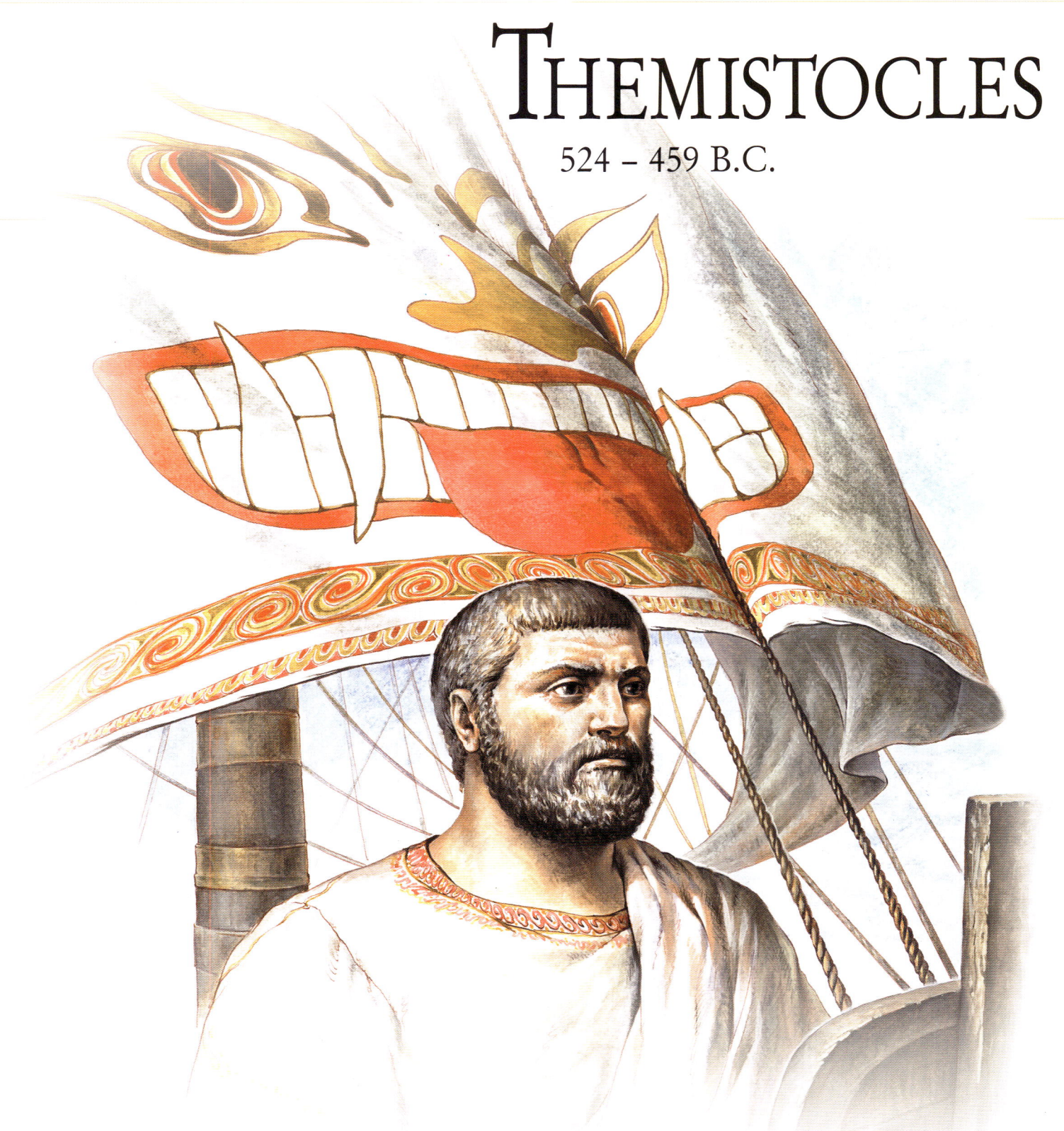

Portrait illustration by Hristo Hadjitanev

ACCORDING TO ancient sources, Themistocles' father Neocles attentively followed his son's development, and noticed early his ambition for glory and grandeur. He once decided to teach him a lesson and took him to the shore to show him the abandoned oar-powered ships. "This is how the people treat their statesmen when they become useless," he said. Nothing, however, could deter Themistocles from his chosen course. Ironically, he was the one to build and command a mighty fleet that would save his country from the disastrous invasion of the Persian king Xerxes the Great.

In fact, his father Neocles was not of illustrious birth; he was not among the eminent dignitaries of Athens. Themistocles' mother Abrotonon was a Thracian, and in those times the children of mixed marriages were not considered legitimate. They were required to exercise at the Cynosarges, a gymnasium outside the city gates. The place was dedicated to Heracles for he, too, was not a legitimate god, his mother being a mortal. The young Themistocles would not accept this tradition. He sought to induce well-born youths to go out to Cynosarges to exercise and compete with him in athletic games. This soon became a daily routine and no longer shocked anyone. With this cunning move, Themistocles removed the distinction between the "legitimate Athenians" and the "aliens." He seemed to be carrying the spirit of Heracles that encouraged him for valorous and heroic deeds.

Although possible after Cleisthenes, the career of newcomers to Athenian politics was far from smooth. They lacked education and erudition, fine manners and speech, and the carefree affluence of the aristocracy. These characteristics would continue to differentiate good statesmen from undependable ones. From an early age, Themistocles was unruly but intelligent and quick to learn. He was particularly interested in those spheres where he could display his natural talents and acquire practical knowledge and skills. Gradually, he was attracted by the philosopher and master of rhetoric Mnesiphilus, an ardent follower of Solon who created a theory of good and practical government. However, infuenced by his willful character rather than by reason, the young Themistocles often displayed unsteadiness and lack of perseverence. He did however embark on every project with much fervour and determination. His teacher once told him that he would never be mediocre; he would either make a great benefactor or a great villain.

The other Athenians regarded Themistocles with mixed feelings. When aristocrats would mock his obscure origin during feasts, Themistocles reacted furiously and rudely. Challenged to play the lute, he admitted that he, indeed, could not play but he could make a small state great. So strong was his thirst for fame and superiority that his relations with many prominent Athenians were strained. But although they mocked him, the Athenian dignitaries were increasingly aware that Themistocles was not speaking empty words, and that he did possess the qualities required to fulfil his promises. One of his earliest and major rivals was Aristides, the son of Lysimachus, a person of kind and noble character who was not seeking fame and recognition but justice and well-being for the entire polis. Odd and great was their rivalry, for although they could not be more different in disposition and way of thinking, the two statesmen would combine their efforts in the most decisive moments of Athenians' complex history.

The people liked Themistocles, for he had the amazing capability to remember the names of all Athenians, young and old alike. Besides, he was a just judge in private matters. His immense ambition was evident in all his acts: the lavish offerings, the organization of dramatic performances, the Olympic games where he attempted to outshine even the legendary rich man, Cimon, the son of Miltiades the Younger. He invited a highly respected musician to his home so that many Athenians might seek admission to it, increasing Themistocles' fame.

The most poignant description of Themistocles was made by the brilliant historian Thucydides who was born around the time of the statesman's death and was, like him, half-Thracian. "Themistocles was a man who exhibited the most indubitable signs of genius; indeed, in this particular he has a claim on our admiration quite extraordinary and unparalleled. By his own native capacity, alike unformed and unsupplemented by study, he was at once the best judge in those sudden crises which admit of little or of no deliberation, and the best prophet of the future, even to its most distant possibilities. An able theoretical expositor of all that came within the sphere of his practice, he was not without the power of passing an adequate judgment in matters in which he had no experience. He could also excellently divine the good and evil which lay in the unseen future. In conclusion, whether we consider the extent of his natural powers, or the slightness of his application, this extraordinary man must be allowed to have surpassed all others in the faculty of intuitively meeting an emergency." (*History of the Peloponnesian War*, 1.138.3)

Themistocles began his political career in the summer of 493 B.C. when the Athenian demos elected him an archon. During his year in office, he launched large-scale construction in the Athenian port of Piraeus. That was the first clear sign of his future policy. It took a lot of effort on his part to overcome Athenians' traditional attitude to the sea as a means of livelihood; that attitude was centuries-old and was deliberately encouraged by the ruling conservative aristocracy. The aristocracy wanted to exercise control over all polis affairs, and that was only possible within the set limits of the barren land of Attica, the traditional Athenian territory. Again, Themistocles managed to find a way out of this paralyzing tradition in order to carry through his innovative political ideas. He took advantage of the Athenians' opportunity to mine the silver deposits at Laurion. In ancient Greece, this precious metal was extremely rare; wealth was measured in silver, and the coins in circulation were silver, too. The deposits were not too rich but they did provide an income to the polis throughout antiquity. Before Themistocles, the income was distributed among the citizens as dividends. He was the first one to dare propose to the Assembly to use the silver for the construction of the highly mobile warships, the *triremes*, instead. The trireme had been recently invented in Corinth. It was a vessel of average size, with sails and three tiers of oarsmen, equally good for trade and warfare.

Themistocles foresaw the difficulties which lay ahead and of which few were aware. In 495 B.C. the Persians crushed the Ionian revolt in Asia Minor, and turned the population into obedient taxpayers. Being allied to the Ionians since ancient times, the Athenians supplied 20 ships to the rebels. According to the historian Herodotus who described the valour of the Hellenes against the Persian barbarians, it was the twenty Athenian warships that caused all the misfortunes for continental Hellas. Every day, the Persian punishment drew closer.

At that time in Europe, hardly any politician imagined building a fleet that could match the Persian one. The Great king of Persia had in his service the famous Phoenicians and, after the Ionian revolt, the Ionians themselves were forced to fight on his side. Among all Hellenes, they had the best naval experience, owing to their conquest of overseas territories. Themistocles foresaw that any waiting and inaction would be disastrous, and that the building of a strong fleet was a must. Athens had an income from the silver mines, and good relations with Macedonia, the source of cedar wood. Tall, straight and light, cedar was the best possible material for the ancient ships. Themistocles was one of the few who realized that the sea provided a means of living for thousands of Athenians in times of both peace and war, and without it there could be no future for Cleisthenes' democratic reforms.

On the other hand, without warships, Athens could no longer maintain its control of overseas markets. The war with the Asian giant Persia would be a matter of life and death, and the far-sighted Themistocles understood that it was inevitable, too. However, the Athenians were not yet prepared to accept this statesman's bold ideas. The Persian threat seemed to them distant, and Themistocles' opponents, mainly hereditary politicians of aristocratic descent, used that against him. They accused him of trying to deprive the courageous warriors of the spear and shield and to reduce them to oarsmen.

Unfortunately, even under Themiscotles' archonship, his worst apprehensions started to materialize. Having crushed the Hellenic revolt in Asia Minor, the Persians took their coastal and island poleis and their huge fleet and army headed for Athens to seek retribution for its support to the insurgents, and to intimidate all Hellenes in Europe. Fortunately, a formidable storm off Mt. Athos hit the Persian fleet. Thousands of Persians died, and hundreds of ships were destroyed. Two years later, in 490 B.C., the Persians launched a second naval operation against Athens, landing in Attica at Marathon. That was the first memorable encounter between the Persian and the Athenian army. Under Cimon's son Miltiades the Younger, until recently a ruler of the Thracian Chersonese, the Athenians defeated the Persians and put them to flight. Only a few of the invaders got back to their ships. The contemporary world was caught unprepared for these developments. Even the Athenians themselves were surprised. Philippides ran 42 km from the battlefield to the Agora to announce the glorious victory. The warriors of small Attica destroyed the myth of Persian invincibility. This victory complicated Themistocles' task to convince the Athenians of the reality of a future Persian threat and an inevitable battle at sea. Themistocles himself was one of the ten *strategoi* at Marathon, but during the feasts and celebrations of the victory he retired into his burning ambition, and stood aside absorbed in thought. He used to say that he could not sleep because of Miltiades' victory.

The trouble did arrive ten years later but in the meantime major changes took place in both Persia and Athens. In 486 B.C., Darius the Great, the son of Hystaspes, the great builder of the Persian State, died. His son Xerxes inherited dozens of conquered nations on a huge territory from India in the east, to the Aegean Thrace in Europe in the west, and from the Caucasus in the north, to Ethiopia in Africa in the south. Darius divided all territory into twenty-three provinces known as satrapies, governed by relatives and people close to the royal family called satraps. Incalculable and unparallelled gifts and gold poured into the royal palace in the newly-founded Persepolis. Darius also built the main roads in the empire, along which the king's envoys, merchants, and armies could travel quickly. His successor Xerxes, unlike his father, was uncertain as to the feasibility of a campaign against the Hellenes in Europe. His resolve to fight followed prolonged discussions with notable Persians and Hellenes, including Athenian supporters of tyranny. One night, Xerxes had a dream in which he was crowned with an olive twig, spreading to cover the whole earth. After that omen, the king called his army to the colours.

At about the same time, around 487 B.C., the Athenians were completely absorbed in warring with their traditional enemies of the nearby island of Aegina. Themistocles who had been following the developments with apprehension for the future, seized the moment and convinced the Athenians of the need of building warships. Time was on his side. In a span of several years, all his political opponents – Megacles, Xanthippus and Aristides - were ostracised for one reason or another. Before that Miltiades, the victor of Marathon, was sentenced to pay an enormous fine for a failed naval operation. Thus, Themistocles finally prevailed and the Laurion silver was used for building a hundred new triremes instead of being distributed as dividends. These were the warships which, under Themistocles' command, were to save the Hellenic world.

In 480 B.C., Xerxes arrived in Europe with a hundreds of thousands-strong army and a fleet of nearly a thousand warships. The Great King himself travelled on a gold chariot pulled by snow-white horses. He made such an impressive sight that the Hellenes thought Zeus himself had come to take away their land. In the face of the threat, the Athenians had to appoint a commander but no one was prepared to shoulder the responsibility for the nation's fate. Themistocles was the only one bold enough to take all risks in the forthcoming dramatic events for which he had been preparing for years. The Persian invasion hit like a natural disaster, throwing the Hellenes into panic. The Thracians, the Macedonians, and all the Hellenes from northern and central Greece

RULERS OF ANCIENT EUROPE 41

Themistocles wisely foresaw the need for a fleet to defend Athens.
The silver from the deposits at Laurion was used to pay for the construction of the triremes.
Illustration by Emilian Stankev

gave "land and water" to Xerxes, submitting unconditionally to his will. Humiliated and threatened with extinction, they opted to bow down before the Persian might. Few Hellenes, including the Peloponnesians headed by Sparta and Athens, dared think of fighting the Persians. The large southern peninsula had long been regarded as a last stronghold, although the entire Hellenic history bore witness to its vulnerability by both land and sea. Again Themistocles displayed remarkable statesmanship. He did not challenge the supreme command of Sparta, and at least temporarily stopped the never-ending conflicts and internecine wars in the face of the invasion.

The most difficult part of his plan, however, still lay ahead. He had to sell his strategy of winning the war and saving the homeland to the Athenians. He wanted the population to evacuate the city, and the women, children and old people to be sent to a safe place, leaving Athens to the Persians to sack. That was unprecedented in Athenian history. Themistocles was planning a decisive battle at sea. He had even chosen the location, the strait between Attica and the island of Salamis. There he wanted to display the uselessness of the many Persian ships, of the lavish gold jewellery of Persian warriors, of their arrogant cries and formidable war songs. The Persians were not sailors by disposition, nor could they match the Athenians in their knowledge of the sea. The long and hardly mobile Phoenician ships used by Xerxes were not suited for a battle in the Salamis strait. Although Themistocles knew well that courage was the foundation of any victory, to most Athenians the evacuation of Athens was a personal drama. Twice the Pythia at Delphi gave sinister oracles. Themistocles was the only one who was never disheartened. In the divine message, he found the hope for survival. The oracle said that "the wooden wall should never be taken." Many of the old Athenians thought the Pythia meant the old wooden wall of the sacred Acropolis, and died there in a hopeless battle against the Persian troops. Themistocles claimed that the "wooden wall" in fact meant the Athenian ships. His plan was underway, and the decisive battle was approaching.

On the eve of the battle of Salamis, the two most valorous and noble men of Athens, Themistocles and the recently recalled Aristides, made peace and swore to compete only in the services they would do to their country. At sunrise, the land and the sea shook as if the gods were boding fateful events. Xerxes was sitting on a gold throne on a nearby hill, surrounded by scribes who wrote down the developments. The battle went on all day, and ended just as Themistocles had predicted. The Persian ships were put to flight, many were sunk and their crews drowned. Defeated and apprehensive that the Hellenes might cut his way back to Persia, Xerxes left the battlefield and retreated from Europe.

The victory was no doubt due to the Athenians' courage, but the clever plan and the leadership belonged to Themistocles. He won glory and recognition not only in Athens but also in Olympia, Sparta, and all Greece. The great battles with the Persians had only just finished when he set about rebuilding Athens, which lay in ruins, and the port of Piraeus, protecting it with a strong wall. Themistocles had a large plan for establishing Athenian dominance at sea. For the first time, unfortified Sparta became suspicious. Themistocles' relations with the Spartans became even more strained after a meeting of the *Amphictiony* (Delphic council). Sparta suggested that all Hellenic poleis who had submitted to the will of Xerxes be expelled from the council. Themistocles opposed the motion as he saw in it Sparta's ambition for domination. Of hundreds of Hellenic poleis, only thirty-one had taken part in the war; moreover, the majority of them were small and insignificant. Because of Themistocles' stand, the rumour spread that he was sympathising with the Persians. It became evident that many Hellenic leaders, including Athenians, recognized the contribution of the victor of Salamis unwillingly and with illconcealed malevolence. They had him ostracized, and Themistocles had to look for a new homeland. He lived in Argos, on the island of Kerkira, with Admetus of Epirus, and in

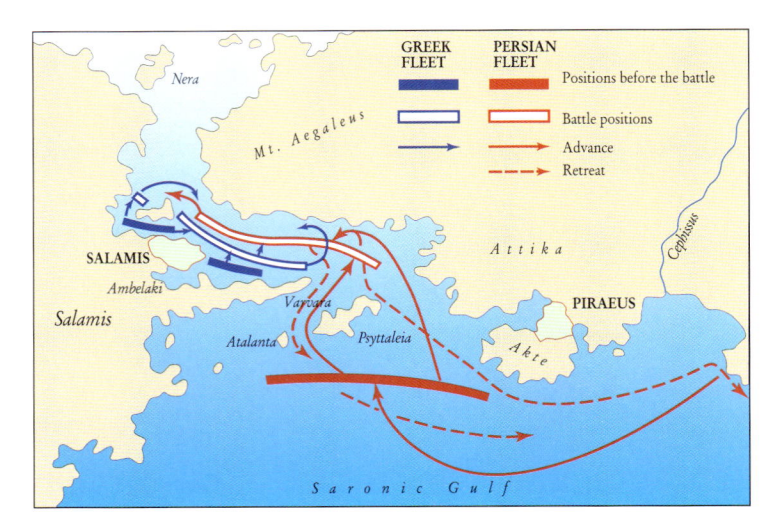

Positions of the Greek and the Persian fleet at Salamis before the battle.

Syracuse, on the island of Sicily, continually persecuted by his opponents. Surprising to all, he finally found shelter at the court of the Persian king. He soon came to wear Persian brocades, and adopted the manners and speech of the Persian notables and could even talk with the Persian king without an interpreter. He became his companion in feasts and hunts, the king's mother confided in him, and he mastered the secret knowledge of the Magi.

The prophetic words of Themistocles' father were coming true, and so was the prophecy of an Athenian who had said that they were treating Themistocles like a chestnut tree: hiding under his branches during storms and breaking them in good weather. When the Persian king asked Themistocles to help him in a new campaign against Hellas, Themistocles committed suicide, preserving the memory of his unparalleled patriotism and courage. He famously said for posterity: "Children, should we not perish, we are bound to perish."

The Persian king Xerxes watches the battle from his gold throne, surrounded by scribes.
Illustration by Rossen Toshev

PAUSANIAS
the second half of the 6th c. – 467 B.C.

Portrait illustration by Hristo Hadjitanev

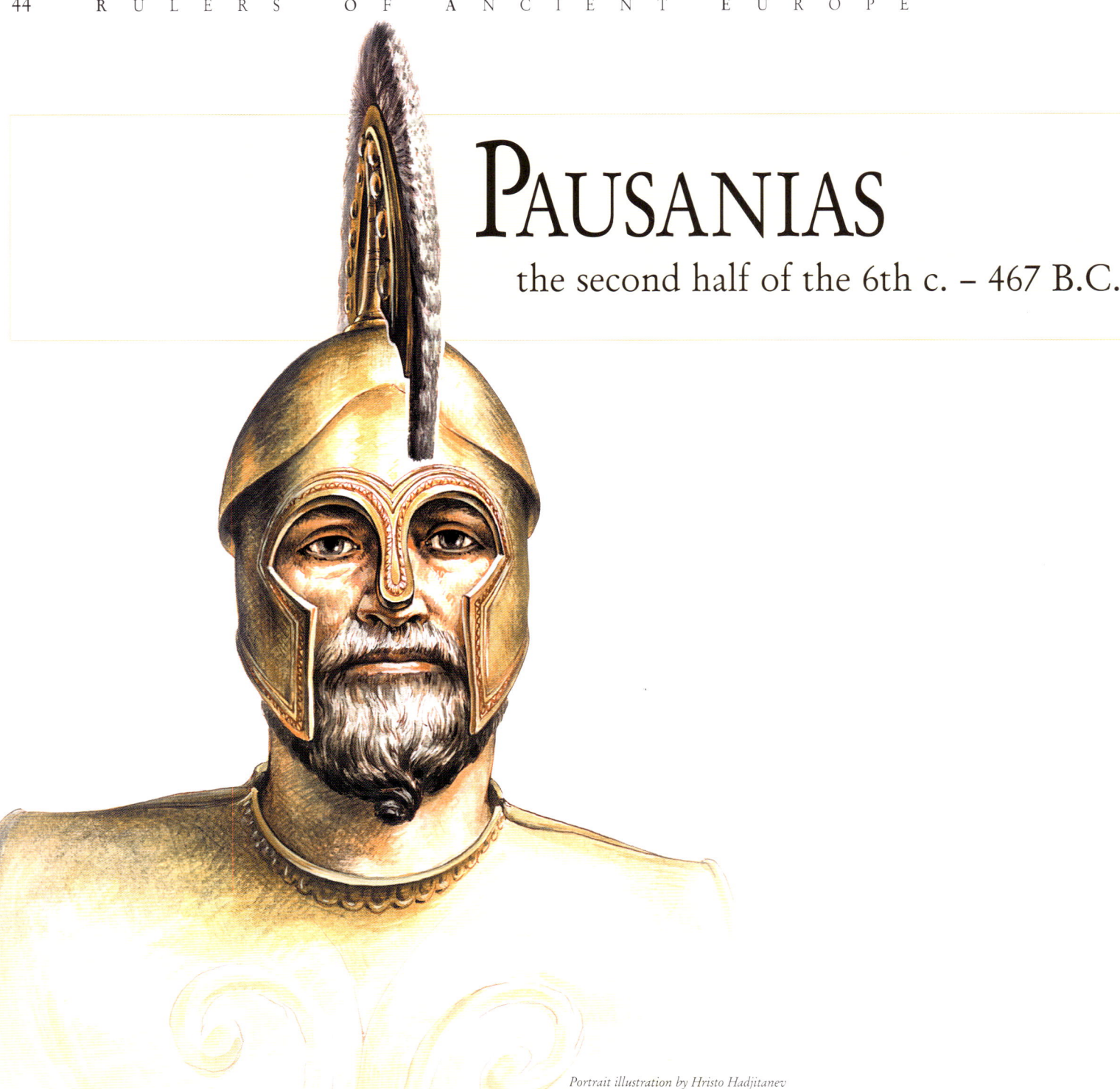

"GO TELL THE SPARTANS, stranger passing by, that here obedient to their laws we lie." This is the Epitaph to the 300 heroes who, headed by their King Leonidas, fought to the last man against Xerxes' hundreds of thousands of Persians at the strategic pass of Thermopylae which blocked the invaders' way to the heart of Hellas and the Peloponnesus. Leonidas and his elite guard could retreat and save their lives but none of them hesitated to die for the glory of their polis and the Hellenic world. The oracle Leonidas had received from Delphi, a prediction he knew well and reflected upon before the battle, came true. The oracle said that either the king of the Spartans had to die, or the barbarians would destroy Sparta. Leonidas wanted the Spartans to get all the fame, and Sparta to be remembered as grand and glorious. He also realized that when the oracle came true, all Sparta would mourn the descendent of Heracles. Indeed, King Leonidas traced his origin to the hero of the heroes. His distinguished predecessors included the lawgiver Lycurgus and King Leobotas. His father's name was Anaxandrides. He had two older brothers who, according to the Spartan law, were to become kings (basileis) but both were killed, leaving Leonidas to become king of Sparta. His younger brother Cleombrotus had a son, Pausanias. It was Pausanias, Leonidas' nephew, who a year after the battle of Thermopylae delivered a crushing blow on the last Persian forces in Hellas (479 B.C.) Unlike his uncle, however, he was not favoured by fortune; he never gained the immortality of a valorous warrior. His life was marked equally by the greatest glory and the greatest drama. This is probably one of the reasons why neither ancient historians nor biographers described his childhood and adulthood. Besides, the Spartans were not in the habit of remembering and putting into writing disgraceful stories.

After the death of the brave Leonidas at Thermopylae, his son Pleistarchus inherited the command of the Spartan army but he was still a minor and his uncle Pausanias was appointed regent. Before long, the naval battle at Salamis made Xerxes retreat, leaving his soldiers in Hellenic lands. Mardonius, the Great King's trusted councillor who had insisted on the campaign in Europe, stayed on undisturbed in the central and northern region of ancient Greece. With much silver and gold and lavish gifts (Xerxes having left him all his belongings on his way back to Asia), Mardonius attempted to dishearten the Hellenes, bribing their statesmen and instigating distrust and discord among the dozens of poleis. He found support in the vast rich plains such as Thessaly in the north and Boeotia in the heart of the Hellenic lands. They provided him with supplies and filled him with hope that his insidious plans might materialize. However, the Persian nobleman was not yet aware of the freedom-loving spirit of the Greeks. The fortresses of the Hellenic spirit were impregnable. An Athenian once dared comment that Mardonius' proposal to buy their freedom was acceptable, and the Athenian men stoned him to death in the city square, while the Athenian women killed his wife and children in the same way. At the same time, the Peloponnesian Hellenes were deeply confused. They feared that Athens might accept the Persian gold and abandon Sparta and its Peloponnesian allies to a cruel fate. This is why, under the leadership of Pausanias' father Cleombrotus, they erected a wall across the Isthmus to block the access to the Peloponnesus. The fortification with the loopholes was almost ready when a decision was made to help Athens and those Hellenes who remained faithful to their homeland and gods. Indeed, ten months after Xerxes had destroyed Athens and had set fire to the sacred Acropolis, Mardonius continued demolishing every wall, house or temple that came his way in Attica. He no longer hoped to reach an agreement with the Athenians. Besides, he heard that the allied army of the Peloponnesians was advancing against him.

Cleombrotus died soon after he returned to Sparta from the Isthmus, and his son Pausanias marched against the invaders. The two camps were set up in Boeotia, on the two banks of the river Asopus, near Plataea. The Persian army, including dozens of conquered Asian tribes, numbered about three hundred thousand men. They were joined by some Hellenes who admired Persia's Great King, believed him to be the ruler of the world, and expected a reward for their loyalty. The Persians had found particularly ardent supporters in the Thebans, the population of the very ancient main city of Boeotia. Those Hellenes who remained faithful to their ancestors and opposed the invaders, numbered only about a hundred and ten thousand men, but every day more and more forces arrived from the neighbouring regions. Upon his arrival, the Spartan king Pausanias made the traditional sacrifice. It was favourable but warn that he ought to stay in defense, without crossing the river. The sacrifices that the arrogant Mardonius made in both Greek and Persian fashion were most unfavourable. However, counting on his superior forces and looking down upon the Hellenes whom he despised, Mardonius grew increasingly nervous about the lack of development. He refused to heed to the wise words of Artabazus, son of Pharnaces, who insisted that they move the entire army close to the walls of the friendly city of Thebes. More than ten days passed, and neither of the armies dared start the battle. The Persians were anxious about the unfavourable omens, and Pausanias heeded to the oracle that advised him not to attack first. The Persian cavalry inflicted heavy losses on the Hellenic camp. Both armies were running out of supplies. Pausanias was one of the last Greek commanders to regard with respect and awe the gods and their prophecies, while preserving the ability to make quick and wise decisions. Contrary to Mardonius' expectations that the Spartans would remain true to their tradition never to leave the battlefield, in the twelfth night Pausanias led his men to a new camp where water and food were abundant. Mardonius could not resist the temptation; he thought that the Hellenes were fleeing in panic, and ordered his forces to cross the Asopus. A fierce battle began in which for the first time Hellenes fought Hellenes, and for the first time the Hellenes met face-to-face Xerxes' famous warriors. Pausanias' Spartans excelled all others, they had the hardest share of the

Battle between a Persian soldier and a Greek hoplite.
Replica of a red-figure drawing, Athens, c. 480 B.C.
Illustration by Hristo Hadjitanev

battle, and displayed an amazing bravery. Mardonius who fought on a white horse died in the battle, and so did his elite guard. Artabazus hurriedly retreated with his troops, and withdrew to the faraway Thracian Bosporus and Byzantium, at that time in Persian territory. For the first time at Plataea, Hellenes from dozens of poleis fought side by side for the liberation of their ancestors' lands. For the first time they managed to set aside their eternal quarrels. Pausanias undoubtedly possessed the talent to unite the diverse Hellenic world in the crucial moment. On that day, Mardonius paid for the death of the Spartan King Leonidas, and the oracle the Spartans had received came true. According to the ancient historian Herodotus, Pausanias' was the most glorious victory the father of history knew of.

Pausanias was not only a remarkable commander; he also knew how to be a victor. He was merciful with the few surviving Persians, and showed respect for their noble dead. There was a Hellene, a notable from Aegina, who, seeking to please him, suggested that he cut off the head of Mardonius and stick it on a pole, just as Mardonius had done with the head of King Leonidas. Pausanias replied with the dignity of a Hellene who found it unbecoming to seek such barbarian revenge. He said that the death of Leonidas and the brave warriors of Thermopylae had been avenged by the many fallen Persian warriors, and asked the alleged well-wisher to leave his tent. He ordered the heralds to announce that no one was permitted to touch the spoil, and sent slaves to bring it all together. He then set apart a tithe for Apollo, the god of Delphi, another for Zeus at Olympia, and one more for Poseidon at the Isthmus. The rest was distributed among the warriors. Pausanias himself got ten times the individual share in women, horses, carriages, camels, gold, silver, colourful fabrics and furniture.

Herodotus also tells the following story. Pausanias decided to teach Hellenes and the few surviving Persians a lesson. He ordered the bakers and the cooks to prepare a dinner such as they were accustomed to do for their lord Mardonius. He then commanded his own servants to prepare a dinner in the Laconian fashion. There was a striking difference between the two meals. The Hellenes were amazed when they saw the golden and silver couches richly covered, the tables of gold and silver and the magnificent service. Pausanias then told them: "I desired to show you the foolishness of the leader of the Medes who, with such provisions for life as you see, came here to take away from us our possessions which are so pitiful."

Pausanias became famous throughout the Hellenic lands as well as in Asia. He was benevolent to those Hellenes who had made the mistake to take Xerxes' side. For a brief moment, he felt as an all-powerful arbiter of victors and defeated alike in times of misfortune. In that, he bore much resemblance to the other leading general from the time of the Persian invasion, Themistocles of Athens, who was his friend. Moreover, these two outstanding Hellenes were to share a common unhappy lot. Pausanias' troubles started with the inscription he made on the gold tripod at Delphi, dedicated by the Hellenes from the Persian spoil at Plataea: "The Mede defeated, great Pausanias raised / This monument, that Phoebus might be praised." As soon as they heard of the couplet, the Spartans had it erased and replaced with the names of the poleis that had contributed to the victory. Pausanias' deed seemed to them deeply immoral. Shortly after the battle at Plataea, the Spartan king was sent to the Hellespont to take back Byzantium, which was still under Persian control. At that time, Pausanias was still respected by most Hellenes. However, their sympathies started to wane while he was still in Byzantium. A rumour spread that he had established connections with the Persian king and had offered him his services. When he took Byzantium, Pausanias spared the Persian king's family, and sent him a letter, proposing to marry his daughter and submit Sparta and the rest of Hellas to his power. Xerxes was delighted and sent Artabazus (the same Artabazus who had fled from Plataea) as a governor of the territory on the opposite shore. In his reply to Pausanias' letter, Xerxes wrote that Pausanias had done his family a great and memorable favour: "Let neither night or day stop you from diligently performing any of your promises to me, neither for cost of gold nor of silver let them be hindered, nor yet for number of troops, wherever it may be that their presence is needed... Boldly advance my objects and yours, as may be most for the honour and interest of us both."

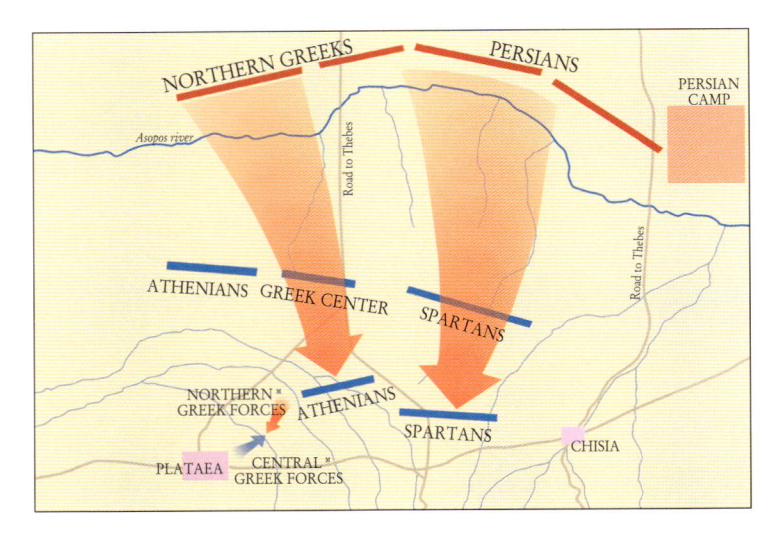

Positions of the armies before the battle at Plataea.

When Pausanias received this reply, he was filled with pride. He could no longer follow the traditional way of life. He adopted the Persian clothing, and travelled with a guard of Egyptian and Persian lancers. He ate Persian meals and was unable to disguise his intentions. He became extremely irritable, made himself hard to reach, and repulsed even his supporters. His conduct betrayed his ambition to act on a grander scale. Claiming that the Hellenes were ungrateful, he even attempted to lure Themistocles to his side while he was still in exile. Themistocles flatly refused, although he was also destined to end up at the Persian court.

As soon as they heard of Pausanias' conduct, the Spartans recalled him and accused him of treason, acquitting him in the end. Pausanias returned to Byzantium but was driven away by Cimon of Athens, the son of the victor of Marathon Miltiades. This time, the Spartans no longer hesitated. The *ephors* – the officers whose prestige was eroded by Pausanias' behaviour – sent him a messenger with the order to go back to Sparta with him. Facing the threat of being declared an enemy of Sparta, Pausanias thought he would be able to buy himself an acquittal. In Sparta the ephors sent him to prison, as they were entitled to do even to kings. Although Pausanias was later released, a former good friend fooled and betrayed him, providing to the ephors evidence of Pausanias' guilt. To avoid capture, Pausanias took refuge in the nearby temple of Athena. The ephors walled the sanctuary and starved him to death. The former glorious victor of Plataea came out of the temple only to expire in the arms of his accusers. At first they thought of throwing him into the chasm – as was the fate of all criminals – but then decided to bury him nearby. The god of Delphi through the Pythia accused them of sacrilege. As redemption for the death of Pausanias, the Spartans dedicated two copper statues at Delphi.

Like Themistocles, Pausanias will be remembered as a tragic character. Both were valorous leaders of the Hellenes in the most crucial moments of the history of Athens, Sparta and all Hellas. Their victories over the mighty Persian empire brought them fame and power for which they were unprepared. Having realized before his contemporaries that the defeated Persians would remain unrivalled in their ability to accumulate wealth, and would continue to instigate conflicts among the disunited Hellenes, Pausanias was ahead of his times even more than Themistocles was. He foresaw the future in which the Hellenes would need the unifying power of a strong monarch to resist Persia. Although he was a king, Pausanias was subjected to the Spartan law created by Lycurgus that gave him very limited prerogatives, and curbed his increasing self-confidence as a victor over the Great King. Aristotle wrote that the Spartans blamed his king for having failed to rule over his own state while aspiring to rule over the neighbours. While he fought, he attained glory, but power was his undoing. Like steel, he lost his toughness in times of peace. For that, however, Aristotle blamed the lawgiver who had not cultivated the ability to live in peace.

Pausanias' Spartans fought valiantly and contributed most to the victory at Plataea.
Illustration by Hristo Hadjitanev

PERICLES
c. 490 – 429 B.C.

Portrait illustration by Hristo Hadjitanev

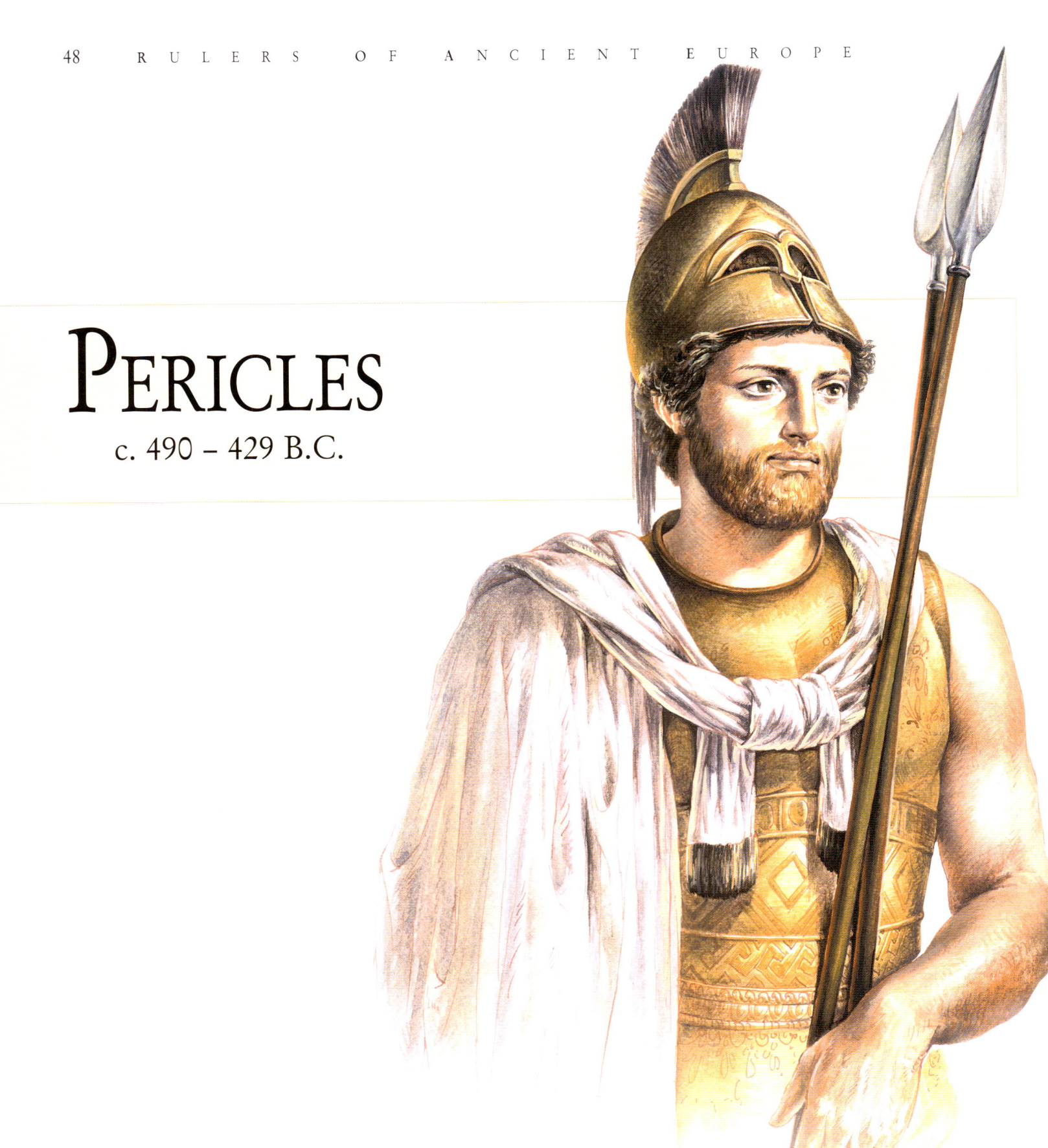

THE TALENTED ATHENIAN STATESMAN PERICLES was born around the time of the glorious battle of Marathon in which the Athenians with supreme effort and courage defeated on their own soil the army of the Persian King Darius the Great, son of Hystaspes. They were the first among the Hellenes to overcome their dread at the very mention of the word "Persians," or at the sight of the richly dressed, haughty Persian warriors. The battle at Marathon was to have a powerful reverberation. For the first time in history, the Persians had succeeded in establishing military control over the lands of centuries-old Eastern civilizations, from India to Asia Minor, from the Caucasus and the Caspian Sea to Egypt, and uniting them into a state. Crucial times were lying ahead – times of the inevitable choice between freedom and the humiliating subordination to Asia.

The decisive battles of the Greko-Persian War (480/79 B.C.) still lay ahead, as did the prolonged period of clearing the Balkan shores of Persian garrisons, and the Aegean of the Great King's heavy battleships (until 449 B.C.). These interconnected events of land and seas, in which Athens was the Persians' main target and the seafaring Hellenes' last and only hope, concentrated a mass of historical energy in this area.

The Marathon Generation – those born after the victory at Marathon – were called to crown the centuries-old Hellenic civilization and elevate Athens as its classical example.

Both of Pericles' parents came from families of Athenian notables. His father Xanthippus was victorious in the battle at Mycale (479 B.C.), the last of the Greko-Persian war at the time of the invasion. His mother Agariste was the niece of Cleisthenes, a talented and determined reformer who consolidated democracy, and eliminated any prerequisites for the formation of future tyrants. To the Athenians' tribal memory, his laws added a lasting involvement in the life of the polis. It is no coincidence that to the end of his life Pericles would combine the qualities of a warrior and a general with those of a statesman of insight and daring. One legend claims that a few days before Pericles was born, his mother dreamed she bore a lion. The child had no physical defects, only his head was elongated and disproportionally large; this is why sculptors always depicted him wearing a helmet.

Pericles studied music with the Sophist Damon, mastered the teaching of Zeno of Elea as well as Zeno's rhetorical skills, but all his life he admired Anaxagoras of the faraway Clazomenae. In his teaching about the structure of the universe, Anaxagoras introduced the principle of primordial, pure and universal reason, and although he shunned the noisy and bustling polis life, he taught Pericles early to seek reason in every public affair, and the explanation of every earthly or celestial phenomenon.

Thus, with the years Pericles came to combine in one person remarkable qualities of the mind, soul and bearing: breadth and nobility of thought, disregard for popular superstition, a serious expression, a poised gait, and modesty in apparel and gesture. His voice was pleasant, and his verbal expression light and lively. For these qualities, the Athenians called him "the Olympian." Pericles' power of speech was so impressive that he was comparable to the thunderer Zeus in defeating his opponents. One thing was clear: Athens had acquired not only a brilliant orator but also a statesman of profound insight and bold ideas for his country.

Many of the Athenian elders followed his progress with awe and apprehension. On his mother's side, as a descendent of the famous Alcmaeon, the young Pericles had inherited considerable wealth. However, the Alcmaeonid lineage bore a heavy burden of guilt: the murder of the rebel Cylon and his followers by the altars to the gods a century and a half earlier. This was believed to be a sacrilegious act.

Pericles had to make his political choice in difficult times. The aristocratic circles from which he came had just been divested of power through the resolute and extreme actions of the democrat Ephialtes (462/61 B.C.). Nonetheless, the best Athenian generals were still of aristocratic origin. By an unwritten rule, all major democratic reformers also came from the aristocracy. Simultaneously, the Athenian people, finding themselves empowered, became – as the philosopher Plato put it – intoxicated with freedom as if by undiluted wine and were particularly sensitive and fickle in mood. The young Pericles justifiably feared his people's rage and was very cautious.

Pericles' predecessor and relative Cleisthenes himself had placed in the people's hands a powerful weapon: ostracism.

Absorbed by the problems of these hard times, with a strong tribal memory of Athenians' deep-rooted traditions, Pericles used his power of foresight and made the right choice, taking the side of the people, the non-notables and the poor. He engaged enthusiastically in politics at an opportune moment: after prominent politicians had died in the Greko-Persian War, Themistocles had been sent into exile, and Cimon was winning battles far from Athens.

By that time Pericles, almost 30, not only knew and took into account but could also foresee the Athenians' predilections. He was well aware that the people could not remain without a leader, and that hard times inevitably called for strong personalities. The significant powers Athenians enjoyed under their laws, and their increasing self-confidence in the Athens-headed Delian League against Persia, could match only Pericles' boundless energy and political will in seeking to implement his ideas. He was the only one capable of taking the helm of a democratic nation and of controling its spontaneous passions with the tools of hope and fear. His biographer Plutarch wrote that Pericles tuned his speech like a musical instrument and was able to inspire his audience with certainty and confidence. He was trustworthy even in the eyes of his political opponents because of his selflessness and incorruptibility. During his long political career, Pericles avoided attending feasts in friends' and relatives' homes, and surfeiting the people with his continual presence, but his strong will inevitably achieved its ends through hand-picked orators.

Before concentrating the entire political power in his hands, Pericles won the Athenians' hearts not only with his courage in battle, but also with insightful ideas that came at the right moment and were implemented with resolution. To start with, he defeated his main opponent, the influential and very rich Cimon, and soon had him ostracised. Cimon had been spending his personal wealth generously to appease the poor Athenians, organising feasts and opening his gardens for them to taste fruit. These charitable acts won him votes in elections, but they did not make the people of Athens richer, nor did they help them exercise their powers more efficiently.

Herodotus reads his History to Hellenic men of letters of Pericles' entourage. Illustration by Emilian Stankev

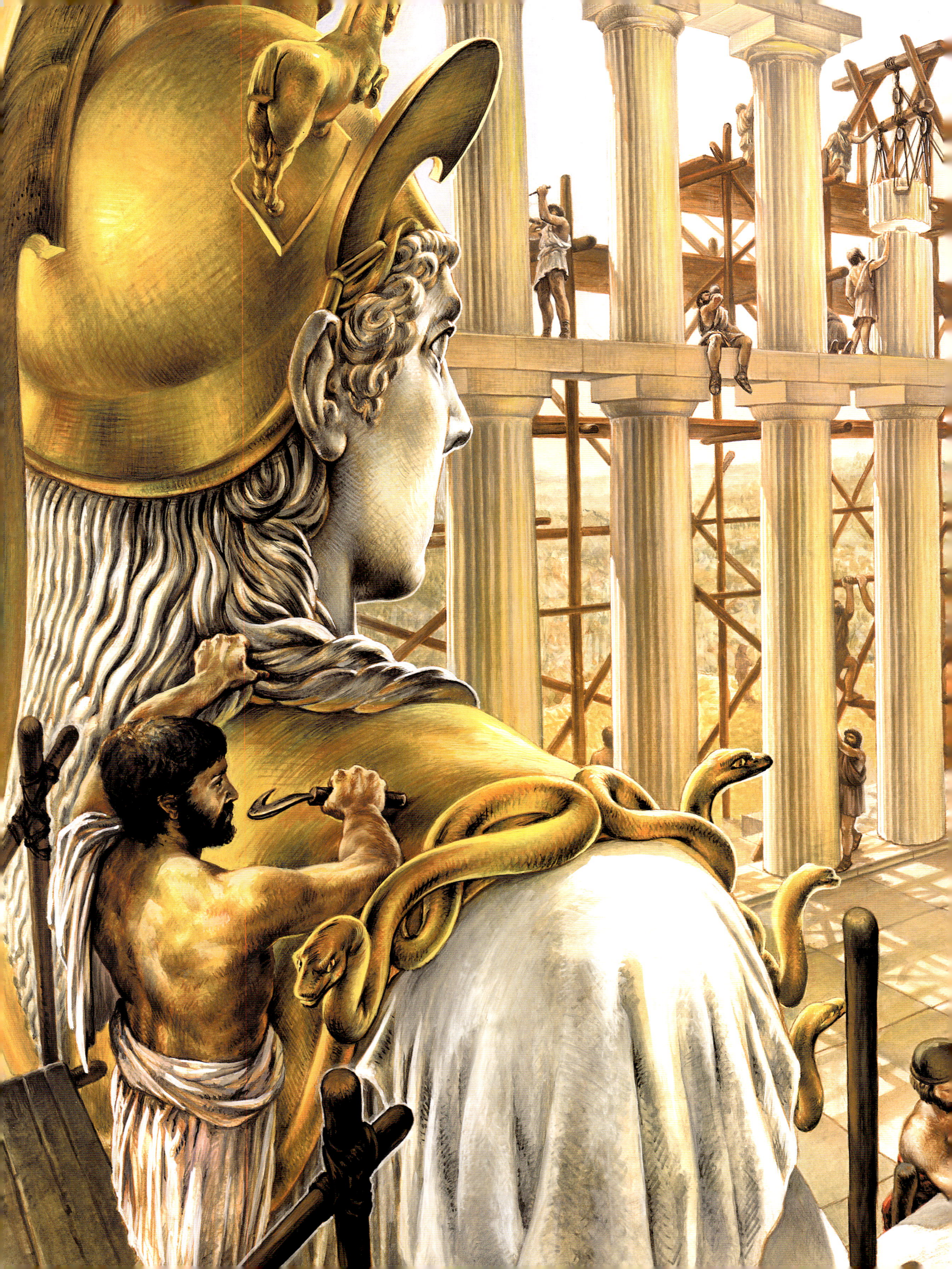

The building of the Parthenon

The main temple at the Acropolis, the temple to Athena Parthenos, was built in 447-438 B.C. by the architects Ictinus and Callicrates and the sculptor Phidias. In the main hall stood the statue of Athena Parthenos by Phidias. In her right hand she held Nike, the goddess of victory, and in her left hand a shield 5 metres in diametre, with images of the Greeks' battles with the Amazons. The statue's face and arms were made of ivory, and the clothes and weapons of wood covered with a thin sheet of gold. The reliefs and the sculptural compositions on the frieze and the pediments were created by Phidias and his disciples Alcamenes, Agoracritus, and Callimachus.

Illustration by Hristo Hadjitanev

Pericles introduced an entirely new practice in human history: the state started paying the Athenians for their participation in the organs of democratic government. Until then, as everywhere in the ancient world, the participation in politics in Athens carried no direct material benefits and was desirable only for the related prestige and eminence. Now even poor Athenians had real access to politics, and could forget the problem of how to make ends meet; thus, they were more willing to abandon temporarily their fields and gardens. This resulted in a higher interest and involvement in public affairs. Pericles harmonized the democratic system in Athens, a goal that previous reformers' laws had never attained. Democracy flourished as never before. In the everyday political parlance, the word "democracy" acquired its full meaning. Social justice and political equality proved possible under Pericles. Naturally, his undertaking was difficult and risky, and he was quick to face furious opposition. His conflict with Cimon divided the Athenians into two camps. The aristocrats were waiting for the opportune moment to take the offensive, although they had no one to match Pericles in abilities. Pericles' contemporary Thucydides, the outstanding historian of that period, wrote that Athens was "in name a democracy but, in fact, governed by its first man."

Pericles was well aware that while the mighty Persian state was their neighbour to the East, not only the Athenians but all disunited Hellenes were faced with a mortal danger. In this he was far superior to orators' petty political concerns, and greatly excelled previous leaders' capabilities. He started considering the transformation of the Delian League, a union including over two hundred island and coastal poleis that stored their tributes and held their meetings on the sacred small rocky island of Delos, into a monolithic Athenian maritime state.

This bold and dashing political plan, however, went against the historical memory, the self-confidence, the deeply-rooted local patriotism and the narrow-mindedness of most of the League's members. Some protested openly, the less courageous fretted secretly, still others envied the advance of Athens. Pericles and his few farsighted followers had to take the whole responsibility for this spectacular upsurge and for the risks of its uncontrollable consequences. From then on, many would regard Athens as a self-imposed unifier and leader – in a word, a tyrant. Thus, Pericles gradually usurped power while extending at the same time the people's prerogatives. This is why no one dared to attempt to ostracise him.

Pericles was aware that for decades the majority of Athenians had been making their living from the sea – from war and trade, as fertile land in Attica was scarce. The creation of a vast and stable market, of permanent crews and coastal garrisons in the lands of the League would take the unemployed off the streets of Athens and provide them with decent jobs. In 454, at Pericles' initiative, the tributes of the League were moved from Delos to the Acropolis in Athens under the pretext that the Persians were planning a new invasion of Hellas. From then on, the Athenians controlled the funds, the tribute continued to be paid annually, and its size was determined by the allies' loyalty to Athens. Administrators were sent to other League members to follow the tribute's collection, and Athenian villages with military garrisons were founded in rebellious lands. During Pericles' rule, some 10,000 warriors were thus provided with land. The Athenian people voted a law that Athenian parentage on both sides was required for a person to be an Athenian citizen. Thus, Pericles secured the subsistence of the now thickly populated polis.

In 449 B.C., after a series of naval victories of Athens and its allies, the Persians agreed to sign a peace treaty – the Peace of Callias, named after the Athenian diplomat who negotiated it. The peace was a triumph for all Hellenes – their compatriots in Asia Minor no longer had to pay tribute to the Persians. The Aegean Sea became a zone of peaceful trade. Soon afterwards, at Pericles' suggestion, 20 heralds carried the message that a congress of all Hellenes, regardless of where they came from – Europe or Asia, large or small settlements – was to be convened in Athens to discuss the damages of the war, the reconstruction of burnt temples, the safety of seafaring and the joint actions for the defence of all Hellas. The congress failed, mainly because of the proud Spartans. However, it was Pericles' ambitious plan that remained in history. He was decades ahead of his time, exhibiting ideas of the following epoch. The plan's failure was just another sad proof that the desired unity would always be hindered by the inevitable and increasing disunity of the Hellenes. Partial unity was possible only for brief periods, and achievable only by coercion. Although flourishing at that moment, Athens was not strong enough to shoulder all on its own the mission of the unifier.

Pericles proved to be a cautious and talented general. He won nine major victories in his life. He praised self-sacrifice and claimed that those who died for the freedom of their land became immortal and god-like. He was particularly efficient in suppressing the rebellious allies on the island of Euboea and on the rich island of Samos which fell after a heavy nine-month siege. Contemporaries compared it with the siege of Troy.

Pericles also strengthened Athens' positions at the strategic Hellespont strait (today's Dardanelles), and took an impressive fleet to the Pontus (today's Black Sea) to demonstrate his military might. Many people thought that with a leader like that the Athenians might overbear the other maritime powers in the Mediterranean: Syracuse on the island of Sicily, Etruria and Carthage. It was no coincidence that in the last fifteen years of his life, Pericles was invariably the strategical chief – a sign that Athenians trusted him to govern them.

During that time, the sound of battle was distant to the Athenians. Peace had reigned in the polis for almost half a century (479 – 431 B.C.) With the passing years, Athens became an attractive place for various talented men. Protagoras of Abdera, a Sophist and a contemporary of Pericles, expressed the unique atmosphere in the city in a single sentence: "Man is the measure of all things"

Pericles was aware of Athenians' innate taste for elegance combined with simplicity. He used the funds of the Delian League to embark on a large-scale construction project, designed to match the power and influence of his state. An unprecedented bustle began in Athens. As Plutarch wrote, where there was stone, copper and ivory, gold, ebony and cypress, where there were craftsmen with a mass of apprentices to work these materials, where there were people engaged in their transportation and delivery by sea or by land – from sailors and large merchants to road builders and ore-miners – there would be wealth to all ages and trades.

Almost the entire work of organising the construction and providing materials, as well as decoration with friezes, sculptures and paintings were shouldered by Phidias, Pericles' close friend and a talented sculptor. In about five years, Mnesicles erected the official entrance to the Acropolis, the Propylaea. The main temple of Athena Parthenos ("Athena the Virgin"), the Parthenon, was designed by the architects Callicrates and Ictinus. It was in that temple that Phidias made a twelve-metre statue of the goddess in gold and ivory. On her shield, he depicted Pericles in battle with the mythical Amazons, and himself as a bald old man, throwing stones on the enemies. In front of the Parthenon, on the way into the Acropolis, stood a colossal statue of Athena Promachos, ready for battle. Another interesting building was the Odeon, erected under Pericles' instructions and resembling in shape the Persian king's wartime tent. There, he initiated musical contests in singing and playing the flute and the kithara. To be able to enjoy the magnificent performances, the Athenians were allotted "theater money" from the treasury. Pericles was also

Under Pericles, an unprecedented bustle was observed at the Athenian seaports of Piraeus and Munychia. Hellenic merchants crowded there, bringing all sorts of rare and expensive building and sculptural materials and decorations.
Illustration by Emilian Stankev

considering stronger fortifications for the increasingly wealthy Athenians.

All these were not just buildings. Indeed, they were immense, but their size was not overbearing; instead, they inspired admiration with their unique beauty and sense of proportion. Even in architecture, Pericles seemed to leave a trace of his ambition to unite the Hellenes under the supremacy of Athens. The stern Doric order of the Propylaea and the Parthenon was skillfully combined with the harmonious proportions, the spaciousness, and the elegance of the Ionic order.

That period of Athenian history was remarkable for the tragedies of Sophocles – an important part of the world's literary heritage – the works of the "father of history" Herodotus of Halicarnassus, and Thucydides, the most talented ancient historian. It was home to the architect Chipodamus of Miletus who designed the straight streets crossing at right angles, and to the philosopher Socrates, credited by many with perfection for his nobleness and wisdom. Pericles' faithful supporter throughout his hard career was his second wife Aspasia of Miletus in Asia Minor. Contemporaries compared her with the goddess Hera just as Pericles was likened to Zeus. As the daily life of Athens became spiritually more and more intense, it became a sort of a capital of all Hellas, and a focus of admiring, curious, and anxious observers.

In a brief span of time, Pericles made the advantages of democracy visible, and left behind monuments of eternal value. The Athenians' supremacy could be felt in their pride. The democratic rule was introduced in many other poleis – either by force of the general political trends, or under pressure from Athens.

Many of the allies, as well as some Athenians, watched the growing splendour of the coastal capital with mixed feelings. The allies accused Pericles of spending common funds on Athens alone; Athenians accused him of spending too lavishly instead of promoting his people's well-being. To the former, Pericles answered that for decades Athens had been paying for these funds with ships, crews, cavalry and the lives of its warriors in the battles against the common enemy. To his own people he declared that he was willing to pay for the whole construction activity from his personal assets but in that case he would put down his name as a donor everywhere. The Athenians then yielded and took their leader's side.

During the years of Athens' grandeur, the aristocrats' political spite towards Pericles and the jealousy of the empowered people who had long become simple executors of the leader's brilliant and incontestable projects were somewhat muted. With the approach of the Peloponnesian War (431 – 404 B.C.), however, things suddenly took a different turn. Sparta and its Doric allies from Peloponnesus were terrified by the increasing might and influence of the Athenians. Pericles' enemies in Athens had nothing to accuse him of openly, and he was still popular with the people. This is why they attacked his closest circle. Phidias was charged with stealing gold from the statue of the goddess Athena. Convicted by his people, he died in prison. Aspasia was charged with impiety and Pericles with great difficulty saved her from a disgraceful trial. Even one of Pericles' sons, Xanthippus, turned against him.

Pericles had to put up a firm and resolute stand that was to the benefit of all Athenians but few understood him. He was unjustly likened to Peisistratus and his friends to the Peisistratids. All his life, however, Pericles had obeyed the laws. He suffered quietly and humbly the humiliations and the hatred. He took the caustic insinuations and the open offenses of comedians and mimes with innate dignity and tolerance. Pericles was no tyrant or usurper of power but a wise statesman. The grandeur to which he raised Athens would protect it in the future from the aspirations of self-styled or influential monarchs. Athens would always command the respect of the outside world, and its democratic system was consolidated for centuries to come.

The inevitable war between Sparta and Athens and their allies finally began. Pericles insisted that the Athenians ought to preserve their dignity, shoulder the burden of their

The Erechtheum: a temple erected in the place where the contest between Athena and Poseidon took place. The city's most ancient treasures were kept there, including a statue of Athena.

The sacred olive tree of Athena

RECONSTRUCTION OF THE ACROPOLIS
Illustration by Atanas Atanasov

leadership and not avoid the war but take advantage of the sea and their markets in Hellas, Macedonia, Thrace, and Scythia. In response to his call, the population of Attica started crowding into Athens. They had no homes in the stronghold and usually lived in their fields. In Athens, they spent the nights with relatives, friends or casual acquaintances, in the streets and temples and even in places believed to be cursed. Very soon, an epidemic of typhoid broke out, taking the lives of thousands of Athenians. Athough Pericles' first battles were successful, the Athenians became discouraged and began to lose confidence. When the Athenians realized they could no longer do without him, in the early autumn of 429 Pericles himself fell victim to the epidemic.

Although even today the history of Pericles is divergent and even conflicting, one thing is certain. The ripest fruits of the Hellenic civilization grew in Pericles' Athens. And the words of Pericles from one of his speeches came true: "I dare say that to Hellas, our entire polis is like a school."

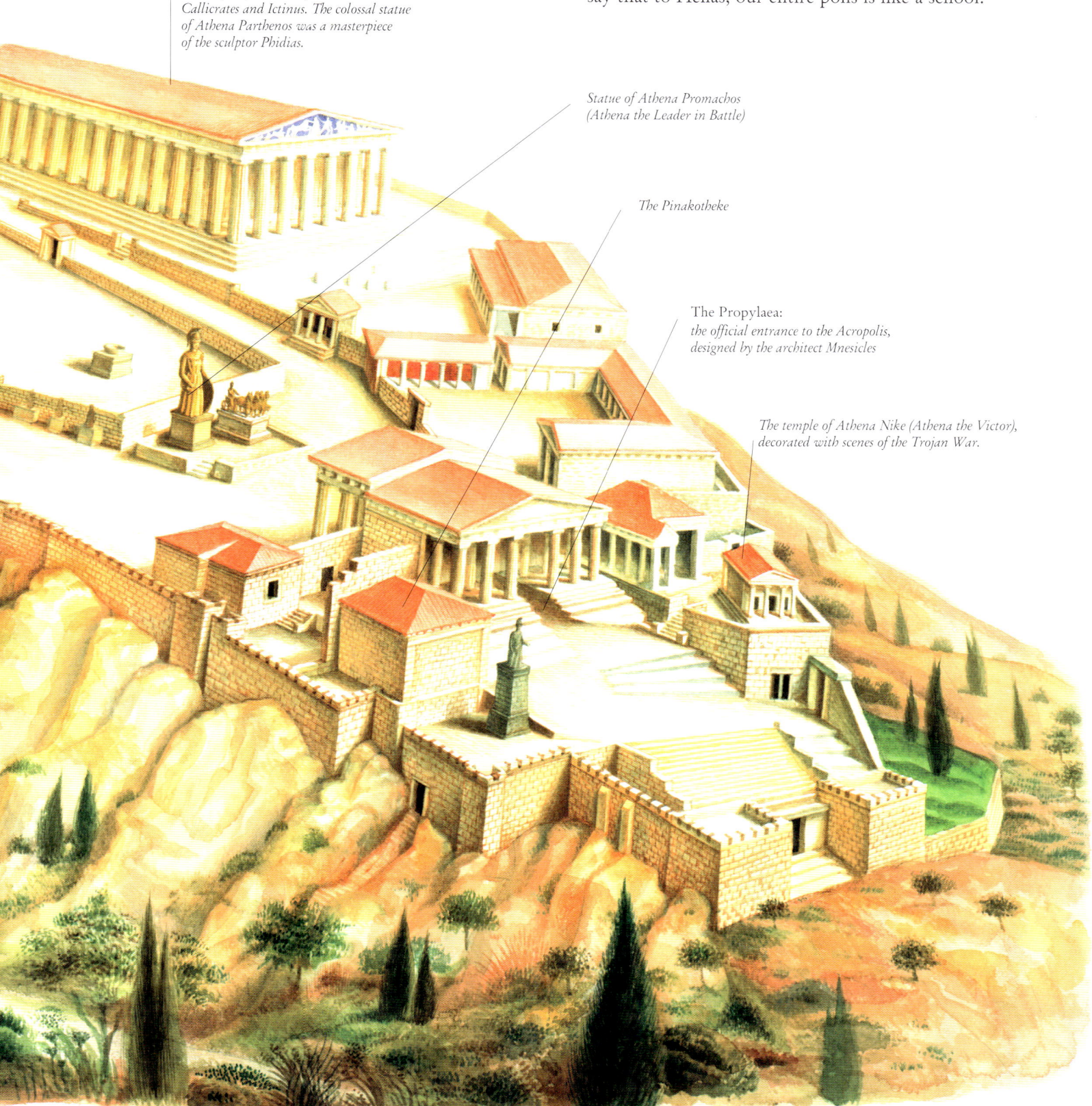

The Parthenon:
the temple of Athena by the architects Callicrates and Ictinus. The colossal statue of Athena Parthenos was a masterpiece of the sculptor Phidias.

Statue of Athena Promachos (Athena the Leader in Battle)

The Pinakotheke

The Propylaea:
the official entrance to the Acropolis, designed by the architect Mnesicles

The temple of Athena Nike (Athena the Victor), decorated with scenes of the Trojan War.

SITALCES
c. 445 – 424 B.C.

Portrait illustration by Hristo Hadjitanev

THE ODRYSAE were one of the many ancient Thracian tribes in Europe. They initially settled in the fertile valleys of the rivers Hebros (Maritsa) and Tondzos (Toundja), from the upper reaches of these rivers to their confluence with the swift-running Artesk (Arda), flowing from the Rhodopes. Nestled between Haemus (the Balkan range), its folds towering above the plains all the way to the sea and to the Rhodopes, that ancient land had always yielded plentiful wheat, barley, hemp and grapes, and had provided rich pastures for the vast Thracian flocks. Even Homer and later Hellenic poets praised the Thracian plains and the magnificent Thracian horses.

Today, no one knows by who the Odrysian state was founded or when. The first Hellenic historian Herodotus wrote that the Thracians were the second most populous people after that of India, and were named after the regions they inhabited, but as they were disunited, they never really acquired much power. This is why the ancient history of the Odrysae was obscure until their brave warriors conquered a few neighbouring tribes and attracted the attention of the inquisitive travelling Hellenes. Unlike the Hellenes, the Thracians were not in the habit of keeping records of the events in historical or epic works. The Athenian historian Thucydides who was of Thracian descent on his father's side was the first one to write competently about the Odrysian state, with knowledge and understanding. According to him, the first powerful Odrysian king's name was Teres. Teres lived ninety-two years, most of which passed in wars, for he said that when he stood idle instead of warring, he was not much different from his own stable-men. Teres was the first to expand the Odrysian state beyond the ethnic Odrysian territories, taking advantage of the military successes of the Persian King Darius I in eastern Thrace and of his son Xerxes in Hellas, and conquering the small Thracian tribes all the way to the Bosporus, reaching the Hellenic city of Byzantium. To the north, he conquered the mighty tribe of the Getae, and extended his state to the mouth of the Danube. His border thus reached the Scythian state, and to strengthen it, he gave his own daughter as a wife to the Scythian king. Octamasades, the future Scythian ruler, was born from that marriage.

Teres' power was not inherited, and was not characteristic of his early rule. He achieved his military successes in the last 30 – 35 years of his life. Teres died around 445 B.C. He had three sons. The oldest was Sparadocus, followed by Sitalces, and the name of the third is unknown. For some reason, Teres chose Sitalces for his successor to the throne – maybe because Sitalces was born in the years of his glory, when he established his dominance over the Thracian tribes and consolidated his throne. Sitalces' coming to power was not without turbulence in the royal family. Teres' youngest son felt neglected and fled to his relative Octamasades' court. At the same time, somebody named Scyles sought refuge from Octamasades at Sitalces' court. When the two armies faced each other on the banks of the Danube, the Odrysian and the Scythian kings exchanged the refugees. Octamasades beheaded the traitor Scyles on the spot, while Sitalces acted as a noble and wise statesman, sparing his brother's life. Sitalces was also kind to his brother Sparadocus who spent years fighting with the Paeonian tribes in the valleys and hills between the rivers Axios (Vardar) and Strymon (Struma). In those foreign lands, far to the south-west of the Odrysian strongholds, Sparadocus established himself as a co-ruler *(paradynast)* while Teres was still alive, and he was the first among Odrysian notables to mint silver coins stamped with his own image on horseback, wearing a Thracian cloak *(zeira)* and holding a pair of spears in his right hand. After the death of Sparadocus, his son Seuthes was well received at the court of his uncle Sitalces, he gradually gained the king's confidence and become his trusted advisor in wars and political affairs.

Sitalces inherited his militant father's throne in difficult times. His legacy included not only valour, power, and glory, but also a host of dangerous enemies and half-developed strategies. To the north the Odrysian state was threatened by the Scythians and by numerous and persistent nomadic tribes from the steppes. They came as fast as the northern wind, they hit and disappeared with the rich spoils without engaging in an open battle. To the east, the south-east and the south, the Odrysae had good commercial relations with the coastal Hellenic poleis, but they also faced the freedom-loving new settlers in those areas. The ambitious Athenians made them members of their powerful naval league which rose to an unprecedented power after the defeat of the Persians, and which effectively turned the Aegean into an

It was an ancient law that whoever sowed and reaped in Thrace, was to suffer oppression. Owing to the fertility of their lands, some Thracian tribes became stronger than others but, as Thucydides wrote, that created disastrous conflicts between them, and they were particularly threatened by invaders' aspirations. The ancients believed that a land cannot produce rich crops and valorous warriors at the same time. That applied particularly to the Odrysae. An ancient tradition from the times of Mycenae and the heroes had survived in that rich and fertile land: the numerous population of the small villages made their living from plant-growing, stock-breeding, apiculture, crafts and hunting, and paid tribute in kind to the few rich warrior-aristocrats who lived in fortified castles on the hills by rich villages. The main body of the Odrysian army was made up of the cavalry; the aristocrats were the only ones who could afford the luxury of keeping war horses and buying expensive sets of a helm, a chain mail, greaves, a pair of spears, a bow, a sword and a shield. Gold and silver ornaments adorned the headstall, the bridle and the saddle as well as the horseman's arms, neck and chest. Indeed, the Odrysian aristocracy lived in luxury from taxes, spoils, and gifts. They kept numerous servants, but they also bore the entire responsibility for order in the state. They protected the fertile lands from invaders, often sacrificing their lives, and gave meaning to ordinary people's peaceful life. To get used to bloodshed and ruthless battle, the aristocrats hunted not only deer but also game that was worthy of warriors: bears, lions and boars that were abundant in Thrace. The dynasty of the supreme Odrysian ruler, called basileus by the neighbouring Hellenes, also came from that tribal aristocracy. Power was inherited by the son or the brother. However, just as the courage of the Thracian warrior-aristocrats was due not only to eager exercise in hunting and warring but also to their deep conviction that they were immortal, so the power of the king did not end in this world. The heirs to the throne were taught to believe that they were the gods' elects: they spent years acquiring spiritual power through exercising self-restraint, they learned how to perform sacred rituals, and finally, in a secret rite, they were initiated into the secret of their divine origin, became the creator-gods' equals and gained immortality. The ordinary Odrysae believed their ruler to be intangible and perfect, they believed that he would live forever in flesh and blood, and their belief was so ancient and strong that no one would think of changing it with an alien faith – until, centuries later, times of fall, destruction and oblivion set in.

Replica of a silver phial featuring four Thracian battle chariots and armed soldiers.
Illustration by Atanas Atanasov

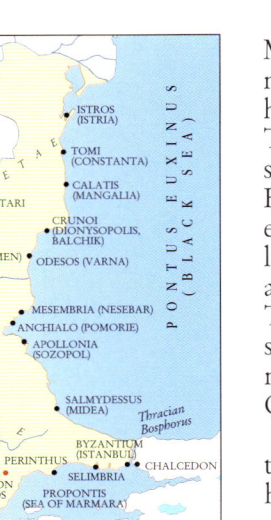

The Odrysian state under Sitalces.

Hellenic sea. Under the leadership of Athens, all these poleis contributed to a fund that was kept at the Acropolis. It so happened that Sitalces' coming to power coincided with the rise of the famous Pericles in Athens. Very soon, the Athenian ambition for complete control over trade with inland Thrace was manifested in the founding of Amphipolis, a settlement on the banks of the Strymon in its lower course, in the strategic area known as the "Nine Roads." For decades, the brave but sparse Thracian tribe Aedonae defended their land from the invaders but the Athenians finally prevailed. Exhausted by the fighting, the coastal Thracians found it harder and harder to collect the ancient paternal tax imposed by their ancestors on the Hellenic colonists for the right to settle in their land. When Sitalces extended his border to the coast, the situation changed. In the face of his military power, many poleis had to pay their taxes regularly to the Odrysae, and the Athenians reduced or revoked the taxes due by their allies. Sitalces followed with particular attention the developments at the Macedonian court. King Perdiccas II was a skillful diplomat, he kept changing his allies among the Hellenes, and guarded jealously his power and his territory from the aspirations within his own dynasty. Over the years, he grew into a dangerous neighbour of the Paeonic lands conquered by Sparadocus. In order to prevail over his internal and external rivals, Perdiccas would stop at nothing to gain control over the rich gold and silver deposits in Paeonia and Thrace. Thus, at the very beginning of his rule, Sitalces had to fight a difficult war with the rebellious Paeonians, blazing a trail through the mountains for his sizable army. His relations with the Thracian tribe Triballi – north of the Balkan range – in today's eastern Serbia and northwestern Bulgaria, were also strained. Of the large Thracian tribes, the Triballi were the only ones to preserve their independence from Teres. Gradually, they grew more and more audacious as they realized that Sitalces was accumulating wealth from taxes and trade with the Hellenic colonies, focusing his attention far south from their lands. Soon, the Triballi demanded a share of that large wealth, and became the mortal enemy of the Odrysian state. At that point, Sitalces displayed remarkable statesmanship and vision in regard to the relations between the Balkan tribes. In order to preserve the integrity of his state, he made a wise decision.

Sitalces invited merchants from the wealthy Aegean colonies Maronia, Thassos, and Apollonia to establish an inland commercial centre in the westernmost part of his state, where the high Thracian mountains formed the narrow pass Suki (today's Trajan's Gate). This is where the main road of the Odrysian state passed, the Diagonal Road, also known as the Eternal Road, for it had been used for centuries by peace-seeking envoys, merchants, and skillful artisans as well as by merciless invaders. The Hellenic settlers called the place Pisthiros and, several times a year, gathered there in a market where Thracian and Hellenic goods were exchanged. Thus, Sitalces satisfied for a while the desire of the Triballi from the far north of Thrace to gain access to luxury goods, similarly to Odrysian aristocrats.

The Odrysian king not only preserved but even extended the heritage of his father Teres. According to Thucydides, his state spread along the coast from the Hellenic polis Abdera on the Aegean to the Black Sea and the mouth of the Danube. It took four days and four nights to travel by sea in a merchant ship, provided that the wind was favourable. By land, it took a trained walker eleven days to go from Abdera to the Danube by the direct route, and thirteen days by the Diagonal Road from Byzantium on the Bosporus to the Scombros (Vitosha) Mountain, so vast was the kingdom of Sitalces. In revenue, it was unequalled among the states from the Adriatic to the Black Sea, and maybe in all Europe of that time. Every year, Sitalces received 400 talents (10,600 kg) of gold and silver and rich gifts of precious objects and colourful fabrics from his Hellenic and Thracian tax-payers. In Thrace, there was a custom to offer gifts not only to the king but also to the local governors and paradynasts, as well as to all nobles at the king's court.

The Odrysian state became so famously powerful that when the Athenians and the Spartans sought allies in the pending Peloponnesian war, they addressed Sitalces. The Hellenes in the Thracian peninsula of Chalcidice, and more particularly the Dorians of Potidaea, were to play an important role in that conflict, as they rebelled against the naval league controlled by Athens. Athens launched a prolonged siege of Potidaea by land and by sea. Pericles' diplomats urged Sitalces to aid the Athenians in that military operation. The Odrisian king had enough trouble defending his own territories across the high mountains and did not rush to respond. In the summer of 431 B.C., both Sitalces and Pericles accepted as a proxenus Nymphodorus of Abdera whose sister Sitalces had married. In the course of the negotiations in Athens, Nymphodorus succeeded in attracting Sitalces, son of Teres and king of most Thracians, and Perdiccas, son of Alexander and king of Macedonia, as allies of Athens. The son of Sitalces, Sadocus, who was of appropriate age, was made an Athenian citizen, and became one of the Athenian adolescents and future warriors. Perdiccas promised to Sitalces some concessions about the one-time territories in Paeonia, provided that the Odrysian king would not support Perdiccas' brother Philip in his ambition to seize the throne. In turn, Sitalces undertook to help Athens with infantry and cavalry so that the siege of Potidaea might end sooner. These were the agreements reached between the diplomats but the war had its own logic and turns.

Perdiccas did not rush to keep his promises to the Odrysae. Sitalces then offered hospitality at his court not only to Philip but also to his son Amyntas, with the intention of installing them on the Macedonian throne. In 430 B.C., a plague broke out in Athens, taking thousands of victims in the polis as well as in the Athenian army in Chalcidice. Sitalces was justifiably apprehensive that the plague might spread in his state, too. The same winter, the situation of the besieged Potidaeans became unbearable. They were so short of food that they resorted to cannibalism. Thus, the rebellious polis finally surrendered without Sitalces' interference. Although the Athenians were still in need of his support, the Odrysian king continued his wait-and-see policy. The exhaustion of Athens and Macedonia was to his best advantage. The right moment to interfere came only in the fall of 429 B.C. when the mighty Pericles also fell victim to the plague.

Having left his son Sadocus who had just come of age as his heir in Thrace, in early winter Sitalces marched against Perdiccas and the Chalcidians to get what had been promised to him, and to fulfill his own promise to the Athenians. They had recently sent to him envoys with gifts and the message that the Athenians and the Odrysae had been related since ancient times. Sitalces called first to his standard his subjects between the Balkan range and the Rhodopes all the way to the Black Sea, then the Getae beyond the Balkan range and, finally, the independent Thracians from the Rhodopes. He paid some generously, while others went for the loot. With his army, of which a third was cavalry, the Odrysian ruler crossed the lands of the Paeonians and headed to Macedonia and Chalcidice. His army grew during the march, reaching the impressive number of 150,000. The news spread like wildfire, throwing even the allies in Athens into panic. To them, the huge Odrysian army looked like "a cloud of locusts" and reminded them of the invasion of Xerxes. Sitalces seized many settlements on his way; others he could not take; for thirty days he ravaged the area between Macedonia proper and the Chalcidian coast but he never got any further. His huge army was getting short of supplies, and the winter also took its toll. Seuthes, the son of Sparadocus who was not only the king's nephew but also the second most powerful man in the state, convinced Sitalces to go back before he suffered heavier losses. Seuthes' sincerity was questionable as it later became known that Perdiccas had promised him money and the hand of his daughter Stratonice.

After the campaign which had thrown the Hellenes and Macedonians into a panic, Sitalces realized that it would be very hard to conquer and keep Paeonia, which lay beyond the mountains, far to the southwest. He opted to maintain good trade contacts with the Paeonians through the Hellenic marketplace of Pisthiros. The aggressive Triballi took this as a sign of weakness, and soon Sitalces had to fight a war on the northwest that took precious victims. In 424, Sitalces himself died in a battle with the Triballi. Seuthes I, the son of Sparadocus, inherited the throne.

Under Sitalces, the Odrysian state flourished for the first time, and saw its greatest expansion. Sitalces was one of the few statesmen of vision in Europe, resolutely walking his path in history, following the voice of his land. The historical continental roads that crossed his state went all the way to the southern coasts. The Odrysian king Sitalces walked them gloriously but, unfortunately, he got involved in the Peloponnesian War in which there was no true victor in the Balkans.

The funeral of a Thracian noble with horse races, military honours, and religious ceremonies.
Illustration by Rossen Toshev

ARCHELAUS
413 – 399 B.C

Portrait illustration by Hristo Hadjitanev

From times immemorial, the most ancient Macedonian lands were inhabited by Elimiots, Orestes, and Lyncestians. Each of them had their own ruling dynasty that rather unwillingly submitted to the authority of the Macedonian king. These vassals often forsook their subordination and took every opportunity to participate with their armies in the bitter struggles for the Macedonian throne in the capital Aegae. The rest of the Macedonian territory had been conquered recently, chiefly under Perdiccas' father Alexander I, and was inhabited by small and once glorious Paeonian and Thracian tribes. To consolidate their power, the sparse invaders moved the local population beyond the river Strymon and to Chalcidice where the new borders of the Macedonian state now passed. With their fertile land and favourable climate the newly acquired valleys touching upon the Aegean had an invigorative effect on the young state, but they also created a feeling of trouble and insecurity. They not only bore rich fruit but were crossed by important roads to the heart of continental Hellas, linking it with Europe and Asia. The surrounding hostile tribes, the coastal Hellenes, the Thessalians, and the Epirots from northern Hellas anxiously followed the rapid Macedonian expansion and consolidation. The new lands were divided among the Macedonian king and his brothers but that seldom assured security to the state. Every inch of that rich land invoked memories of the past and incited new fratricidal conflicts.

In order to preserve his supreme power and the integrity of his kingdom, Perdiccas II managed to keep at his court two of his brothers, Alcetas and Menelaus, and later unscrupulously took away their heritage. However, the third brother, Philip, who was installed to rule over the fertile region of Amphaxitis along the river Axios (Vardar), succeeded in breaking loose from the overbearing Perdiccas, and embarked upon a prolonged struggle for the throne. The tumult encouraged other vassals who did not belong to the Argead dynasty to seek independence. In order to cope with the internal troubles in his state, Perdiccas kept searching for allies: at one moment Athens, at another Sparta, then the Odrysian king, but he never remained faithful to any of them. He would stop at nothing: false agreements, perjury, bribery, promises of royal marriages and generous gifts in land, even conspiracy and murder. After his death in 413 B.C., his successor Archelaus faced a difficult heritage.

MACEDONIA ONLY APPEARED to be a unified state. King Perdiccas II (454 – 413 B.C.) had to use all diplomatic and military means to defend the integrity of his state.

Perdicca's legitimate son by his wife Cleopatra was still very young, and Archelaus was appointed regent. Archelaus was also the son of Perdiccas but his mother was a slave of Perdiccas' brother Alcetas. Facing the threat of spending his whole life as a shadow of the growing heir, Archelaus followed the voice of his royal blood, and conceived a sinister plan. He once invited his uncle Alcetas to a dinner at the pretext that he wanted to give him back his power, allegedly usurped by Perdiccas, along with Alcetas' son Alexander, Archelaus' own cousin, who was of about the same age. He served them undiluted wine until they got drunk, and in the darkness of the night, led them out of the palace and killed them. No one saw them or heard of them again after that night. Soon afterwards, another wicked deed followed: Archelaus threw Perdiccas' seven-year-old son, the legitimate heir, into a well, and told the boy's mother Cleopatra that her son had fallen there and died while chasing a goose. He then proceeded to marry Cleopatra, the unfortunate queen who had inadvertently assisted her son's murderer in legitimizing his power. The events in the Macedonian royal house shocked Archelaus' contemporaries; they were so horrible that even Perdiccas' wickedness paled before them, and was soon forgotten.

Over the years, however, Archelaus proved to be a strong and talented ruler. According to the brilliant Athenian historian Thucydides who resided briefly at his court, Archelaus did for Macedonia more than all his eight predecessors together. He erected strongholds that had been scarce in the Macedonian land, he built roads and improved the army: he developed the cavalry of aristocrats in chain mail, and he was the first one to create and arm elite land forces. Having realized that the future of united Macedonia lay in the conquest of foreign shores, Archelaus moved the capital from the ancient Aegae to Pella. The site was perfectly chosen: it was inaccessible to enemies, being surrounded with marshes. Archelaus divided Macedonia into regions and started getting a regular income in the form of taxes. He also introduced a new coin whose significance was comparable to that of Aegean and Persian coins. He put seafaring on the Macedonian agenda, and linked the country's future with coastal and island states. In 410 B.C., he besieged and seized the coastal settlement of Pydna that had been trying to throw off the Macedonian rule. He was assisted in this by his Athenian allies. Having seized Pydna, he moved its population to inland Macedonia, and forever crushed the city's commercial significance.

Both Athens – hesitating over the choice between the return of the banished Alcibiades and its disastrous pride – and Archelaus needed their alliance. The Athenians declared the Macedonian king their friend, and entertained him lavishly; Archelaus in his turn sold them precious timber for ship oars and organised royal feasts for the Athenian envoys. He sought to make his court a centre of Hellenic culture, and although that culture had been born of the freedom and equality in the Hellenic poleis, Archelaus spent quite some money and put a lot of effort to adjust it to his ambition. His generous promises attracted poets, writers, playwrights, sculptors, painters, and musicians. Archelaus was thus the forerunner of a tradition that would become universal a century later, under Alexander the Great. Agathon, Choerilus, Timotheus, Thucydides, and Zeuxis stayed at his court. However, the king's greatest pride was the presence of the famous Athenian playwright Euripides, the winner of many contests. To appease his important guest, Archelaus

Theatrical performance at the court of the Macedonian king Archelaus.
Illustration by Emilian Stankev

was willing to neglect even his closest associates, making bitter enemies among Macedonian notables. In response to his kindness, Euripides wrote the drama *Archelaus*, dedicated to the descendent of Temenus, in which he glorified the king and his dynasty. Soon, a strong friendship developed between the king and the playwright. It so happened that Euripides died at Archelaus' palace; in his overwhelming grief, the king cut his hair, and personally attended the funeral.

Generally, Archelaus sought to prove his Hellenic origin more eagerly than his predecessors; he seemed to be more proud of it than of being the king of Macedonia. On his coins, he stamped the image of the hero Heracles; he won the Pythian games at Delphi and the four-horse chariot race at Olympia. Following the Hellenic tradition, he organised lavish musical contests dedicated to the Olympian Zeus and his daughters, the Muses at the foot of the divine Olympus, at the site of the ancient Thracian settlement Dion. However, Archelaus' pride and ambition did not end there; very soon, his aspirations extended to lands that belonged beyond doubt to the Hellenes. Taking advantage of the power struggles in neighbouring Thessaly, immediately after the exhausting Peloponnesian war he seized the region of Larissa, installed a vassal ruler and took eight noble young men as hostages. Archelaus' insidious plans suddenly became obvious. Larissa lay on the road to the heart of Hellas. When with the typical unpredictability of his ancestors the Macedonian king demanded admission to the Peloponnesian League after the war, the victor Sparta flatly refused. By that time, many Hellenes were regarding Archelaus as a dangerous neighbour, and were recalling the circumstances of his coming to power. In his passionate speeches in defence of Larissa, Trasymachus pointed out with bitter indignation that the Hellenes would now become the slaves of the barbarian Archelaus.

Soon after these dramatic events, Archelaus was assassinated by his former favourite Crateus while hunting. The rumour went that the murder had been organised by three conspirers who had felt neglected and humiliated by the king. Although Archelaus was a talented ruler, he did not leave behind a worthy successor to the throne. The situation in the Macedonian state was more unstable than ever. Crateus held the power only for a few days, falling victim in his turn, and Archelaus' underage son Orestes was murdered by him, just as Archelaus had killed the legitimate heir of Perdiccas II. History repeated itself, only in darker colours. The disorder at the Macedonian court was to continue for four decades, until the coming to power of the famous Philip II of Macedonia (359 – 336 B.C.).

Even before the death of Archelaus, Athenian philosophers discussed the Macedonian king's life in the shadow of their cool porticos. Most of them placed their confidence in him as, despite his ugly and sinister actions at the time he seized power, he was successful: from a slave he rose to a king. Socrates was the only one to claim that Archelaus and his kind were the most unhappy men on earth, for it was those who did evil, not those who suffered it, that killed all that was good and noble in their own character. Socrates was alone in his effort to convert the Athenians to the ancient and eternal virtues. He was the only one who dared decline Archelaus' invitation with the excuse that he had no reason to leave his homeland while the grain was still cheap there. He was also the only one to decalare that the Macedonian king's guests were there not because of the king himself but because of his lavish palace. It so happened that Socrates died in the Athenian prison in 399 B.C., the same year when Archelaus was assassinated. By accepting with humility the greatest injustice of the Athenian court, Socrates announced the irreversible decline of virtues in the polis world. Archelaus in his turn symbolised the road of painful compromises that Macedonia, Hellas, and most Balkan peoples would take – and that sooner or later, for good or bad, would bring to prominence the Macedonian rulers.

Map of Macedonia under King Archelaus.

ALCIBIADES
c. 450 – 404 B.C.

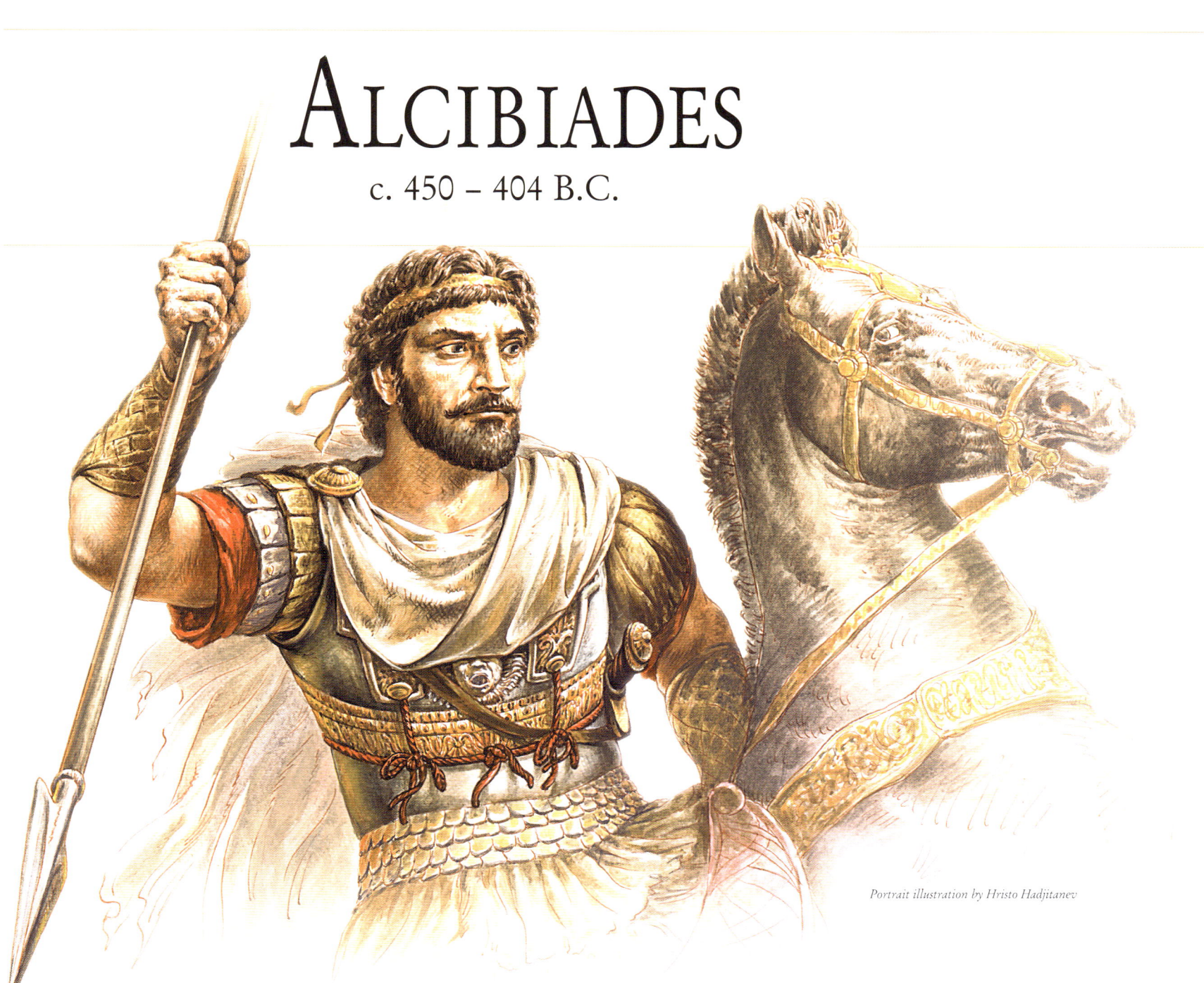

Portrait illustration by Hristo Hadjitanev

ALCIBIADES OF ATHENS saw his days of glory and disgrace at the time of the Peloponnesian War, the fierce war between Athens and Sparta for supremacy in Hellas. It brought to the surface a painful problem that had its roots deep in the past: the Hellenes' need to name an undisputed leader to defend their interests by land and by sea, preserving at the same time the integrity, the dignity and the ancient laws in each of the hundreds of poleis scattered on three continents, each of them an independent state. The Hellenic land lacked a ruler (whom all the Hellenes secretly or openly awaited) yet none of the poleis opened its gates wide for him. After the Persians were driven out of the Hellenic lands, Athens under Pericles shouldered the role of a unifying force by sea. However, its excessive power brought it first to glory and then to a fall. It acquired the reputation of a self-imposed tyranny. This is why many poleis participated in the Peloponnesian War. The interests of dozens of poleis and a number of smaller and larger neighbouring states were brought together as if in a kaleidoscope, and were defended fiercely. Practically all Hellenes wished to live in peace yet the Peloponnesian war broke out, bringing suffering and ruin (431 B.C.) Some Hellenes found out that the war was wasting the rich harvest of their land and became active peace-seekers while others realized that the war had been going on for a very long time, and that it was imperative to put an end to the ancient conflict, immediately and permanently. In 421 B.C. the Athenian Nicias prepared and signed a peace treaty with the Spartans. The Hellenes used to say that Pericles had started the war and Nicias had ended it.

The peace was commonly referred to as the Peace of Nicias. Alcibiades was one of those who proved that the peace treaty was no more than a truce, a breath of air before a greater peril.

Alcibiades' father Cleinias was an aristocrat who achieved glory in the war with Persia. He died in 447 B.C. in the battle of Coronea where the Athenians were defeated by their neighbours, the Thebans. Having lost his father at an early age, Alcibiades was raised by his maternal relatives. His guardian was Pericles himself – the son of Xanthippus during whose time the Athenian democracy and might reached their peak. Born in the most influential Hellenic polis, himself of noble birth, inspired by the ideas and the deeds of the most prominent Athenians, Alcibiades realized early that he possessed manifold natural talents and started to cultivate and display them.

Alcibiades stood out among his peers with his physical beauty, his strong build and his fitness. He was adroit, dexterous and brilliantly intelligent. His charisma and eloquence helped him talk his way out of any situation without making bitter enemies. Being excessively rich, he did not conceal his taste for indulgence and luxury, his dissipation and irresponsibility. He was also bright, resourceful in his relationships, but sometimes outright insolent. He once hit a tutor in the face for not having Homer's poems with him. His quick reaction, his wit, and his sense of humour disguised his arrogance. The Athenians quickly got used to regarding leniently Alcibiades' behaviour – they believed him to be harmless and saw the funny side of his acts. His company was sought even by those sons of Athenian aristocrats who secretly envied him and despised his self-confidence and impunity.

Whenever the situation so required, Alcibiades manifested his physical and mental abilities. He was very strong and vigorous, and had been taught endurance from an early age. It was no coincidence that his nurse Amycla was a Spartan. Alcibiades was ambitious, he always aimed high, and sought to display superiority in everything. An event from his childhood testifies that from an early age his soul was torn by deep and fiery passions that he attempted to bring under control. In a wrestling bout he felt that his adversary was getting the upper hand and bit so fiercely into his arm that he almost tore it off. His unfortunate adversary accused him of unfair play and told him he bit like a woman. "No, like a lion," Alcibiades retorted wittily.

Socrates also contributed much to Alcibiades' fame. The Athenian philosopher surrounded the young man with attention and care, for he quickly saw his abilities and virtues. Alcibiades regarded Socrates' kindness and benevolence as a divine gift, as an opportunity to escape from banality. He admired Socrates' wisdom so much that he began to despise himself and to feel guilty before the wise man's supreme virtuousness. Socrates' care inspired in him love and a sincere

Socrates and Alcibiades feasting with noble Athenians: an usual form of intellectual exchange for the ancient world's cultural elite. The participation of Socrates and Alcibiades in such philosophical discussions on the eternal subject of love was immortalized by Plato in his famous dialogue The Feast.
Illustration by Atanas Atanasov

desire for righteousness. It fuelled his ardent patriotism and his innate courage, and dignified his aspirations for excellence. When Alcibiades grew to maturity, a strong friendship developed between the two eminent Athenians. They even fought side by side in the first fierce battles of the Peloponnesian War, each of them saving the other's life.

Still, Alcibiades continued to combine two strong opposites in his character. He proved to be a passionate patriot and repeatedly demonstrated that he had all the necessary qualities to attain glory for himself and his homeland. He was such a strong and outstanding individual that he often prevailed over the desire for collective life and uniform morality in the polis. The Athenians themselves praised his rare abilities and believed there was nothing he could not handle, an attitude that only fostered the development of some of his negative features. It was amazing how a man could have such unrivalled abilities and such contradicting characteristics. According to his biographer Plutarch, Alcibiades was like iron: softened by fiery passions, he became sensitive, haughty, and dissolute; then, as if cooled by water, he regained his humbleness, the sense of his imperfection and of Socrates' unattainable virtuousness. The fame Alcibiades strongly desired became palpable. He paid no attention to the vicious remarks that he ate in gold and silver vessels, that he wore an unusual long purple garment in public, and that his private life was a permanent public scandal. He knew well that deep inside the Athenians admired his fine manners and his boldness; that despite the established rules he was just the man they needed. Alcibiades won even more admirers throughout Hellas by entering seven chariots at Olympia – no one, not even kings had ever done that before. Alcibiades won the first three prizes, and received great honours wherever he went. Ephesus, Chios, and Lesbos competed for his friendship.

Although still very young when he went into politics, Alcibiades soon outshone his rivals. The speeches he delivered to the Ecclesia were passionate, his phrase and gestures elaborate, his thoughts were clear and well substantiated with unexpected arguments. His daring plans for his country's future moved and enlightened everyone, the young people of Athens in particular. However, many feared him because he gave up neither wickedness nor virtuousness. He led a dissipated life, and he went to extremes in drinking and womanizing. Contrary to all traditions, he carried a gold-plated shield with no genealogical symbols on it in battle. Alcibiades was believed to be responsible for the massacre of all adult inhabitants of the island of Melos by the Athenians – an act which today (as well as at the time of its perpetration) seems sinister and needless atrocity. The problem was that it was easy to lay at Alcibiades' door acts that he had not even considered. Rumours and slander took their toll. On one occasion, going home in triumph from the Ecclesia, Alcibiades was addressed by the elderly Timon who said: "Good for you, son, that you prosper, for a great evil for all these people grows inside you."

Alcibiades' only worthy rival was the peace-maker Nicias who after the death of Pericles in 429 B.C. and particularly after the signing of the peace with the Spartans won the Athenians' sympathies with his moderation. To beat his wide influence, Alcibiades made his best to strain again the relations between the Hellenes, for it was his firm belief that the inaction was unfavourable to Athens. Earlier, Pericles had attempted to convince the Athenians to conquer the rich island of Sicily, taking first the strongest Doric polis there, Syracuse, an old Corinthian colony. It was Alcibiades, who grew up in Pericles' home that resumed the promotion of

The Erechtheum in a reconstructed shape of the Acropolis shown here. At the site of the contest between Athena and Poseidon, a temple called the Erechtheum was erected. It was named after the legendary ancient king Erechtheus. In the temple there was a statue of the goddess Athena which, according to the legend, fell from the sky. An opening on the floor revealed the mark of Poseidon's trident, and in front of the temple grew Athena's sacred olive tree.
Illustration by Maya Buyukliiska

the grand project. He suggested that the island be taken not gradually but all at once, by a large fleet. He regarded Sicily not as the final goal but as the beginning of an ambitious campaign against Carthage, Italy, North Africa, and the Peloponnesus. He believed Sicily to be an excellent base and source of supplies in such a major undertaking. The fertile island yielded a rich grain harvest, and could provide all kinds of supplies for both the fleet and the army. Its position in the heart of the Mediterranean was of utmost strategic significance as well. Alcibiades managed to convince the Athenian demos to vote for his grand project that would make Athens a unifying centre of all Hellas. A talented strategist, Alcibiades actually possessed all the qualities required for the project's implementation, and could very well have brought it to fruition changing ancient history, had it not been for the usual discord and political intrigues in democratic Athens. As strategoi with unlimited prerogatives, the Athenians appointed Nicias, who was against the campaign and did his best to obstruct it, Alcibiades, and the elderly Lamachus who like Alcibiades enjoyed risk and courage. Thus, discord was innate among the leaders in the risky military undertaking.

It was a warm summer night in 415 B.C. The mighty Athenian fleet was to set sail from Piraeus to Sicily the following morning. Unfortunate events during the night caused a dramatic turn in Alcibiades' bold dreams and in the Athenians' boundless faith in his success: the sacred roadside statues of Hermes were vandalized. Alcibiades was wrongly accused of being an accomplice in this sacrilegious act. Witnesses conveniently recalled his previous manifestations of disrespect. Alcibiades defended his innocence brilliantly before the crowd, and claimed that it would be outrageous to send him as a commander of the huge fleet with the shadow of an unproven charge cast upon him. The fleet sailed off but the inquiry – as well as the suspicions – remained in the hands of Alcibiades' opponents. One Andocides who was among those arrested and who claimed to be a descendent of the famous Odysseus, was weak-willed and they talked him into testifying against Alcibiades. Meanwhile, Alcibiades was winning battle after battle in southern Italy and Sicily, where he was reached by the vessel *Salaminia* with the order for his recall. After Alcibiades' departure, morale plummeted. The campaign had to be continued by Nicias who was quite unprepared for that, and in a few months the undertaking failed in the face of the hardships in those foreign lands.

Knowing clearly what awaited him, Alcibiades escaped on his way back to Athens. A man recognized him and asked whether he did not trust his homeland. "I trust everyone but, when it is about my life, I don't trust even my own mother," Alcibiades replied. From that point on, he lived outside the law and even outside his time, for more than ever before he appeared to be the forerunner of future events and personalities. Although he sincerely shared Socrates' ideals, the two prominent Athenians made opposite choices. Wrongly accused, Socrates appeared before the court, and chose death to the option to leave his homeland and go into exile. Alcibiades opted for life. He realized he could only rely on himself at a time when the good laws were no longer alive in the statesmen's hearts but had instead been turned into a terrible weapon against political opponents.

Before long, Alcibiades settled in the enemy camp – in Sparta. Again he was unrivalled and as resourceful as ever. He inspired admiration with his physical beauty, his courage and his endurance. Without a moment's hesitation he offered his recent enemies his valuable ideas on the future course of the war, thus helping them to the victory. Alcibiades suggested that they take the otherwise minor stronghold of Decelea that guarded Athens' all-important supply line by land. He also suggested that the Spartans initiate closer contacts with the Persian satraps in Asia Minor and build a fleet to fight Athens with Persian funds. Although he changed more easily than a chameleon, intrigues overtook him again. His influence in Sparta aroused the jealousy of the Spartan basileus Agidus. As soon as he was told of Agidus' secret order to kill him, Alcibiades took refuge with the Persian satrap Tisaphernes who welcomed him cordially – not because he was such a very kind person but because he was amazed by the Athenian's fickleness.

Soon Alcibiades felt homesick. He delivered his new plans for Athens to the Athenian fleet at Samos. They proclaimed him their strategos. He inspired a political coup in Athens that was to pave the way for his return and for a treaty with the Persian satrap Tisaphernes, but he wished to return in glory instead of empty-handed. Under his leadership, the Athenian fleet restored its supremacy in Ionia and in the Hellespont to the Bosphorus. Alcibiades arrived at Piraeus with dozens of captured Lacedaemonian ships, loaded with spoils. With tears of joy and sorrow from the endured hardships, the Athenians crowned their long-suffering strategos with a wreath of gold, revoked his death sentence, and restored his confiscated property. The priests who had cursed him now praised him aloud. Filled with hope, the people reelected Alcibiades as a commander – but again the result was doomed. Rarely was there a statesmen who suffered so much from his own reputation of being able to achieve a victory in any circumstances. When, for lack of funding, Alcibiades acted somewhat slowly in the campaign in Asia Minor, the Athe-nians became apprehensive that he might be plotting against them, and again banished him. This time Alcibiades escaped to Thrace where he had won the friendship of some local rulers, and lived in his coastal strongholds. Later he sought a safer shelter with the Phrygian satrap Pharnabazus. However, after Sparta's victory in the Peloponnesian war, the word spread that Athens was not dead as long as Alcibiades was alive. Alcibiades' life ended in a small Phrygian village where hired assassins set fire to his home, as no one dared face him in an honest fight. He was buried secretly by his mistress with whom he had spent his last days.

Long before these dramatic events, one Archestratus had said that Hellas could not survive another Alcibiades. Indeed, it was unprepared for him but his entire life was a warning that one day Hellas would badly miss him.

At the Olympic games Alcibiades once entered seven chariots, and three of them ended up in the first three positions. The Hellenes praised the victors like heroes from the Trojan War, and showered them with honours.

Illustration by Hristo Hadjitanev

SEUTHES II
c. 407 – c. 386 B.C.

Portrait illustration by Hristo Hadjitanev

THE FROSTY WINTER of the year 400 B.C. was approaching. The south wind was giving way to the biting north wind Boreas, bringing thunderclouds over coastal Thrace and the Bosporus. It was no coincidence that the Odrysian noble Seuthes had chosen as his stronghold a stone tower by the rich Hellenic settlement of Perinthus, the site of a lively market and a convenient port. Seuthes was expecting the arrival of the Athenian strategus and mercenary Xenophon to discuss issues of friendship and war.

Seuthes kept a handpicked army of brave and loyal cavalrymen, sharing his difficult lot as a stranger in that land. In the supply-rich nearby villages, several thousands of experienced peltasts stayed in permanent readiness to go into battle. Well armed for both close and distant fighting, carrying light wooden shields, clad in fox-skin caps and boots and long woolen cloaks, these foot soldiers were to gather within hours from the horn and fire signal. By day, Seuthes let the horses graze freely around the fortress; by night, he had them saddled as if he could lead them into battle any moment. Indeed, he had reason to be apprehensive. The rumour went that many years earlier the Odrysian king Teres had tried to conquer that region with a numerous army but had lost many of his men in the battles with the locals, and his supply train was plundered. The locals in question were the Tyni, a tribe that was believed to be the most belligerent among all Thracians, particularly by night.

Although he was not welcome in that foreign land, it was the only place where Seuthes felt that he was the lawful ruler. His ancestors had shed blood for that land. His father, the Odrysian Mesadus, had ruled over the local tribes:

Melandites, Tyni, and Tranipsians. That was the time of the powerful Odrysian king Seuthes I (424 – c. 410 B.C.) Untold wealth was flowing into the treasury from the king's Thracian lands, from the coastal Hellenic poleis, from foreign envoys, and from loot: money, gold and silver, fine objects, fabrics, carpets, and purebred animals. Seuthes remembered that time, for part of the wealth came to his father, the co-ruler (paradynast) in the coastal region. As the Odrysians' power declined, however, Mesadus was driven away from his land, and soon fell ill and died. The orphan Seuthes was raised at the court of the next Odrysian king, Medocus. When he grew up, he could no longer accept to be a hanger-on, and asked the king for men and horses to take revenge on the coastal Thracians for his father's suffering.

Seuthes thus returned to live among enemies, and established a home that differed little from the court of Medocus. Medosadus became his trusted envoy to the neighbouring regions and even to Asia across the sea. His loyal service was rewarded with several rich villages that provided him with sustenance and wealth.

A Hellene of the name of Heraclides from the famous Aegean city of Maronea was authorised to sell the taxes and the loot from the rebellious Tyni. Heraclides was a skillful merchant and guarded jealously his position. Although Seutes was fluent in their language, he used a trusted interpreter, Hebriselmus, in his official negotiations with the Hellenes. Seuthes kept cooks, bakers, cup-bearers, jesters, musicians and dancers. He gave lavish banquets for guests from near and far. He had a daughter, and offered her hand to anyone who could support his effort to gain sovereignty over the rich Thracian land. However, the years passed, and the desired success never came. Seuthes got used to living in permanent war and anxiety, ravaging his father's land. It was little solace that the great Alcbiades stayed shortly with him, and they even became friends. Seuthes gave him three of his best coastal fortresses, but driven by his unhappy situation, Alcibiades went to Asia where he met his death. An overwhelming lust for power, might and absolute submission was growing in Seuthes' ambitious heart. The moment was most favourable for his daring plan. Power was materialising in his hands, and he still lacked the resources to seize it.

Seuthes realized he could no longer rely on King Medocus' help. He also knew well that success in war came only to the strong and the bold. Over the years, they even started referring to Medocus as "the upper king." The center of the Odrysian state was far away from the sea, as many as twelve days' walk away. All envoys from Asia and the European coast of the Sea of Marmara passed through Seuthes' land, and many of them, having realized how far away Medocus' power and influence were, went no further and presented their gifts to Seuthes. The Odrysian king himself had much trouble ruling his state, continually facing the threat of the militant and insiduous Triballi from the north-west. He focused on defending the mountain passes and the rear of his state, but he paid little attention to the warm coastal region and the strategic roads, and they became increasingly controlled by Seuthes, and former dependent. Seuthes witnessed the final dramatic event of the exhausting Peloponnesian war, the battle of Aegospotami which ended with an unexpected Spartan victory at sea (405 B.C.) In the aftermath of that battle, chaos set in. The coastal Hellenic settlements in Seuthes' land no longer had the support of Athens, the Spartan officials in the major trade centers were incapable of getting the aftermath of peace under control, and soldiers of fortune wandered about, selling expensively and unscrupulously their martial skills – their only gain from the long years of the war. On top of this, news came of the bloody conflict in the Persian court between Artaxerxes II and Cyrus the Younger who claimed his brother's throne. Cyrus who became the governor of all satrapies in Asia Minor and who, until recently, had been willing to dismantle his gold throne to help Sparta build its victorious fleet, now raised an army of ten thousand Greek mercenaries, most of them Peloponnesians. He was killed in the decisive battle at Cunaxa, not far from the ancient Babylon. The mercenaries had to force their way back through the lands of dozens of hostile tribes and poleis in Asia. After many difficulties they reached Byzantium on the Bosporus, the gate to Europe. In the face of the coming winter, the hungry and miserable army was not only pursued by the Persians but also unwelcome in any of the Hellenic poleis. The mercenaries' general was Xenophon of Athens.

As soon as he heard of the mercenaries' difficult situation in 400 B.C., Seuthes realized that he was closer than ever to the success of his plan. Three times he sent his envoy Medosadus to persuade Xenophon and his men to take his side. Finally, the general agreed to meet with the Thracian paradynast. After the usual sacrifice, Xenophon headed to Seuthes' fortress in the middle of the night. When he approached the place, he saw fires burning but not a soul around them. He first thought Seuthes had not kept his promise and had moved with his men; then he heard noises and signals and realized that Seuthes had made the fires before the guards so that neither their number nor their location could be detected, while he was clearly visible in the light. Soon, two hundred peltasts came forward and invited Xenophon and his men to Seuthes' home. As they entered the strictly guarded tower, Xenophon and Seuthes embraced and, as was the Thracian custom, drank wine from a horn. Seuthes had heard that the Odrysae and the Athenians were related since ancient times, and that contributed to the friendly conversation. The Thracian promised Xenophon and his men abundant food in the winter months, and the generous pay of a piece of gold monthly for each of the mercenaries. To Xenophon he offered four pieces of gold a month, and if their plans should succeed, the honour of being his brother and companion. He also promised him his best coastal fortress Bizate as a gift, and offered him his daughter in marriage, should Xenophon wish to become his son-in-law. Seuthes expected the Hellenes to help him gain absolute control over his lands by mounting a surprise attack on the rebellious Tyni, and to force them to pay him a tribute.

Xenophon was thus employed by Seuthes. The Odrysian invited all the strategoi and the officers to a feast. The Hellenes sat at three-legged tables. As was the ancient Thracian custom, Seuthes himself broke the unleavened bread and served it with meat to his guests. A cupbearer carried around a horn full of wine, and all guests drank from it to celebrate the alliance. The Hellenes then offered rich gifts to the host, for in the Thracian tradition that act of courtesy to the ruler was a must. Then musicians came in: some blew horns, others beat drums. Seuthes jumped up, as if he had not been drinking the undiluted Thracian wine, gave a loud cry and made an inspired performance of a Thracian war dance. The same night, after the feast, he led his numerous army against the rich villages of the Tyni. The roads were covered with a thick blanket of snow. The Hellenes started to realize the hardships of the harsh Thracian winter, and to understand some of their northern neighbours' weird ways.

For about two months Thracians and Hellenes fought side by side. During that time, Seuthes captured many of his enemies. Some of them he sold into slavery, others he gave to his allies. He piled up a huge loot which he sold at the Hellenic markets for gold and silver. He became so powerful that he started conquering coastal areas that had never belonged to his father Mesadus. Attracted by the loot, Odrysae joined him, and their combined forces became more numerous than Xenophon's mercenary army. Maybe because the spring was near, or because Seuthes' treasurer Heraclides had been delaying their pay for two months, the mercenaries soon rebelled and demanded Xenophon to let them go their different ways, or to find them another patron. Seuthes II had achieved his goals. He felt powerful enough to split off from the Odrysian state, and called himself basileus. The relations between the upper king and the coastal king of the Odrysae became strained. Based on violence, Seuthes' power could not last. About the end of his rule, he was driven away from his country, and returned only briefly to power thanks to another Athenian mercenary, Iphicrates. A firm hand and much talent were required to put an end to the disunion of the Odrysae. For those with foresight, the situation and the prospects of the Balkans were as grim as ever. The time of the remarkable statesman Cotys I was arriving.

In the meantime, Xenophon the Athenian settled in his estate in the Peloponnesus, embarked on a historian's career, and became famous. In his writings, he included a description of the events in Seuthes' kingdom in that cold Thracian winter.

Seuthes II performs a Thracian war dance to the astonishment of his guests.
Illustration by Emilian Stankev

COTYS I
384/83 – 360/59 B.C.

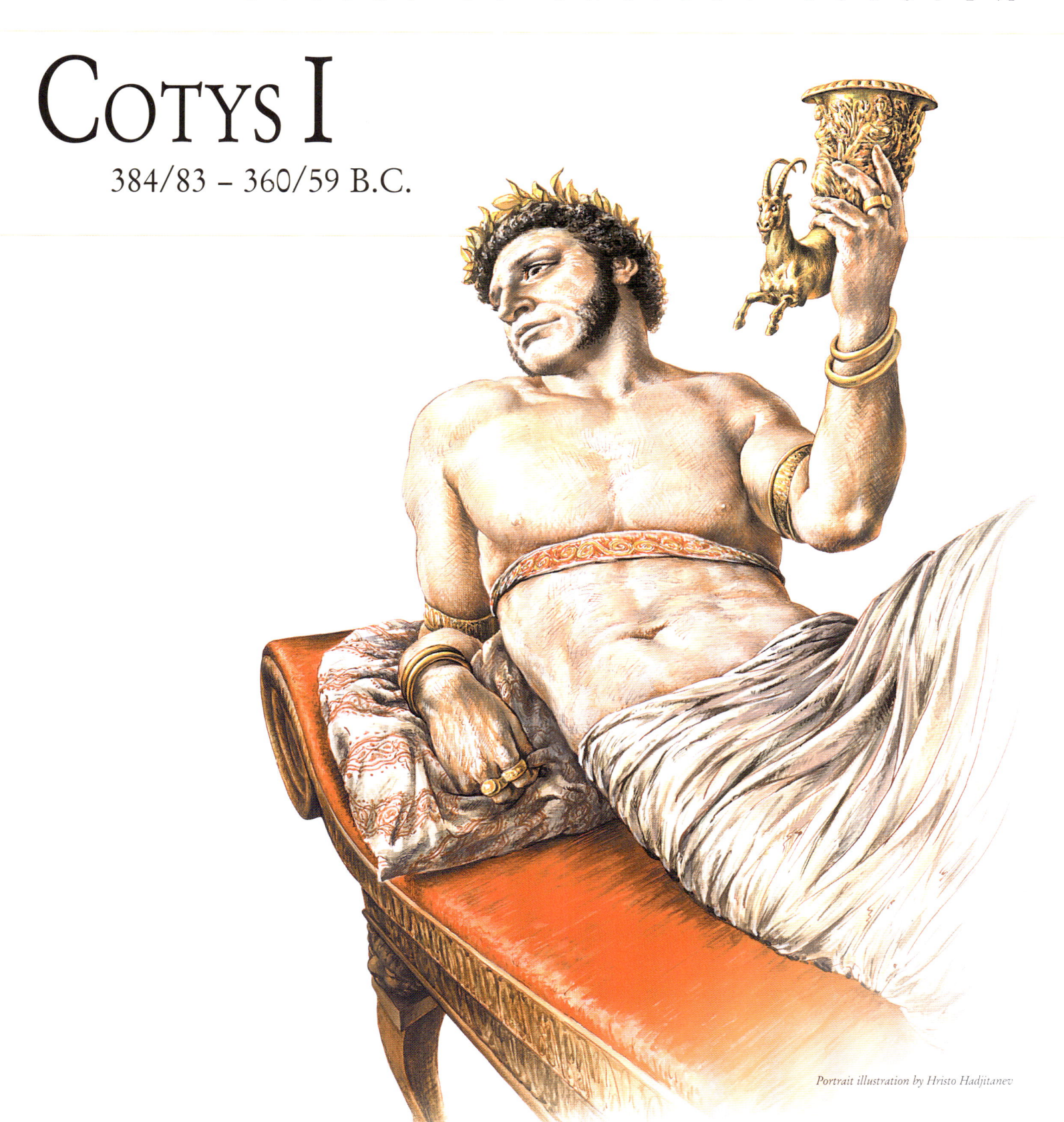

Portrait illustration by Hristo Hadjitanev

COTYS I QUITE unexpectedly ascended the Odrysian throne in 384 B.C., and stayed in power for as many as twenty-four years. The ancient authors fail to mention his father's name, therefore it is generally believed that he ousted his predecessor Hebriselmus (387/86 – 384/83 B.C.). Although he was the first of the eminent Thracian kings of that name, it was at least as ancient as the names of the heroes who had taken part in the Trojan War. Cotys was named after the great mother goddess Cotys or Cotytto, worshipped since times immemorial not only by the Odrysae, and not even only by the Thracians. The cult to Cotytto, creator of all visible and invisible, guardian of the vital and reproductive energy, had spread to some Aegean islands, far to the west to the island of Sicily, and even to large Hellenic poleis such as Corinth and Athens. The noble Thracians were taught that the ruler was the son of the Great Goddess and had, therefore, the gift of immortality. They also believed that the king would obtain from the goddess immortality for them as well. In his sacred matrimony with her, the ruler himself became a god and acquired omnipotence after his death.

The ancients believed the name to be an embodiment and mainstay of the human character. This is why, from the moment of his birth, Cotys asserted his noble lineage and took the long and dangerous road to immortality.

Cotys was born and grew up during the reign of Seuthes I (424 – c. 410 B.C.), soon after the dramatic events at Sitalces' court, while the Peloponnesian War was still raging south of Thrace (431 – 404 B.C.), and he was permeated by the sublimity and the folly of his age. Before his enthronement, he witnessed perhaps every turn and vicissitude in a state's development. The tales of the vast and powerful Odrysian kingdom of Sitalces, spreading from the Aegean Sea to the mouth of the Danube and from the Bosphorus to the upper course of the Strouma river, blended with his childhood memories of the magnificent treasury of Seuthes I and the first losses of territory under his rule. In his adolescence, Cotys witnessed the disunion between the "upper king" Medocus who retired into the ancient Odrysian lands and defended his state's western border, and the "coastal governor" Seuthes II who, with the help of Hellenic mercenaries, gained his father's old territories along the coast of the Sea of Marmara back from the Thyni, and grew increasingly independent of the Odrysian king's central power. He styled himself king and minted his own coins. Cotys learned from both Medocus and Seuthes: he would be wary of both isolation and separatists.

Cotys' early political views were also influenced by his predecessor. Hebriselmus apparently achieved a certain territorial unity as he was known in Athens as "king of the Odrysae." He minted his own coins in Cypsela, near the mouth of the Maritsa river, and had good control over the south-western borders of the Odrysian state where the Straits lay. Hebriselmus entered into negotiations with the Athenians, and had their recognition as a faithful ally, but he also imposed his conditions for the ships passing by his Thracian coast. It seems that the finalization of the treaty was forestalled by the humiliating peace of Antalcides with the Persians which banned the formation of alliances between the Hellenes and left the traditional Athenian market to the mercy of fate. Fairly soon, Athens started looking for ways to skirt the treaty with the Persians, and made preparations for the establishment of a second naval league of free and independent coastal and island city-states. In that undertaking, however, they needed the support of a faithful ally among the Odrysians, as they were beyond the scope of influence of the Persian capital.

Thus, for a brief period of time, some strategic areas between Europe and Asia were left undefended. That offered a historic opportunity to the Balkan monarchs of Thrace and Macedonia through whose lands passed the main roads between the two continents. It was at that crucial moment that Cotys came to power in Thrace, and was quick to grasp the opportunity to claim a share in world affairs. This is the reason why his rule became a remarkable historical drama. Even though today Cotys' significance as a ruler is attenuated by the suspicious silence or the biased assessments of his contemporary historians, by the deliberated political vilification of Demosthenes, by the comedians' purifying laughter, and by entertainers' frivolities, shortly afterwards remarkable personalities such as Philip II of Macedonia and Alexander III the Great would walk in his steps.

The new Odrysian ruler was clearly aware of his advantages. The ancient Diagonal Road that eventually led the ancient traveller to the Hellenic colonies on the Straits and to the northern coast of the Sea of Marmara passed through the Odrysians' lands. Many of the coastal Hellenes profited from their farm produce and their human resources. Artisans, middlemen, merchants, and usurers accumulated wealth from them. Cotys also realized that more than ever the Athenian politicians sought alliance with a unified and orderly Odrysian state in order to convince as many Hellenes as possible of the advantages of a common market. The fine objects from countries near and far that were sold by the Hellenes were well received in the mansions of the Thracian aristocracy. With the intuition of a mature and farsighted statesman, Cotys capitalized on the foreign political situation. At that point, the interests of Athens and its allies fell in perfectly with his own interests. He was granted Athenian citizenship, and crowned with a gold wreath. He was probably also reminded – as were his predecessors – of the distant kinship between the Odrysae and the Athenians. Cotys reacted with pride, dignity and perhaps some concealed irony. A late Roman author quotes his answer to the great honours: "In turn, I shall grant the Athenians my people's rights."

To consolidate his position, Cotys gave his daughter in marriage to the famous Athenian general Iphicrates. The royal wedding was lavish and did not remain unnoticed by the contemporaries. Setting aside the sardonic laughter of Cotys' political opponents in Athens, we find that Iphicrates was presented with generous gifts: strongholds along the Thracian coast, gold and silver vessels, two studs of white horses, and innumerable cattle. Being one of the most talented generals of his age, Iphicrates became Cotys' right-hand man in his military campaigns. During his numerous missions as an official or as a mercenary, he followed closely the political attitudes in Athens, Thebes, the Peloponnesus, along the Aegean coast and on the islands, at the Macedonian and the Persian court.

This successful start to his foreign policy allowed Cotys to dedicate nearly two decades to the internal organization of his state. The Odrysian treasury received taxes in kind from the subordinate Thracian lands, and they were exchanged for silver and gold coins on the markets of the coastal Hellenic settlements. After 377 B.C. when Athens headed the second naval league, the revenues from the so-called "paternal tax," paid by Athens' allies along the Thracian coast in order to preserve the peace and the trade contacts with inland Thrace, increased considerably. The wealth of the Odrysian king also grew from the many lavish gifts presented as a rule by anyone invited to the royal table: foreign envoys, mercenary commanders, passing merchants. Yet Cotys did not have the historical chance to keep his treasury intact. Very soon, in 375 B.C., a large army of the Triballi invaded his lands from the north-west, passed through it and plundered the Aegean coast by the rich Hellenic city of Abdera. The Triballi were a dangerous enemy. In the last years of Sitalces' rule they had done much to diminish the power of the Odrysae, and were probably involved in the king's death (424 B.C.) They insisted on their share of the Odrysian benefits from their access to three seas: the Black Sea, the Sea of Marmara and the Aegean Sea.

Cotys was compelled to fortify his kingdom's borders and roads. Under his rule began the construction of the strategic settlement Cabyle at the Toundja river, as well as of a settlement at the foot of three hills at the upper reaches of the Maritsa. That settlement Philip II of Macedonia would later call Philipopolis (today Plovdiv). Cotys put much effort into

RULERS OF ANCIENT EUROPE 73

*To the Hellenes, the Thracians' mystical
rites were quite unfathomable. Only vague tales
of the Thracian King Cotys' desire to enter into
a marriage with the goddess (which they compared to Athena)
found their way into Hellenic literary sources.*
Illustration by Emilian Stankev

Replica of a relief on a silver jug from the Rogozen Treasure, featuring a Thracian goddess riding an Amazon lioness. Between the two mirror images of the goddess is the scene of a lion attacking a deer.
Illustration by Atanas Atanasov

the revival of the large Hellenic market town Pisthiros in the westernmost corner of his state, between the Rhodopes, Rila and Sredna Gora, where the Diagonal Road entered the Suki pass (present-day Trajan's Gate). This Hellenic market on the Aegean coast was supposed to shield the state from invasions by the belligerent neighbours to the west and north-west. Even today, the remains of the heavy fortifications testify to this. In a formal treaty Cotys guaranteed to the merchants of Pisthiros the safety of their lives and property. He granted them the right to collect taxes from some of the nearby mountain roads that ran south through the Rhodopes to their native cities.

To facilitate further the home market, Cotys started minting silver and bronze coins, using the Hellenic mints in Maronea on the Aegean coast and in Cypsela. Apart from everything else, he asserted his royal prestige and reached lands that he could otherwise never reach during his rule. Instead of the traditional divine images, he had his own image stamped on them. What we see is a man of mature age, with a short curly hair, a thick beard and moustache. A massive forehead, big and deep eyes, prominent cheek-bones, a straight, slightly tapering nose with graceful sensual nostrils, a thick lower lip and a strong jaw: all his features betray the character of a ruler and, at the same time, suggest some unpredictability: a strong mind, an inflexible will, determination, pride, dignity, and nobleness. The moralist Plutarch points out that Cotys was quick-tempered and merciless to those who erred; as he was well aware of this tendency, he made a conscious effort to curb his fits of cruelty.

It is also known that he often travelled his lands. On some coins, he is depicted on horseback, his right arm raised in greeting. His contemporary Theopompus wrote that more than any other Thracian king, Cotys liked indulging in pleasures and luxury. When he saw shady places with trees and water, he ordered that they be made into "reception sites" where he would converse with his closest associates, receive envoys, and make sacrifices to the gods. Cotys took every occasion to point out his divine origin. He once had a room furnished with a conjugal bed for the goddess Athena and, after quite a few drinks, started sending servants to check whether the goddess had appeared. Those who came back with a negative answer he killed with his own hand, until finally one of them proved resourceful enough to report that the goddess was there. To the naïve Hellenic chronicler, that was a most atrocious and barbarian act. In fact, however, the chronicler inadvertently reveals the most important in the ancient Thracians' matrimonial rites: the sacred marriage of the ruler to the Mother Goddess through which he became immortal.

It is also known that the representatives of the Odrysian dynasty to which Cotys belonged were highly respected at the ancient pan-Hellenic and Balkan sanctuary to Apollo at Delphi. The generous royal gifts were not the only reason. Until the time of Cotys' successors, at Delphi there was a priestal clan of the name of Thracidae. In ancient times, the Thracians played an important role in the erection of the oracle. On the other hand, Delphi was the source of many of the early religious ideas and beliefs adopted by the Thracian kings who were also priests. It is an indicative fact that Cotys, with the typical straightforwardness and directness of his age, revealed his divine origin in a gilded inscription on a silver vessel: "Cotys, son of Apollo." A brick building in Epidaurus – the largest sanctuary in Hellas to the god of healing Asclepius (also son of Apollo) – is also attributed to the Thracian king.

In those years of anxiety, Cotys seemed to be the only ruler to consolidate his power, and amass political experience, influence, and self-confidence. The Odrysian realized that Athens, although still claiming full control over the Straits, was losing its leading position. It became an undependable political partner when many of its allies among the poleis in coastal Thrace fearlessly claimed full control over their own affairs, neglected the principle of mutual benefit in their relations with the inland Thracians, and some even started fighting with each other. These events portended the impending disintegration of the second naval league. With a statesman's remarkable intuition Cotys realized that the centuries-old conflicts in the area were entering their decisive final phase, and was quick to claim his share. Around 365 B.C., he made an abrupt turn in his foreign policy, from Athens' faithful ally to its fiercest opponent. Giving up the role of an observer of the dramatic events that systematically impaired the Odrysian statehood, he became the driving force of historic events.

Through open pressure or military stratagems, Cotys started collecting money from the rich coastal poleis to pay his mercenaries. Before that, these contributions had been flowing into the Odrysian treasury under an agreement with Athens. The strongest resistance was put up by the large market city of Perinthus where the Odrysae traditionally sold the agricultural produce from inland Thrace and the loot. It seems that Cotys successfully increased his influence over the cities of Byzantium, Aenos, Maronea, Thassos, and Abdera. To the west of the river Mesta he made an alliance with Olynthus, the leading force in Chalcidice, in the war against the Athenian colony Amphipolis. More than once, he sided with Pausanias, one of the main claimants to the long-contested Macedonian throne. Pausanias, however, consistently failed. Cotys' situation was rapidly acquiring a dramatic aspect. His vigorous military campaigns and his ambitious strategic plans, bordering on adventurism, won him numerous enemies, even at his own court and among other Thracian rulers. Having gained control over sections of two major historical arteries – the Diagonal Road and the Aegean (Royal) Road – Cotys had difficulties uniting and controlling his territories. They were rich and favourably located but also dissimilar and conflicting. Cotys greatly resembled the Persian king who stood, with all his might, before the closed gates of the rich Miletus. That meant war, a life-and-death war. He was to walk the two major roads to their junction in the most neuralgic point of the Balkans – the Thracian Chersonese.

The narrow peninsula was densely populated because of its fertile land and the advantages of the sea. There, Europe was closest to Asia, which lay just across the Hellespont (today the Dardanelles). For centuries, Hellenes and Thracians contested that strip of land. Three times Athenian statesmen erected walls to protect the Hellenic population from Thracian raids. From that peninsula, the Persian king Xerxes embarked upon his offensive against Hellas. It was the place where Xanthippus who defeated the Persians by sea at Mycale took up a position at the end of the war. That was where the Peloponnesian War ended with the Spartans' victory over the Athenians. Finally, the Chersonese was the place through which Philip II of Macedonia would pass before invading Odrysian Thrace, and so would his son Alexander on his way to Persia.

In the winter of 362 B.C., Cotys invaded the Thracian Chersonese and conquered it. His son-in-law Iphicrates supported him in that undertaking. Only Critote, Eleunt and Sestos remained under Athenian control. Just when the Odrysian king was anticipating the final victory, the noble Thracian Miltocites rebelled at his rear, and paralyzed Cotys' campaign for a year. Miltocites took the highest spot north of the peninsula, the so-called "sacred mountain" where Cotys kept his treasury. Moreover, the rebel promised the Athenians to give them back the Chersonese. Fighting on two fronts, Cotys led a nomad's life, changing his residences almost every season. The difficult situation in which he found himself fostered the claims of the rulers of northern Thrace. To resist against their pressure and keep their neutrality, Cotys had to offer them rich gifts. These included splendid gilded silver sets onto which his name was inscribed. Cotys realized how short-lived and dangerous these friendships were, and hastened to write to the Athenians, offering peace. Abandoned, Miltocides surrendered. Cotys spared his life but did not give up the war with Athens. December came in the year 361 B.C., and another incompetent Athenian commander was appointed in charge of the Hellespont. Fierce sea storms cut off the access to the Pontus, the Propontis and the northern Aegean. The Odrysian king used the winter to prepare his next strike. In 360 B.C., the men of Abydos in Asia Minor who were traditionally in conflict with Athens took Sestos and immediately handed it over to the Odrysian king. It was a moment of triumph in Cotys' rule. For the first time, the vital Athenian trade with the northern seas and with inland Thrace was cut off. Very soon, another event added to the Athenians' misery. Philip II came to power in Macedonia and immediately entered into vigorous negotiations with Cotys.

One day in the spring of 359, the news spread of King Cotys' death. He was murdered by the brothers Pytho and Heracleides of Aenos, who claimed that they had done it by divine guidance. Demosthenes praised them, the Athenians crowned them with wreaths and showered honours on them, just as they had once done with the Odrysian king; the Byzantines welcomed them cordially. In just a few months, Cotys' unified state broke up into three parts, ruled respectively by Berisades, Amadocus and Cotys' son Cersobleptes. The disunity only facilitated the mission of Philip II of Macedonia who, in 342 B.C., not only took up his predecessor's strategic position on the Hellespont but also developed further his ambitious plans.

A remarkable strategist and diplomat, Cotys left behind a flourishing Odrysian state. History has yet to stumble in its assessment of his role and significance and, as it inevitably speaks in the terms of his fiercest political opponents, will forever remain indebted to him. Indeed, Cotys recalls of those leaders in human history who, with resolution and talent, paved the way for the new age and set the landmarks of the future but inevitably fell victim to narrow-mindedness at home or abroad. While Philip II would render homage to Apollo the Delphian with a laurel wreath on the battlefield and thus seek to win to his side the united Hellenes, Cotys did not hesitate to sign with Hellenic letters as the god's son. Much later, Alexander the Great would demand recognition of his own divinity.

EPAMINONDAS
late 5th c. – 362 B.C.

Although it seems that the exhausting Peloponnesian War was a war for supremacy between the two seekers of hegemony, Sparta and Athens, in fact, all neighbouring states in the Balkans as well as in Asia were involved in the conflict, either directly in the hostilities, or in distant diplomatic missions and strategic plans. The large-scale war only deepened the painful crisis. During the Classical Age, in the 5th c. B.C., Persians, Odrysians, the Hellenes in the Delian League, and the Peloponnesians enjoyed relatively stable development and success: they had vast and stable markets, regular revenues, good laws, and a balanced social structure, the last years of the century held many surprises in stock. In 405 B.C. the previously unrivalled naval force of Athens was defeated by the newly built and inexperienced Spartan fleet. That was the end of Athens' prestige although it soon returned to its traditional democratic system, restored its fortifications, and rebuilt its fleet. The situation was aggravated further when it became evident that the Spartans were not worthy of their victory. Having accepted the corruptive Persian gold to build a fleet and train crews, the Spartans found themselves unintentional heirs to the Athenian foreign policy after the war: they had to protect the Hellenes in Asia Minor from encroachments by the Great King and his satraps. Possessing neither diplomatic tact, patience, tolerance and commercial intuition, nor seafaring skills, and tending to commit outrages outside their own state as well as having a taste for demonstrative cruelty, they soon made enemies even among their recent supporters. With every passing day, the polis ideals of freedom, justice and equality before the law were falling apart. Unscrupulous people and self-seekers were making their way into politics. The talented and influential politicians were increasingly displaced by prosperous orators, capable of presenting any personal or party opinion as something of public benefit. The collective polis consciousness and the fervent patriotism gradually gave way to individualism and cosmopolitanism, transforming individuals into self-sufficient and adaptable personalities. The notorious Alcibiades was an early example of this new personality type. Mercenary strategists made their living in foreign armies, and were ready to fight – for a good pay – against their home countries where they had found no recognition of their abilities or a means of livelihood.

At the same time, the disunity spread to the large monarchies in the Balkans and in Asia. In Persia, the conflicts between the Great King and the satraps in Asia Minor were aggravated. The satraps themselves competed for more power, riches, influence over the Hellenes, and political independence. Only a few years after the Peloponnesian War, Persia saw a bitter struggle for the throne between the two brothers Artaxerxes II and Cyrus the Younger. Cyrus, supported by well-paid Hellenic mercenaries, the future historian Xenophon among them, was killed in the decisive battle, and Sparta suddenly went into a war with the lawful king Artaxerxes. In 386 B.C., the two belligerents agreed upon a peace treaty, and Sparta found itself compelled to surrender its compatriots in western Asia Minor to Persian rule, thus rendering pointless not only its victory in the Peloponnesian War but also the Hellenes' heroism in the Greco-Persian War. It is understandable why the Spartan diplomat who negotiated the peace treaty, Antalcides, committed suicide, while Sparta gradually restored its conservative ways and would, later on, isolate itself from Hellenic affairs. The Persians had no reason to rejoice, either. The Great King's gains were due not to his talent as a commander but to the gold he paid to instigate conflicts among the Hellenes, and to buy off – dearly – the peace in his own state.

An important consequence of these dramatic events was the Hellenes' increasing confidence that the Persian state was internally fragile and unprotected. Tales of the Persians' might and invincibility were no longer more than a legend. In the 380s B.C., the far-sighted Athenian orator Isocrates even expressed the idea of reconciliation and unification of the Hellenes for a campaign against the barbarian Persians to conquer their vast lands and untold wealth. Several more decades, however, had to pass in eager expectation of a unifier. He could not be one of the polis tyrants, nor any of the demos leaders, by then derisively referred to as demagogues. After decades of open or concealed enmity, the Hellenes and the Persians were considering – each in their own way – their historical prospects. Certainly, that encapsulation and calm did not mean that the antagonism was over. Epaminondas the Boeotian, the son of Polymnis, realized that clearly. Listening to his heart, which beat with the rhythm of the new epoch, he headed to his glory.

DURING THE YEARS of the devastating Peloponnesian war, an ancient city in the central region of Boeotia had its share of the vicissitudes of fate in Hellenic history. Despite this, it always stood in the shadow of Sparta and Athens. The name of that polis was Thebes. Back in ancient times the foundations of its statehood were laid on the hill of Cadmea, surrounded by refreshing springs and a fertile plain. The plain bore a rich harvest, and warhorses and cattle grazed there. Later, Thebes grew to cover the plain around the acropolis on Cadmea. The acropolis was named after the mythical founder Cadmus who, according to the legend, came across the sea from faraway

Portrait illustration by Hristo Hadjitanev

Phoenicia to look for his beloved sister Europa who had been carried off by Zeus. In fact, the settlers were attracted by the fertility of Boeotia. Several centuries before the Trojan War, Cadmus erected a strongly fortified castle with seven gates on the hill. His successors expanded the stronghold, and amassed wealth from the surrounding land and from trade with the East. Thebes along with a dozen other Boeo-tian settlements inevitably took part in the Trojan War on the side of the Mycenaean commander Agamemnon, as the war was to decide the supremacy at sea and to provide peace-ful trade roads through mainland Europe. The busy central road from the north to the heart of Hellas and the Pelopo-nnesus passed just by Cadmea. It was used not only by peace-ful merchants, messengers in a hurry and gift-loaded envoys to the poleis, Delphi and Olympia; ruthless invaders advanced along it as well. Thus the Thebans became active partici-pants in historic events early on, instead of passive onlookers.

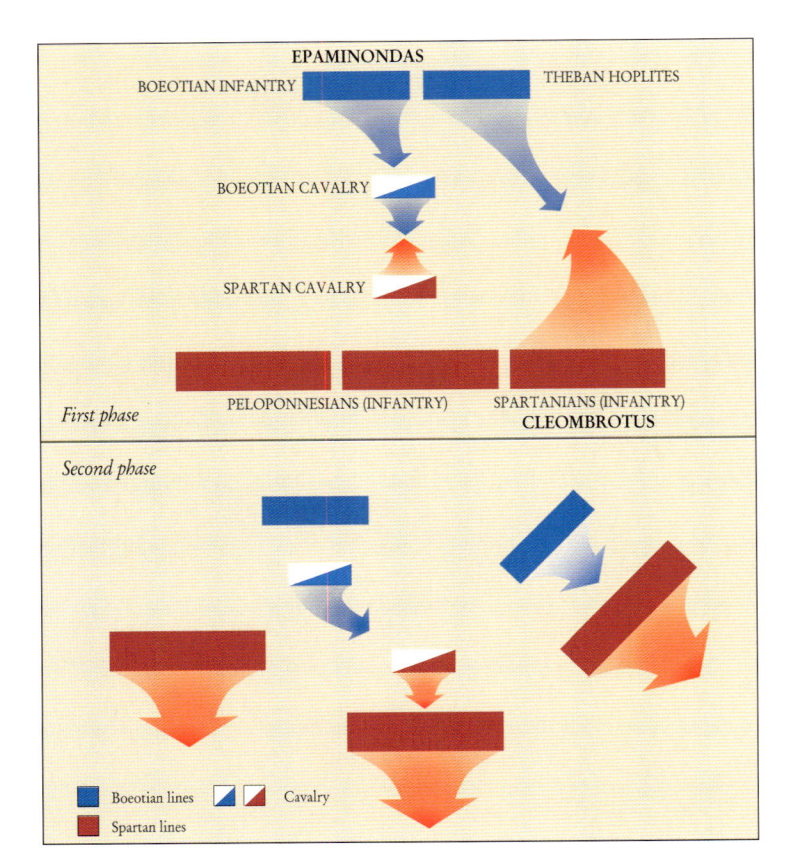

Plan of the battle at Leuctra, 371 B.C.

Although strong enough in itself, and aware of its forthcoming glory, Thebes never quite managed to keep Boeotia under control and to gain the Hellenes' recognition. This is why the Thebans used every dramatic event in Hellenic history to have their say for the future of that ancient land.

The opportune moment arrived after the Spartans signed the humiliating peace of Antalcides in the Persian residence in Susa. The Theban diplomats firmly opposed Sparta's desire to impose the unquestioning observation of the clause according to which all poleis in Hellas, large and small alike, became independent. The Thebans had either to assert their claim for domination in Boeotia or to be satisfied with that imaginary freedom in the shadow of Sparta. To be on the safe side, in 382 B.C. Sparta occupied the Cadmea, installed supporters of the oligarchy into power, and sent dozens of open critics of the new Spartan order into exile. Only in Athens were there more than a hundred Theban exiles. Only twelve of them, however, had the courage to liberate their native city. These were led by Pelopidas whose life, years earlier, had been saved in battle by Epaminondas, with whom they had become close friends and political associates. Dressed in peasants' clothes and accompanied by hunting dogs to avoid raising suspicion, the conspirers entered the city at dusk and, during the night, sent the message of their bold intentions to the country. A crowd gathered that ousted the usurpers and their supporters, and the people took over the government. In the dramatic hours of the coup, Epaminondas stayed at home. When they asked him why he neither defended nor stained his hands with the blood of the "patriots" who had turned their land over to the Spartans in exchange for power and wealth, Epaminondas answered: "Any victory over compatriots is lamentable".

In his childhood, Epaminondas was much different from his peers. Even though he descended from a noble Theban family, he learned to live modestly. The famous musician Dionysius taught him to sing and play the lyre. Olympiodorus taught him to play the flute, Caliphronas taught him to dance, but the teacher with the greatest influence over him was his teacher of philosophy, Lysias the Pythagorean. He inspired him with faith that the soul was immortal, and that military prowess was the supreme virtue. He also taught him temperance in regard to luxury and temptations. Epaminondas was diligent in athletic exercises but he sought to attain agility and skills for the future battles rather than physical strength. Epaminondas grew up with a fine physique, intelligence, prudence, extreme honesty and bravery. He had excellent self-control. Kind and patient, he endured with equal forbearance his rivals' and his friends' insults. He guarded the secrets with which he had been confided and was a talented public speaker, but he also had the gift of listening because he believed that it was by listening that one learned most easily. He was so interested in aged Thebans' talks on state affairs that he always listened to them attentively to the very last word. For him, that was a source of invaluable wis-dom from history, and of knowledge of the Thebans' most daring ambitions.

As he later became an associate of Pelopidas in his political actions, and was elected among the strategists of the Boeotian army, the so-called *Boeotarchs*, Epaminondas set about turning these ambitions into reality. Although kind in his relations with the Thebans, he was one of the few to try to blaze a trail to the future, beyond the idleness of his anxiety-ridden time. Epaminondas often spoke of the Boeotian plain as a "military ground" that would be controlled by him who always had a shield in his hand. His opponent Meneclides who possessed the gift of eloquence, urged the Thebans to prefer peace to war. Epaminondas addressed the crowd with the following words: "You only fool your fellow-citizens with empty talk, dissuading them from the war because, for the sake of peace, you condemn them to slavery. Peace can only be obtained through war. He who wishes to enjoy it for a long time, should be prepared to go to war." The words of Lysias the Pythagorean were forever engraved on his mind, and he taught his warriors that death in battle was a sacrifice to the gods. He never allowed them to panic, and scorned those of them who, like the Persians, lolled on couches, eating and drinking without moderation. Even as a strategist he led such a modest life that once, having been invited to a lavish dinner, he left with the words: "I assumed the gods would be honoured here, not abused".

The war for which Epaminondas had long been preparing the Thebans was drawing nearer. In 371 B.C., the Hellenes gathered in Sparta to sign a peace treaty. The Thebans were not recognized as representatives of all Boeotia, so they refused to join the peace and walked out indignantly. This time, the war between Thebes and Sparta was inevitable. It so happened that at that precise moment one of Sparta's greatest command-ers, Agesilaus, had fallen ill, so it was king Cleombrotus who led the army. The decisive battle took place the same year near Thebes, in the plain at Leuctra. Epaminondas was appre-hensive that in case of failure, the Boeotian allies of Thebes might claim their independence; on the other hand, Cleom-brotus' opponents accused him of sympathizing with the Thebans. The tension reached its peak. According to their ancient tradition, the Spartans lined up in long straight ranks. Epaminondas displayed intelligence and tactical excellence. Surprising his enemy, he ordered a depth of 50 ranks on his left wing against the traditionally strong right wing of the Spartan army. The cavalry was the first to go into battle and, as expected, the Boeotians proved superior. Soon the Spartan infantry was disgracefully put to flight. King Cleombrotus himself, his son, and about a thousand noble

Spartans fell in the battle. The outcome was miraculous. For the first time the invincible Spartan army was defeated by land. The news resoun-ded throughout Hellas. The name of Epaminondas became known in all poleis, and raised faint hopes for a new order and a new freedom. Hellas had found its new leader; strangely enough, many lamented the ideal that had been crushed in dirt and blood.

Epaminondas, who consistently and deliberately suppressed his bursts of joy, said that the best of all that fate had allotted him was that his parents had lived to see his famous victory at Leuctra. To an opponent who jealously claimed that he had been trying to match himself with Agamemnon, Epaminondas answered boldly: "You are wrong because it took Agamemnon and his allies from all Hellas ten years to take a single city while I, with only the forces of our polis, in a single day liberated all Hellas by defeating the Spartans."

The following decade in Hellenic history was the time of Epaminondas' glory. After a series of campaigns against Laconia, he threw the ancient Peloponnesian League into confusion, devastated the Spartans' land, and for the first time in 500 years they faced the horrible threat of extinction. Epaminondas also won the highlanders of Arcadia to his side, built the stronghold of Messene that had been demolished by the Spartans two hundred and thirty years earlier, and attracted the famed Argos as an ally. Thebes became a force to be reckoned with – even for the tyrants in the northern region of Thessaly and for the Macedonian kings. The future Macedonian king and talented statesman Philip II spent some time there as a hostage. Epaminondas urged the Thebans to build a fleet to challenge the now precarious naval supremacy of Athens. Faced with this growing threat, the Athenians and the Spartans forgot their old enmity and joined their forces for a decisive battle.

It was harvest time in 362 B.C. The sun scorched the Peloponnesian land. Theban and Spartan allies were preparing for battle at Mantinea. By Epaminondas' order, the soldiers' shields and helmets were polished and shone sinisterly in the sun. The Theban commander lined up his force as a trireme, its prow facing the enemy. He hoped to make a breakthrough with his attack and subsequently destroy the enemy army, so he sent his best forces ahead, leaving weaker ones in the rear to avoid their defeat, which might dishearten his own men and inspire confidence in the enemy. Thus, Epaminondas attacked with a spearhead of cavalry and foot soldiers, and his plan proved good. The attack put the enemy army to flight. The Spartans realized that their state's survival depended on the death of one man, so they all dashed on Epaminondas who fought bravely but, unfortunately, was wounded in the chest by a spear. He endured the pain as long as he could so as not to discourage his warriors, but as he felt he was dying, he uttered his last words: "I have lived enough if I die undefeated." Thebes would never again have a remarkable commander, and Epaminondas realized that clearly. His life was a proof that a single man can often have more significance than an entire state.

Epaminondas never married nor fathered children. With his typical wise sense of humour, he used to say that the battle at Leuctra was his daughter, and it would not only outlive him but would remain immortal.

Almost all Hellas took part in the battle at Mantinea, and both sides believed that the victor would dominate and the defeated would be subordinated. However, it was so destined that each side erected monuments to the victory but neither obtained more land, more cities or more power than before. The battle only added more to the Hellenes' suffering.

The crucial battle at Leuctra.
Illustration by Marin Marinov

Philip II of Macedonia
359 – 336 B.C.

THE ASSESSMENTS of contemporary authors of the twenty-four-year reign of the Macedonian king Philip II vary widely. Apparently, even the time when he was destined to play the leading role in a series of historical events and vicissitudes was reminiscent of the blaze of glory and the bitter end of a neighbouring Balkan monarch, the Odrysian Cotys I. However, while the Odrysian was just an outstanding forerunner of the approaching new epoch, Philip's resolute and large-scale undertakings broke the impasse in which Europe and Asia had been frozen for decades.

Archeologists recently discovered by the town of Vergina (Greece) – where the ancient Macedonian capital Aegae once lay – a large royal tomb with murals, lavish gold, bronze and ivory gifts, and a full set of weapons of the deceased. Most scientists are unanimous that Philip II of Macedonia was buried there. The remains that were found in the tomb show that the king was rather short but, according to his temporaries' description, he was good-looking, with regular features, thick curly hair and beard, well-built and stately, with a royal bearing. Philip preferred the simple life of a soldier to luxury, and battles to lavish banquets. This is why the immeasurable wealth he acquired through much fighting and admirable diplomatic efforts was used only for military purposes. He often walked out of feasts to go into fierce battles. More than once, he received serious wounds, or was overtaken by illnesses, but he inevitably retained his presence of mind, and recovered quickly and acted so firmly and unexpectedly that he immediately disproved the rumours of his alleged death. He was moderate in both serious and jovial matters. He never yielded to anger but hid it skillfully in view of more distant objectives. He always sought to win, no matter the means. This is why his bitter enemies often accused him of insidiousness. He once intended to seize a fortress, and his spies reported that it was inaccessible. "Is it so inaccessible that a mule loaded with gold would not pass," Philip asked. His inexhaustible energy was infectious, and it affected his associates. In his personal contacts he was so charming and understanding that he captivated all. Yet, he would not attach himself easily, he repeatedly tested his associates' loyalty, and he measured friendship in interest. It was no coincidence that he said he envied the Athenians who were able to elect ten new strategoi each year while he, in all those years, managed to find only one, Parmenion. Philip also had the remarkable gift of expressing his thoughts understandably while his words were not devoid of sponta-neous wit and imagination. That gift brought him much diplomatic success and helped his military exploits. He was compassionate and perfidious at the same time. When he was told that he ought to do away with his key enemies, the Athenians, Philip answered that it was silly for a man who

Portrait illustration by Hristo Hadjitanev

was prepared to do anything for glory to deprive himself of his best audience. Having many gifts that his contemporaries could only boast sporadically, Philip inevitably showed many weaknesses as well, particularly in his private life. One of his historians, Theopompus of Chios, who never passed over the ruler's weaknesses of character, wrote: "Europe had never born a man such as Philip, the son of Amyntas." His enemies often acknowledged his qualities, and many became his enemies in the first place because they felt neglected and underrated by him.

Philip was the third son of the Macedonian king Amyntas III (394/93 – 370 B.C.) and Eurydice, daughter of the Lyncestian noble Siras (Lyncestis was a region populated predominantly by the hostile Illyrians). After the brutal murder of King Archelaus in 399 B.C., the Macedonian court became an arena of bloody power struggles. Self-proclaimed rulers ascended the throne only to hold it for a couple of days or a couple of years before dying a violent death. That encouraged the ancient enemies of the Macedonian kingdom. Moreover, there was no longer a personality strong enough to put an end to the tumult in the Balkans. After the death of Amyntas III, his eldest son Alexander II (370/69 – 368 B.C.) ascended the throne.

That was the beginning of the most sinister and confused decade in Macedonian history. Only a year had passed from the enthronement of Alexander II when his own mother Eurydice and her brother-in-law and lover Ptolemeus made a plot and killed him during a feast. Ptolemeus on his behalf failed to do anything remarkable while in power. Particularly important for the future was an apparently minor event. Ptolemeus made a military alliance with Thebes and sent fifty young boys as hostages there, the young Philip among them. The boy lived in the home of the great philosopher and commander Epaminondas. The three years as a hostage in that city of stern ways, and the personal contacts with one of the military geniuses of humanity, left an indelible mark on Philip's mind, and inspired him with bold ideas and plans that would soon surpass Epaminondas himself. In 365 B.C., the second son of Amyntas III, Perdiccas, avenged his brother Alexander's death by killing Ptolemeus, and ascended the throne. Perdiccas III befriended the people of Amphipolis and managed to station a Macedonian garrison there, exposing his state to great peril. In 359 B.C. the belligerent Illyrians again attacked Macedonia. In the fierce battle, Perdiccas was killed together with 4000 elite soldiers. Western Macedonia was seized by the Illyrians. The Paeonians were raiding from the north. As an ancient author put it, it was a critical moment for Macedonia's fate: as if all tribes had conspired to attack it from every side and demolish it.

Hope loomed when the youngest son of Amyntas III, Philip, stepped forward. For many, he was the last hope for the fulfillment of an ancient oracle that said that one of Amyntas' heirs would lead Macedonia to greatness. One thing was certain: Philip's heritage was war on all fronts. At first, as a regent of the young son of Perdiccas III, Amyntas, he had to cope with three new pretenders for the throne. Philip, who was only twenty-three at that time, had but a few days to make his decision, and could not afford a mistake. One of the pretenders he eliminated, the other he killed in battle, capturing many of his loyal soldiers, and the third he rendered harmless by making an alliance with his supporter in the ambition to reign, the Odrysian king Cotys I. With bribes and promises, Philip persuaded the commanders of the invading Paeonians to withdraw from Macedonia. His first quick successes restored the Macedonian army's self-confidence, and soon Philip was placed on the throne. He kept the young Amyntas with him, and later had him married to one of his daughters.

The first project the new Macedonian king embarked upon energetically was a reform in the army. Until then, it consisted mainly of cavalry made up of heavily armed nobles, sometimes supported by recruited infantry, but that small elite army was no longer serviceable. It did not take a clairvoyant to hear the sinister rattling of the weapons coming against Macedonia on many fronts simultaneously. Every day of idleness could cost the country its independence. Some weird historical vacuum had been forming there, due to both the half-way measures of Philip's predecessors and the vain attempts of the Hellenes from Athens, Sparta, Thebes, Pherae, and Olynthus to gain dominance in the absence of authority. Philip retained the famed elite cavalry of about 800 close companions or *hetairoi*. According to the old tradition, they were armed with helmets, chain armour, shields, swords, and spears. Among them the king selected his guards who accompanied him in everyday life as well as in battle. Philip then created a light cavalry made up of lancers in flaxen shirts. It was organized in squadrons, and was the most maneuverable force in battle. Later, this light cavalry was reinforced with the experienced Thessalian cavalry units when the plains of Thessaly were finally annexed by Macedonia in 343 B.C.

However, Philip's most remarkable military innovation was *the Macedonian phalanx*. The phalanx as a military formation had been known in the Balkans at least since Homeric times. Its length and the number of ranks often decided the outcome of the battle. The phalanx was an appropriate formation for a frontal fight in a flat country. Philip armed his soldiers with long Macedonian pikes called *sarissas*. The deeper the rank in the phalanx, the longer the sarissas. When extended, the deep ranks' pikes reached before

From his youth Philip II of Macedonia pondered the military traditions of nations near and far to create the victorious Macedonian phalanx.

Illustration by Plamen Vulchev

the first rank. The Macedonian phalanx made an overwhelming striking force. Surrounded on all sides by the spearheads, trained in harsh discipline and hardened in continual battles, the Macedonian phalanx knew no retreat. To be prepared to fight with various enemies on various grounds, Philip included in his army light infantry, archers and slingers. He succeeded in uniting all the different troops into an organic whole, displaying his genius as a commander. For the first time in Macedonian history, the country's fate was in the hands of a numerous army raised not only from among the nobles but from among the ordinary population as well. Representatives of all tribes that inhabited the ancient Macedonian land were enlisted. The infantry even included many poor and migrating shepherds from the mountainous regions. Some joined the army for the loot and the subsistence; others were paid for their military services. Thus, under Philip, warring became a major source of income, regardless of the soldiers' social stand or tribal origin. To prevent the notables' aspirations for the throne, Philip had their children sent to the court as soon as they reached a certain age, and there he raised them and conversed with them daily, referring to them as "the king's children". According to ancient sources, Philip talked casually with his soldiers, and visited them often, unaccompanied by guards. In battle, he was second to no one in courage and stamina. He never did anything without a purpose. Along with his own rise, he mobilized his people's resources and raised its self-confidence. His firm will, however, was invariably supreme.

Philip knew well the weaknesses and the keenest desires of his major enemies in Hellas, Thrace, Illyria and Paeonia. Having first consolidated his state internally, he decided to beat them one by one. To gain time and resources while fighting with some of them, he did such great and unexpected favours to the others that many patriots shuddered in horror while those who grew rich from his gestures never forgot his generosity and expected to continue to reap its benefits. It was remarkable that it did not take Philip years to mature as a monarch; he started implementing his strategy immediately as he came to power. This is why the chronicle of his great achievements is so long.

Philip first addressed a letter to the Athenians, stating that he gave up the strategic Hellenic city of Amphipolis at the mouth of the Strymon, and asking to renew the good relations his father Amyntas had once established with them. The exhausting war the Athenians were waging against Cersobleptes, son and successor of the Odrysian king Cotys I, for the Thracian Chersonese forced them to accept the proposal. Philip took advantage of the favourable situation and immediately fended off the threat from the north. In 358 B.C. he subdued the Paeonians whose king had just died, and defeated the unyielding Illyrians in a bloody battle, regaining Western Macedonia. Thus, the next year Philip could turn his gaze on the vital Aegean coast to which the Macedonians had lost almost all access during the changes in the royal house. Without a moment's hesitation, he went for the most contested city for which Athenians and Spartans had been fighting fiercely: he besieged and seized Amphipolis. That put him in a state of war with his recent allies, the Athenians. However, while in the democratic Athenian assembly talented orators argued for or against Philip, in the winter of 357/56 the Macedonian ruler took the coastal city of Pydna. In vain his enemies claimed that he had been helped by bribed traitors. Meanwhile, Philip won to his side the powerful Olynthus, which continually sought to incorporate the large trade centre of Potidaea into its league – and never succeeded because of the Athenian garrison there. Philip not only seized Potidaea but let the surviving Athenians go and turned over Potidaea with its surrounding land to Olynthus. That noble gesture further confused the Hellenes who could not quite figure out the Macedonian's true intentions, while his bold plans multiplied with every passing day. Philip needed to keep the Olynthians happy for a while so that he could cross the Strymon unopposed, while the tales of the Athenian survivors would bring confusion in their fellow-citizens. It so happened that at that time Athens was waging a hopeless war against several strong former allies: Byzantium and the islands Chios, Rhodes, and Kos. The continuation of that war was advantageous to Philip. The blood of his future enemies was being shed.

At that point, what the Macedonian ruler needed most was money to keep his sizable army going. The richest silver and gold deposits lay across the Strymon, in the Thracian Mount Pangaeum – just opposite to Amphipolis. After the death of the mighty Cotys I, his unified state soon split into three separate kingdoms, and their rulers had neither the abilities nor the resources of the famous Odrysian, while the news of Philip's military achievements spread far and wide. In 356 B.C., oppressed by the local Thracian governor Cetriporis, the population of Crenides – the site of rich gold mines, fertile lands and dockyards – asked the Macedonian king for help. Philip seized the region of Pangaeum, drove out the Thracians, and founded a new settlement named after himself, Philippi, on the site of Crenides. This happened for the first time in the history of that ancient land, but was to become a tradition in the new epoch. Philip blazed his trail with fire both in the land and in his contemporaries' minds. His actions showed that he was prepared to walk the ancient Aegean Road all the way to the Straits, and the affected neighbours were beginning to guess his intention. Thus, the Thracian Cetriporis, the Illyrian Grabus, the Paeonian Lipeus, and Athens made an alliance against Philip, but with his characteristic aggressiveness the Macedonian routed them one by one, before they had ever managed to combine their efforts. His resolve was so immense that where the ground did not allow him to go into open battle, he sent hunting dogs after the fugitives.

Having brought the situation under control, Philip increased the output of the gold mines in Mt. Pangaeum. Soon, they yielded about 1000 talents per annum (1 talent = 26.5 kg). Philip used it to mint coins with the image of the Delphian god Apollo stamped on them (but called them *philippeioi*), and with them he paid his mercenaries and his agents in the Hellenic poleis, bribed traitors to seize fortresses, and built a small fleet in Amphipolis to defend the sea from pirates. Before Philip's time, gold coins were a rarity; only the Persian kings could afford them. Philip was considering even greater and more glorious achievements.

The ancient historian Pompeius Trogus wrote: "While each of the Hellenic poleis separately fought for hegemony, they only drained their own resources. Darting rashly to their mutual destruction, they realized only after they had been subdued that their separate losses had led to their common ruin. As if from the top of a tower the Macedonian king Philip was watching for every opportunity to take away the freedom of these small states, and fuelling their struggles by helping the weaker, he forced defeated and victors alike to bow before the Macedonian king." This time trouble for the Hellenes came from the ancient land of Phocis where Apollo's Delphic Oracle lay. The Thebans, who had become highly confident of their strength under Epaminondas, managed to impose through the Amphictiony an immense fine on the Phocians because of an old enmity between them. Facing a

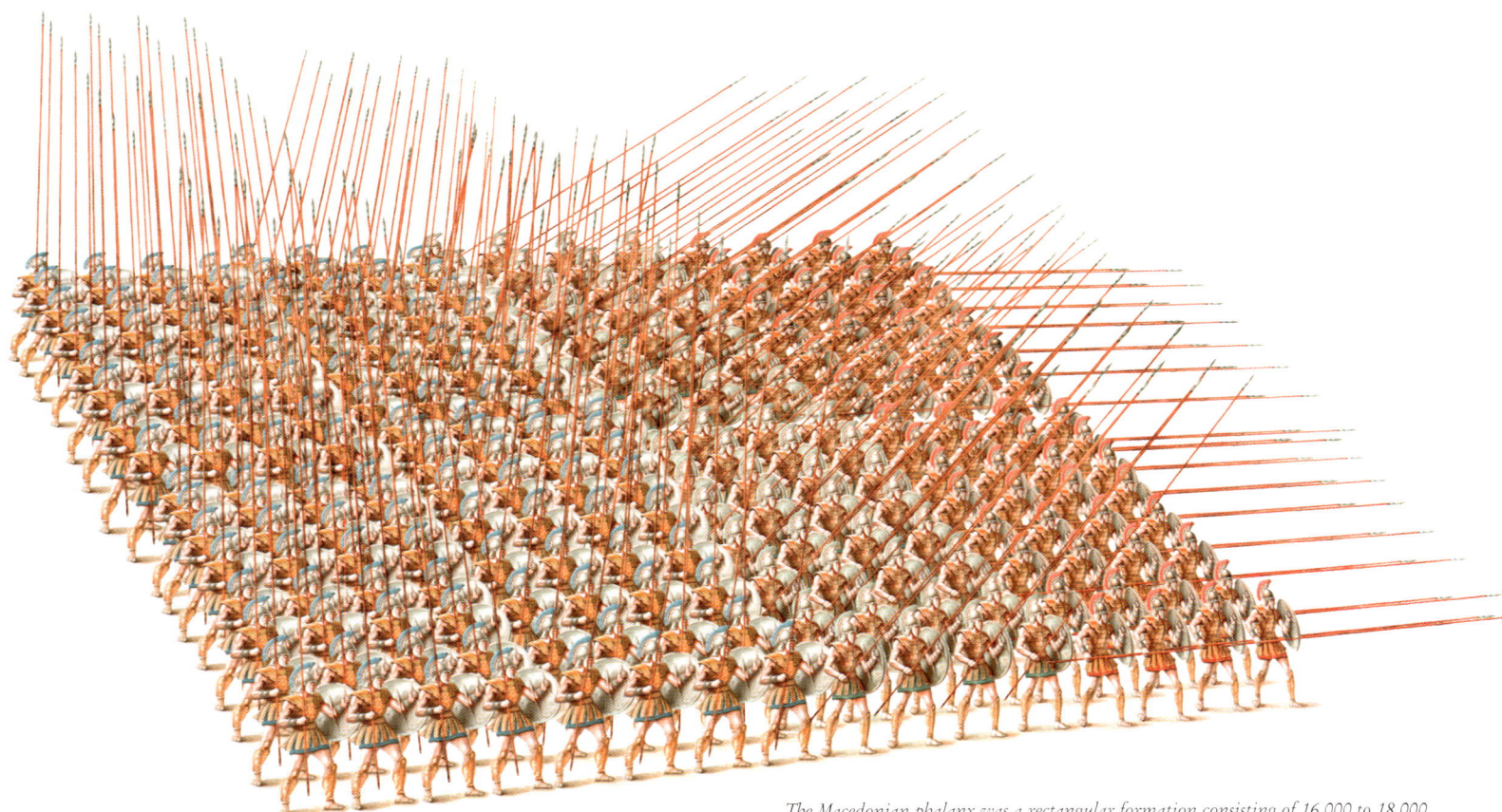

The Macedonian phalanx was a rectangular formation consisting of 16,000 to 18,000 heavily armed soldiers standing shoulder to shoulder. The smallest unit was the syntagma, made up of 16 rows of 16 soldiers each. They were armed with swords, shields and long spears – sarissas. The sarissas were shorter in the first row and longer in the back rows, so that they could project and several rows could act simultaneously.

Illustration by Atanas Atanasov

fine they could not pay, the Phocians took Delphi and plundered its immense wealth. The situation became intolerable when the profaners headed by Onomarchus hired a large army and won to their side the corrupt and power-loving Thessalian tyrants from Pherae. Philip was following closely the course of the war in Hellas and did not remain idle. In the spring and the summer of 353 B.C., he took the large Aegean cities of Abdera, Maronea, and Methone. He lost his right eye in the siege of Methone but was not embittered and treated the defeated Methonians leniently. At the time, any useless cruelty would only win him dangerous enemies. Philip's army invaded Thessaly and suffered two defeats by Onomarchus. The following spring, with his characteristic perseverance, Philip fought a new battle with the Phocian army. This time he acted with the self-confidence and the daring of a ruler who came to free the world of the impious. He ordered his soldiers to wear laurel wreaths, dedicated to the god whose sanctuary had been profaned. Onomarchus himself and six thousand mercenaries fell in that battle. Philip ordered that all survivors be drowned in the sea. His victory saved Thessaly from tyranny and the arrogant profanation was punished. From that moment on, Philip's fame and boldness grew irresistibly. To prevent any further attack from the Phocians, Philip appeared – much to the surprise of the Hellenes – before the Thermopylae, causing as great a horror as the Persian invasion had caused. Hellenic freedom and independence were hanging by a thread. At the last moment, the Athenians managed to block Philip's advance. This is when Demosthenes started delivering his passionate speeches, warning of the growing Macedonian threat.

Philip retreated but those who knew him realized that his was not a shameful withdrawal. He himself said that he was like a ram who always came back for a second, even more crushing strike. Time was on his side, and he was well-advised to let the Hellenes think seriously about the event. In the fall of 352 B.C., he moved the front to Thrace. There he allied himself with the Thracian king Amadocus and the population of Byzantium who were forced to cede lands and pay tribute to the Odrysian ruler Cersebleptus. Philip reached the coast of the Sea of Marmara and laid siege to the Odrysian's main stronghold. Left without support, Cersebleptus sued for peace, and sent his son as a hostage to Pella. Philip would have probably attacked the much-disputed Thracian Chersonese as well but he fell ill and rumours of his death spread. Very soon, however, those whose hopes had revived, were to suffer his blows. In 350 and 349 B.C. he fought successfully with Illyria and Paeonia. He consolidated his influence in Epirus, from where one of his wives, Olympias, came. Meanwhile the Olynthians felt opressed by the Macedonian king's actions in the region and, as they felt sufficiently rich and strong, they turned against him. At that time, Chalcidice was like an island under siege amidst Philip's coastal lands. The implicit threat pushed the Olynthians into an alliance with Athens – a belated one, in any case, as Philip already had his paid supporters in all poleis, and Olynthus was no exception. The Athenians' help for their allies in Chalcidice was in vain. It took Philip only a year to seize all poleis in the area. After a prolonged and desperate defence, in the fall of 348 B.C. Olynthus fell – with traitors' help. The city was plundered and razed. All citizens were sold into slavery, and their

Before the battle with Onomarchus' Phocian army, Philip ordered his soldiers to wear laurel wreaths, and became known in Hellenic history as a benefactor and protector of Apollo's sanctuary at Delphi.
Illustration by Plamen Vulchev

evaluation was entrusted to the traitor Euticratus. Olynthus' lot was to serve as an example to the disobedient Hellenic poleis. After paying generously to his army, Philip celebrated the victory with contests, performances and banquets, distributing generous gifts.

At that time, Hellas was exhausted by internal fighting and the ten year of fruitless warring with Philip. It was so impoverished that in Athens there was even no money to pay the court. Sparta turned a deaf ear on the misery of those Hellenes who were still defending their independence. The Phocians' mercenary army had almost depleted the gold and the silver at Delphi. In the spring of 346 B.C. Philocrates of

Athens made a draft for a peace with the Macedonian king. Philip welcomed the embassy of ten Athenians in his palace in Pella. Rumour spread that he had managed to buy Philocrates himself and the renowned Athenian orator Aeschines to his side, and they became his ardent supporters. However, his hospitality, his generosity and his charisma were so great that even Demosthenes was dumbfounded and lost his tongue. Philip expressed readiness to grant all of the Athenians' wishes except those that offended his dignity. Philip needed that peace treaty as acknowledgement of his victories. This is why, during the three months of discussions on the issues of peace in the democratic poleis of Hellas, before taking the sacred oath, he decided to consolidate his positions in Thrace. He crossed the Hebros (present-day Maritsa) and conquered the Thracian coast all the way to the Straits with the exception of the Thracian Chersonese and the lands of Byzantium. Defeated, Cersobleptus withdrew deep into his land as a vassal to Macedonia. Again, Philip was not rash in his conquests in order to avoid the making new enemies and alliances in his rear, but he always made it known that he would find a reason to come back. This gradually exhausted his enemies and they lived with a feeling of doom and inevitable ruin by their own fault. Philip's numerous victories on the battlefield proved that he ruled by right and by divine law.

When, after his expedition in Thrace, he returned to Pella, he found there embassies from almost all Hellenic poleis that were still arguing bitterly in anticipation of the oath and its consequences. Philip rightly felt he was a peace-maker and an arbiter in Hellenic affairs. He insisted, however, in excluding from the peace Cersebleptus and the Phocians who were still holding the strategic Thermopylae pass.

Left without allies and without hope, the Phocians soon surrendered, and Philip got hold of the Thermopylae. No one and nothing could now stop him from marching against the heart of Hellas, Athens, or even to the Peloponnesus, but instead he headed to Delphi to restore order in Apollo's sanctuary. No one and nothing could stop him from throwing all Phocian soldiers from the steep red cliffs in punishment for their impiousness – the Hellenes themselves suggested that he do so – but again he avoided useless cruelty, and ordered that the Phocians' weapons be smashed and burned, and their war-horses sold. Philip and his successors were given the Phocians' place at the Amphictyonic Council with the right to two votes. Along with the Thessalians and the Boeotians, he was also given the right to preside over the ancient Pythian games dedicated to Apollo. All these honors were not for the Macedonian tribe but personally for Philip. He realized well how precious these prerogatives were, how they gave him an exceptional opportunity to influence the events in northern and central Hellas however, and to avoid hurting the Hellenes' pride, refrained from styling himself "king of Macedonia." He did not even stamp that title on his coins, and they bore the image of the Delphian Apollo. It sufficed that the Hellenes were grateful to him for having punished the outrage of the Phocian mercenaries and for having put an end to the suffering of the war.

The more farsighted contemporaries, however, realized that Philip was not yet done with Hellas. They foresaw dramatic future events beyond the apparent peace. The Macedonian king made it clear that he could not tolerate idleness and delusions. The elderly famous Athenian orator Isocrates saw in Philip the saviour of the Hellenes. He wrote to him, reminding him of Philip's descent from Heracles, and calling on him to put an end to the hopeless and useless conflicts between the poleis, and to lead the Macedonians and the Hellenes together against the common enemy, Persia. It was not this correspondence that decided Philip's plans but it did help him realize how far the realistic attitude of some Hellenes had gone, and how desperate his worst enemies in Hellas were. In 343 B.C. he finally annexed all Thessaly and, as was the old tradition, installed there four governors among his political followers. The same year he made a nonaggression pact with the Persian king Artaxerxes III. In the language of diplomacy, however, that pact betrayed precisely his distant plans for a war with Persia. It was not an empty rumour that his spies had accurate information about the numbers of the Illyrians, the Thracians and the tribes in Asia Minor.

Protected by the peace, Philip soon occupied the lands of the Odrysians. He spent the harsh winter of 342/41 B.C. in Cotys' one-time kingdom, crossing it all the way to the Marichina Valley where the high Thracian mountains drew close and important roads crossed, and installed Macedonian garrisons in four strongholds. He also sent many of the vagrants in his state there as settlers. That part of occupied Thrace became known as "the land of the four strongholds." A long and exhausting siege of the coastal fortress of Perinthus followed, the place where the Thracian kings had once been selling their country's produce. The Perinthians were supported by Byzantium, Athens, and Persia. The Thracians from the occupied territories rebelled, too. Philip felt that the outcome was near, and acted boldly. Surprisingly, he gave up the siege of the Bosporus and went against the Scythians in the north, and on his way back to his capital invaded the lands of the northwestern Thracian tribe Triballi. It was the spring of 339 B.C. The Scythians were hostile to the Macedonian king for having disrupted their grain trade by the prolonged siege of Perinthus and Byzantium. They were at the same time under pressure by their neighbours. The Triballi were also hostile because Philip had cut off their vital access to the southern coasts along the rivers Strymon and Heres and the roads across the Rhodopes. In the battle with the Triballi, Philip not only lost his loot but received a bad wound in the thigh. The rumour even went that he had died in Pella. Philip decided that the time had come to punish his enemies among the Hellenes.

An Athenian embassy to the court of Philip II at the time of the signing of the Peace of Philocrates. Illustration by Atanas Atanasov

In the meantime, Demosthenes had asserted his dominance in Athenian political life. With promises, he had even managed to attract the Thebans as allies against the Macedonian king, even though they had previously been on his side in the punishment of the profaners at Delphi. Philip was not surprised by that turn, and he accepted the challenge of war. In August 338 B.C., at Chaeronea in Boeotia, he fought a decisive battle with the Hellenes. The two enemy armies were about equal in size, around 30,000 men. Philip commanded the right wing while Alexander, his eighteen-year old son by Olympias of Epirus, led the cavalry on the left wing against the Thebans. The Hellenes were routed. Demosthenes himself fled to save his life. Philip punished severely his recent allies, the Thebans: he made them buy off each of their prisoners and even the bodies of their dead. Surprising to all, however, he treated the Athenians considerately, winning the sympathies of many that had been in doubt about him. According to the ancient sources, Philip's greatness was evident even in the way he celebrated his victory: he remained serious and grim during the feast, as if he lamented the useless bloodshed.

Philip decided to announce the conditions of the new common peace at Corinth. He invited there representatives of all Hellenic poleis except Sparta. It was no coincidence that he chose Corinth. Philip had repeatedly proved that he had an excellent knowledge of Hellenic traditions and mentality. More than once in their tumultuous history, the Hellenes had succeeded in contemplating their future at Corinth and joining their efforts to find the right solution. Philip proclaimed the independence of all Hellenes and the common peace, and created and headed a council. He was unanimously proclaimed general plenipotentiary of the united Macedonian and Hellenic forces. His office was not created specially for him; it came from the historical traditions of Hellas and had once adorned Alcibiades when his country had been in a difficult situation. Now the Macedonian king was to direct the cumulative energy and aspirations. Soon after the conference at Corinth he sent his *hetairoi* Parmenion and Athalas to the Hellespont to prepare the forthcoming expedition against Persia. The Hellenes in Asia Minor held their breath in hope for their coming liberation.

Meanwhile, Philip focused on his private life which was no less dramatic than his rule. Having married six times during his military campaigns, he decided to marry again, this time the beautiful Macedonian aristocrat Cleopatra. The wishes for a worthy successor soured the otherwise good relations between the king and his grown-up son Alexander. With his mother Olympias he retired to Epirus and then to Illyria. Later, Philip and Alexander did make up, but that did not improve the situation at the Macedonian court. In the fall of 336 B.C. the king prepared to celebrate the wedding of one of his daughters. In the crowd that was pushing to take a glimpse of the greatest of the kings, Philip was stabbed by the young Macedonian noble Pausanias, supposedly because of a personal grievance, and died. Similarly to Cotys I, Philip I died an unexpected and violent death that seemed to reflect the interests of his numerous enemies. However, their malicious triumph was short-lived. The words of the famous commander Phocion to the Athenians proved prophetic: "It is dishonorable to rejoice at the death of an enemy. The force that fought against you at Chaeronea was reduced by just a single man."

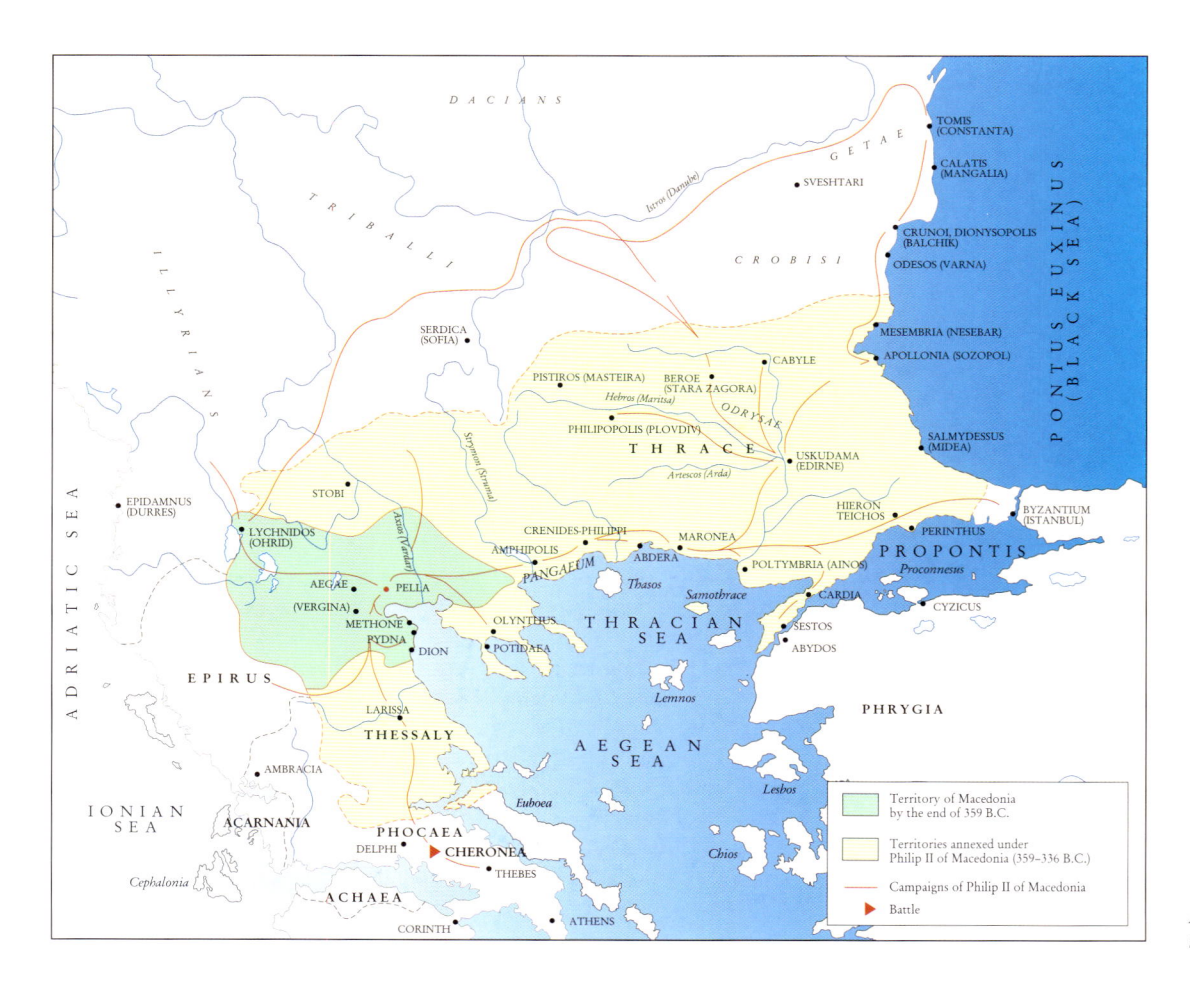

Macedonia before and after the conquests of Philip II.

SYRMUS
4th c. B.C.

Portrait illustration by Hristo Hadjitanev

SYRMUS, the king of the Thracian tribe Triballi, had pitched his camp by the swift-running river Lyginus, which flowed down the slopes of the Haemus with its snow-covered peaks, and meandered in its northern foot. The mountain that reached far east to the Euxine (Black Sea) was only seemingly a strong wall, protecting his country from the advance of the disturbing new times. The spring of 335 B.C. had just arrived, and its gentle warmth was drifting over the vast plains of the Triballi from the River Brongos (present-day Morava) on the west to the lands east of the River Oxius (Iskar) that cut its way through several Thracian mountains before it flowed wide to water the Triballi's lands. To the north, their state bordered on the Danube. Roads and waterways linked it with the other Thracian states that were closer or even had an outlet on the sea, with the Illyrians, the Celts and the Germans, the Getae, the Scythians, and the Sauromatae across the Danube. The rich harvest yielded by the land of the Triballi filled the king's and the notables' homes with agricultural produce that could only be seen in Thrace. In the king's stables, there were many purebred horses: stout, short-legged, and quick in both hunting and battle. Abundant game and fish were served at the banquets offered to the guests from near and far. Silver and gold came from trade, from the mines in the mountains, and from the river sand. Skillful artisans used the precious metals to make vessels and plates decorating the king's weapons and clothes and his horse's saddle and straps. Syrmus only lacked one thing: neither he, nor his predecessors had ever had direct access to the southern or the eastern seas, to those famously bustling coastal Hellenic cities with their rich markets. All important roads that had been controlled by his royal house for decades entered into neighbouring territories. Syrmus sometimes felt stifled, the wings of his plans crushed in the high slopes of the Haemus or drowned in the deep waters of the Danube. Even to the east, the coast of the Pontus was hopelessly far. Between Syrmus and that sea lay the vast plains of the Getae with their proverbially brave soldiers and battle-hardened cavalry. The roads could only bring him unwanted guests with treacherous plans; for himself, there was no real way out.

Syrmus' predecessors had to fight difficult and almost incessant wars to defend their independence and gain access to the common wealth. In older times, it came rather accidentally in the form of captures, loot or gifts from faraway lands, and it fired the imagination. This is why the Triballi had been good warriors for generations. It was the tribe's ancient tradition to have their military formation arranged so that the first ranks were made up of light infantry, particularly good in hand-to-hand fighting. Next came the heavy-armed infantry, followed by the cavalry made up of aristocrats who kept the formation orderly and stopped the first ranks from fleeing. For the same reason, the army was followed by the women and the children who shouted to encourage their husbands and fathers. Syrmus' aristocrats were inspired by the belief that their king was immortal and divinely appointed. Syrmus remembered the tales of his predecessors' achievements in hunting and in war. He himself passed voluntarily through numerous ordeals as soon as he reached maturity to prove that he was worthy for a king. Then he spent years in silence, abstention and fasting before he was initiated into the secrets of the Great Gods of the Triballi, his creators according to his predecessors' secret teaching and faith. To these gods he was priest, to them he prayed for the future of his tribe, and to them he would go after his death to become immortal. That spring day, however, Syrmus needed the gods' help more than ever, and he sought support in his faith.

This time Syrmus had turned his back to the field and watched the pass through the Haemus intensely. He was expecting messengers. Part of his army together with women and children had taken up positions in the pass to defend it from the Macedonian Alexander, the son of Philip. Less than a year earlier, the 20-year-old Alexander had ascended his famous father's throne after Philip had fallen victim to a plot. The news had reached Syrmus that ten days earlier the Macedonian king had led his army from the mouth of the Nestos on the Aegean shore towards the kingdom of the Triballi. Syrmus was relatively prepared for these events. He was thinking intensely, recalling past events – some he had witnessed, others he had heard of. Many rulers had been compelled to accept the fact of the Triballi's increasing power. Even the rich and mighty Odrysian king Sitalces whose lands spread from the southern slopes of the Haemus to the Euxine and the hot Aegean coast had been forced to fight an exhausting war with the Triballi in which he was defeated and died. Four decades before the battle with Alexander, the Triballi had thrown the Aegean Hellenes into panic and confusion. Their commander Chalis had led an army of 30,000 men that reached the rich coastal city of Abdera, blocking the vital trade of northern Thrace. All the men were about to be killed but their lives were finally spared. Ambitious and farsighted, Cotys realized the threat of a never-ending war along his western border and turned the Hellenic city of Pisthiros in the Marichina Valley by the Suki Pass into a lively market, offering luxury goods from across the sea. As they saw Cotys absorbed by the war for the Thracian Chersonese far to the southeast, the rulers of the Triballi achieved even greater concessions. The Odrysian king pronounced them allies and friends, and started sending them rich gifts, but that favourable situation ended with his death.

Soon Syrmus came to know that the Macedonian king Philip, the son of Amyntas, who had recently inherited the throne, was winning a series of glorious victories along the rich Aegean coast of Thrace, and that he had installed a garrison in Maronea where the Triballi effected much of their trade. Then came the defeat of the Odrysian kingdom, and even the good old market centre of Pisthiros was transformed into a Macedonian military camp. Indeed, the Triballi defeated Philip in a memorable battle on his way back from an expedition against the Scythians. The Macedonian king was badly wounded in the thigh, and his horse was killed. The rumour even went that Philip had died in the battle with the Triballi. After his recovery, he squared accounts with his enemies in Hellas once and forever. The roads to the southern markets were thus cut off for the Triballi. Even the old road along the Strymon now led to the heart of Philip's state, and its upper reaches were controlled by Langarus, the king of the Agrianes and Philip's faithful ally. Syrmus could now feel the pending threat of the invaders from the north, the Celts and the Sauromatae, attracted by the loot looming in the ruins of old glory. Syrmus could not accept that situation while Alexander, surprisingly, did not delay his expedition. Indeed, Syrmus had counted on that: if the son of Philip was planning a

Alexander III of Macedonia concludes a peace treaty with King Syrmus of the Triballi and the Celtic envoys from faraway lands. Illustration by Atanas Atanasov

campaign against the vast Persian Empire to the east, he was not likely to take his time in Thrace.

Syrmus was waiting for the messengers on his white horse, bareheaded, dressed in a linen shirt and chain armour, with finely crafted silver greaves, holding a pair of spears. Gilded plates adorned the straps on the horse's chest and head, and they looked as if they were made of solid gold. Similar to his predecessors, Syrmus did not have his image stamped on his coins. This expensive adornment was the symbol of his royal authority and his faith.

Soon the messengers came, bringing anxiety. Alexander the Great had crossed the pass. He had ordered his soldiers to lie prone on the ground with their shields locked together above their heads so that the heavy carts the Triballi were sending crushing down upon the Macedonian ranks had bounced over the top of them. Poorly dressed and poorly armed, many of the Triballi had been killed, and the invader had captured the women, the children and all the stores.

Syrmus decided to protect his people even if he was to violate some of the ancient traditions. He diverted Alexander's attention from the Triballi's traditional lands and settlements, and ordered that all women, children and old people move to the large and inaccessible island of Peuca in the Danube river near the lands of the Getae. The island's shores were steep, and the river ran quick in the narrows. Syrmus himself withdrew to the island with his army. A single unit of lightly armed soldiers stood behind to slow down Alexander's advance. Many brave men were killed in the battle with the Macedonian to assure the tribe's survival. Syrmus' plan worked. The ambitious Alexander insisted on fighting with him but his few ships did not manage to secure a landing on the island. As was the Thracian custom, Syrmus sent him rich gifts and asked for peace. Alexander agreed and they took an oath of friendship.

The future conqueror of the world thus gave way before the wisdom of a king who saw the last years of the Triballi's glory. In the following years of bloody wars, many ancient authors would admire the nobleness and the ingenuousness of Syrmus who, although undefeated, chose peace.

ALEXANDER III THE GREAT
336 – 323 B.C.

Portrait illustration by Hristo Hadjitanev

A LEXANDER, the son of the Macedonian King Philip II and Olympias, was born in the summer of 356 B.C., in the month of July which the Hellenes called Hecatombaeon and the Macedonians Lous. It so happened that the same day an evil man of the name of Herostratus set fire to the famous temple of Artemis at Ephesus in order to become famous. The temple burned down, and the Ephesians cursed Herostratus and ordered that his name never be mentioned. Naturally, the ban was not observed, as even among the contemporaries there was already a historian who was too garrulous, and who had a liking for curious events: Theopompus of Chios. On the other hand, the name of Herostratus has forever become the symbol of wild and futile desire for fame. That was not, however, the fate of Alexander who was born the same day. Shocked by the coincidence, the Hellenes thought that the temple burned because at that time its mistress was absent, assisting at the birth of Alexander in faraway Macedonia. The Persian priests – the Magi – who witnessed the fire, thought the ruin of the temple to be the forerunner of some other calamity, and beat their faces, crying that this day had brought forth something fatal and destructive to all Asia. From that moment on, with the tales that – true or invented – were spread hectically from mouth to mouth, the world seemed to live in a state of expectation, pulsating with the rhythm of Alexander's heartbeat. For it was him, the Great, who would create the history of their day faster and more brilliantly more than any other statesman in human history.

Philip II of Macedonia had just taken Potidaea when he received three good messages at one time: that his general Parmenion had defeated the Illyrians in a great battle, that his race-horse had won the course at the Olympic games, and that his wife had given birth to Alexander. The diviners said that a son whose birth was accompanied with such successes could not fail of being invincible.

Alexander's mother Olympias played a special role in his life. She was a princess from the region of Epirus in northern Hellas, neighbouring on Macedonia. Orphaned at an early age, however, she grew up excessively ambitious and jealous, and after her marriage with Philip she quickly became one of the most influential figures at the Macedonian court. While she was fairly tolerant to the whims of her famous husband, where Alexander and his lawful right to succession were concerned, her jealousy was unbridled. The rumour went that before leaving on his expedition against Persia, Alexander was told by his mother the secret of his divine origin.
On the night of his conception, a serpent embodying the all-powerful Zeus was found in the bedroom of Olympias. Neither Philip's glorious victories during his lifetime, not his likening to Zeus after his death could quite unveil the queen's secret about her son's mystical conception – as if it was not enough that on his father's side Alexander traced his descent to the hero of the heroes, Heracles, and on his mother's side to Aeacus, the ancestor of Achilles. In those distant times, however, the peoples of the Balkans were still more or less willing to accept the kings' divine and earthly descent without finding a contradiction between the two. Another legend was born, and it would help Alexander along the endless roads of the ancient Orient.

In fact, Alexander was not a pure-blooded Macedonian, but in those times only the biased few reflected upon that fact. In his veins was a mixture of Macedonian, Illyrian and Epirot blood, which was probably the reason why he adapted so easily to any land where he came as a conqueror or as a liberator, depending on the point of view. His contemporaries described him as having a very fair complexion and rosy cheeks. His body and his clothes were always fragrant. His body was hot, and so was his temper. His posture was poised, with his head slightly tilted to the left. His gaze was captivating. His features were regular and manly: a massive fore-

Replica of a relief featuring the battle at Gaugamela. The sarcophagus of Alexander. Hellenistic age.
Illustration by Hristo Hadjitanev

head, a straight nose, large expressive eyes and mouth, and a chin betraying a strong will. Unlike his father, Alexander was clean-shaven, and advised his closest associates to follow that fashion, as it was best in battle. Many attempted to imitate his conduct but few succeeded, as his character was quite complex. Alexander himself trusted only the sculptor Lysippus, and it is thanks to him that we have knowledge of his appearance today.

Philip was a considerate father, mindful of his son's education and upbringing. Leonidas, a relative of Olympias, was invited to the Macedonian court as a tutor, and so was one Lysimachus who was not too well-read but appealed to the young Alexander as he compared him with the hero Achilles. Alexander studied rhetoric with Anaximenas, a Hellene from Asia Minor. He not only developed his talent for verbal expression but also inspired into him an interest to the intransient wisdom of Homer's poetry. Later, as this interest developed into a passionate love of philosophy, Philip found himself compelled to invite to his court the famous philosopher Aristotle from the nearby Chalcidian city of Stagira. It was no coincidence that life brought together two personalities who were to gain universal fame. Indeed, later the roads of the great philosopher and founder of the Lyceum in Athens, and of the conqueror of the world parted, but Alexander cherished the memories of those years when he had been devouring Aristotle's teaching of the divine structure of the world and of the boundless capacity of the immortal human spirit, of supreme ethics, politics, poetry and medicine, and of the reason behind every terrestrial or celestial phenomenon. The people of Mieza long showed the nymphs' sacred grove, and the stone seats in the shadow where the tutor and the student used to converse. From Aristotle, Alexander received a corrected copy of Homer's *Iliad* which he kept under his pillow during his long march to the east. For him, the *Iliad* became a guide to military prowess and virtue. Alexander used to say that he loved the great philo-sopher no less than his own father because, although it was thanks to Philip that he lived, it was thanks to Aristotle that he lived a worthy life.

Over the years, Alexander grew stronger physically. He went hunting regularly, and was an excellent runner although he was not interested in boxing and wrestling or in the pan-Hellenic games that had so much attracted his predecessors. When Philip once asked him whether he wished to compete at the Olympic games, Alexander answered: "Alright, but only if I should compete with other kings." He had an acute feeling of honour and dignity. His passionate nature fuelled an ambition for glory which he never concealed even in his father's lifetime. His increasing self-confidence was based on his own achievements. Once, he was presented with a very expensive horse of the famous Thessalian breed. The horse turned out to be strong and spirited. No one at Philip's court could ride it. To everyone's amazement, Alexander himself tamed him. According to his biographer Plutarch, Philip exclaimed: "O my son, seek out a kingdom worthy of thyself, for Macedonia is too little for thee." That stallion, Bucephalus, carried Alexander almost to the end of his expedition, and brought him much luck in battle. When he died, Alexander mourned him as he would have mourned a brother, and gave him a royal funeral.

Philip was proud of his son and in no way showed any intention to deprive him of succession to the throne of Macedonia, despite Olympias' suspicions. He repeatedly demonstrated his great confidence in his son. When he was leaving for the siege of Byzantium, he left Alexander in charge of the royal seal, although the boy was only sixteen. In his father's absence, Alexander even received an embassy from Persia, and not only gave the envoys the usual hospitality and kindness but questioned them in detail about the roads in their state. He also reduced to obedience the neighbouring Thracian tribe Maedi, and founded in their lands a new settlement, calling it after his own name. He was only eighteen when, in the decisive battle at Cheronaea, his father put him in charge of the Macedonian cavalry on the left wing against an elite unit of Theban soldiers. From an early age, Alexander thus lived with his father's bold strategic plans, and in his youthful imagination they acquired unprecedented proportions. He often complained to the young hetairoi that his father's victories would leave nothing great for him to do. Fate, however, was kind to him. His father's sudden violent death faced him with a host of unfinished projects.

As was the ancient Macedonian tradition, the Council of the Hetairoi convened to elect a new king. Philip's loyal commanders installed his twenty-year-old son Alexander on the throne. Olympias was triumphant. Alexander had a lion's heart but that no longer sufficed: his father had paved the way for the new epoch, and he had no other alternative except to step forward into it. The situation in Hellas, Thrace, and Illyria was so turbulent that Macedonia suddenly became the

---

Plutarch relates the story that many statesmen and philosophers went to Alexander to congratulate him on his election as leader of the Hellenes. Alexander expected Diogenes of Sinope to do the same. At that time, Diogenes lived near Corinth. As he did not show up, Alexander decided to visit him instead. He found Diogenes basking in the sun. They greeted each other and Alexander asked the philosopher if there was anything he could do for him. "Step aside," Diogenes replied. "You are standing in my light." Alexander was amazed. On his way back, he told his retinue who were mocking the philosopher: "If I were not Alexander, I would wish I were Diogenes."

*Alexander III the Great with the philosopher Diogenes.
Illustration by Emilian Stankev*

target of all of Philip's enemies who saw in Alexander's youth an opportunity to regain control over their own countries. Alexander rapidly called another conference at Corinth, and gained – as if with his father's heritage – the title of *strategos autocrator* (supreme commander) in the future expedition against Persia. In the spring of 335 B.C., he was already fighting far north against the Triballi under king Syrmus, against the Getae and then against the Illyrians. During that time, rebels in Thebes spread the rumour that Alexander had been killed in the war in the north. Soon, the rumour encouraged many Hellenes to split off from the alliance with Macedonia. Alexander was quick to act. In just a few days, his army was at Thebes. The ancient polis was razed to the ground. There was no mercy even for the women, the old people and the children. Thousands of Thebans were killed in their homes and in the streets, tens of thousands were sold into slavery. However, even Alexander's rage was measured. He spared the lives of the priests and of his loyal friends, and ordered that the home of the famous poet Pindar be left intact. Again he found a way to express his reverence to the immortal Hellenic spirit. They say that he long mourned the tragedy of Thebes, and dared not deny a Theban's request. This time, embassies from all parts of Hellas were sent to him to plead for mercy. Again Athens was treated considerately. Alexander's had a sound judgement. He was not only appre-hensive of leaving behind a dangerous and embittered enemy in the face of Athens; he also realized that Athens would be the measure of his achievements. He actually told his allies that he was setting out on that campaign to punish the Persians for the evils done to Athens and Hellas under the Great King Xerxes.

Plutarch wrote that before the expedition, Alexander went to Delphi to make sure that the gods were on his side. However, it happened to be time when oracles were not given, while Alexander's thoughts were already focused on the vastness of Asia. Any delay could be misinterpreted by his enemies as a sign of weakness and doubt. He actually tried to drag the priestess to the temple, and all she managed to say was that he was invincible. That was all Alexander wanted to hear.

It was the spring of 334 B.C., having left as his deputy in Europe Antipater, one of Philip's experienced and loyal commanders, Alexander led some 30,000 foot soldiers and over 5000 cavalry to Asia. His army consisted mainly of Macedonians and Hellenes, but it was joined by many elite units from the allied and the subjected Balkan tribes: Agrianes, Paeonians and Odrysae. Alexander advanced along the same coastal Aegean road once used by Xerxes in his invasion of Thrace and Hellas. While he was crossing the Hellespont, Alexander ordered that his ship stop in the middle of the sea, sacrificed a bull to Poseidon, the god of the seas, and made a solemn libation from a gold goblet. He was the first to descend on the Asian shore, clad in full armour. As his army met no organized Persian resistance, Alexander decided to visit the ancient city of Troy where the tombs of the Achaean heroes could still be seen. He made a sacrifice to the Trojan King Priam, begging him to no longer bear grudge against the descendents of Neoptolemus to whom Alexander was related on his mother's side. He also anointed the gravestone of Achilles whose fame he wished to equal, and suggested that his close friend Hephaistion do the same with the gravestone of Achilles' faithful friend Patrocles. He took from the local temple weapons from the time of the Trojan War and ordered that they be carried ahead of him in battle to bring him the luck of the old heroes.

From the very beginning, there was nothing accidental about Alexander's actions, and his contemporaries were convinced that he was pursuing a well-devised strategic plan. He soared not only with the daring of youth, which was as natural as the sunrise and the spring, nor with the dauntless resolve of those great conquerors that humanity had seen through the ages: his greatness was in his ability to find his way on the dusty roads of the ancient Orient, and having taken them, to become the motor of dramatic events that were to open new horizons before the peoples of three continents. Luckily, the demands of time were in harmony with Alexander's talent. Philip's political heritage was a heavy burden for a young king to carry. To obtain recognition of his control over the Central and the Southern Balkans, Alexander's father had to fight the same enemies two or even three times. He often had to buy his way out with bribes, or to apply crafty moves and military stratagems, and that emptied the Macedonian treasury. Alexander relied on quick victories, embarking on many different projects that offered the materialization of at least a fraction of his hopes. With time, he shouldered several historical roles, very much like those ancient actors who would change clothes and masques and play several characters at the same time. Although an embodiment of his time, Alexander was very lonely. He transformed the conscious-ness of all peoples, regardless of their origin or past.

It behooved to remember that he was a descendent of Heracles, and was – openly or not – compared with the ideal image of the hero. He was thus the first and only ruler who was expected to bring justice and peace. It is no coincidence that, as soon as his expedition ended in India, the rumour spread that Heracles had also reached that distant and exotic country in his travels. It suddenly became evident that many believed Alexander to be an embodiment of Heracles, just as the Hellenes had once compared Xerxes to the all-powerful Zeus. Alexander was also extolled as a mythical son of Zeus. Although this curious story of Alexander's divine origin was regarded ironically by the practical Hellenes, it was beyond doubt taken seriously by the young Macedonian king and guided many of his actions. Born and raised near the sacred Mt. Olympus, he knew clearly that he would only gain true recognition of his divine origin in Egypt where Zeus had been worshipped for ages under the name of Ammon, and the pharaoh was his acknowledged earthly embodiment.

Alexander's relationship with the heroes Achilles and Neoptolemus, immortalized by Homer, filled him not only with pride but also with a burning desire for epic achievement. While in its time the Trojan War was perceived and, above all, described in epic works as a war of Europe against Asia, and only decades before Alexander a similar war had been fought with a brilliant beginning and a disastrous end by the Spartan King Agesilaus, Alexander managed to reproduce it on an unprecedented scale. Therefore, he armed himself with his ancestors' fame, although their war had been but a prolonged siege of a single stronghold. Alexander knew that while he was shedding blood for Hellenic dignity, behind his back in Athens they staged comedies in which he was mocked as a fool assuming to be Achilles; he also realized, however, that in times of contradictions and conflicting feelings, his real-life historical drama was unfolding before a huge audience. Despite the ridicule, his contemporaries were expecting great deeds from him. Any retreat was equivalent to suicide and eternal disgrace. Alexander's first steps in Asia, however, showed that the "youngster" had outgrown the mistakes of both the Achaean heroes and his celebrated father. With his attention focused on his distant goals, he made no attempt to seize the straits – the Hellespont and the Bosphorus – i.e., he refrained from obstructing Hellenic trade with the northern seas, and thus appeased the Hellenes' concealed anger about their forced alliance with Macedonia.

Another historical role that Alexander played in Europe on his way to the heart of Persia was to liberate the Hellenes from the centuries-long Persian oppression. The Macedonians themselves were not overly eager to seek retribution. Centuries earlier, they had not only let the army of Xerxes pass through their land, but had also taken advantage of the universal confusion after their retreat to conquer neighbouring territories, which allowed them to exert pressure on the coastal Hellenic cities. This is why Alexander now needed to present his expedition to Asia as a noble mission. He was not only preparing to face Darius III (336 – 331 B.C.), but was mustering his strength, abilities and self-confidence to ascend the throne of the Great King, the lord of the world.

Having come to power the same year when Alexander succeeded Philip to the throne of Macedonia, the Persian king evidently paid little attention to the Macedonian advance. The Persian satraps and commanders in Asia Minor were to go into battle first. They gathered to discuss the developments. Among them, there were many Hellenic mercenaries, including one Memnon of Rhodes, a bold and talented general who, at that point, was even more dangerous to Alexander than Darius III himself. Memnon suggested that they avoid going into battle with the Macedonian army but instead retreat deep into Asia, burning the harvest and their own settlements. Alexander would not stay long in a barren land without supplies for his infantry and cavalry, he assumed. The Persian pride and arrogance, however, prevailed. The satrap Arsitas whose land Alexander was treading said he would not let a single Persian home be burned down.

Deciding to face Alexander in battle, the Persian commanders did not yet realize that they were setting upon one of the most glorious expeditions in human history. From that moment on, the boomerang of history would return with a frightening might. The ancient East that had been the source of human achievement for thousands of years, would have to bow before the victorious army of the young West.

The first battle took place by the river Granicus (334 B.C.). The Persians took up better positions on the steep bank. For a brief moment, the two armies stood facing each other in silence. Then Alexander led his cavalry ahead into a sweeping attack, to the sound of trumpets, so as to let his infantry cross the river. A fierce battle began. Attacked on several sides, Alexander fought bravely not only for his first victory but for his life, too: his spear broke in his hand, his horse was killed under him, a Persian split his helmet. His life was hanging by a thread when the satrap Spithridates raised a knife behind his back, but Clitus, the son of Driopidus, cut off his arm. Many Persians fell at the Granicus, including close relatives of Darius III, while Alexander lost twenty-five hetairoi. He ordered Lysippus to cast their statues in copper. The ancient sources mention that the king sent as an offering to Athena to the Acropolis in Athens hundreds of Persian armour sets and weapons with the inscription: "Alexander the son of Philip, and the Grecians, except the Lacedaemonians, won these from the barbarians who inhabit Asia."

The same summer, Alexander's army reached Sardi in Asia Minor. There, Alexander ordered that a huge temple to Zeus be erected in the place of the ancient Lydian kings' palace. He also restored the freedom of the Lydian population and their ancestors' laws. In Ephesus, he restored the democratic government, and he called on the Ephesians not to kill inno-

Plan of the battle at the river Granicus, 334 B.C.

RULERS OF ANCIENT EUROPE 97

The decisive crossing of the river Granicus and the ensuing victory over the Persians allowed Alexander of Macedonia to march gloriously into the rich lands of the centuries-old Eastern civilization.
Illustration by Emilian Stankev

cent people along with their enemies. He embellished the temple of Artemis, made a sacrifice and a parade. He now had the fame of a liberator and restorer of the traditional order. Increasingly, representatives of cities in Asia Minor sent embassies to him, surrendering to his authority, and he restored their liberty. He only had to take the coastal cities of Miletus and Halicarnassus by force as they fought fiercely under Hellenic commanders in service of the Persian king. As soon as he took Halicarnassus and the region of Caria, Alexander re-installed Queen Ada, the rightful ruler of these lands, and she proclaimed him her "son" as was the local custom.

Then the Macedonian headed to the southern coast of Asia Minor, and took dozens of settlements. By concluding friendship agreements with the small inland tribes and solving justly their ancient land disputes, he rendered meaningless the subversive actions of the Persian fleet in the area, and disbanded his own expensive navy. Occasionally he left behind garrisons to be governed by his closest hetairoi. From some cities he took money, from others war horses. He also sent all newlyweds from his army to spend the winter with their wives in Macedonia, demanding that they come back in spring with new recruits. The tales of the king's kindness and virtue won the admiration of his supporters, and fuelled the fears of his opponents.

In the winter of 334/33 B.C., the Macedonian army reached Gordium, the ancient capital of Phrygia in the heart of Asia Minor. On the hill where the palace of the fabulously rich King Midas had once stood, was the famous chariot. Alexander was attracted to it by an ancient tale that whosoever should untie its fastened cords, for him was reserved the empire of the world. Without hesitating, he slashed the knot with his sword. Wasn't that the only way to conquer the vast reaches of Asia? In the meantime, one of Alexander's most dangerous enemies in Persian service, Memnon, was preparing a war in his rear in Hellas and on the islands, but it so happened that he died in the course of the preparations. Alexander could now continue even more confidently to the east. He soon added to his conquests the regions of Paphlagonia, Cappadocia, and Cilicia where he installed loyal governors.

The first battle with Darius took place at Issus, in a gorge between the Taurus Mountains and the sea, near the Cilician Gates. That was where Asia Minor ended, and Asia began. Confident with his huge army, knowing that Alexander was taking his time in Cilicia, Darius thought that the Macedonian was afraid of facing him. Actually, Alexander was delayed by an illness that nearly killed him. It was most unwise of Darius to accept a battle in the gorge. It was in November 333 B.C. The massacre continued until dusk. In their panic-stricken flight, tens of thousands of Persians were killed, and their dead bodies filled the mountain chasms. Darius himself had to flee for his life, leaving behind his chariot with his cloak, arrow and shield. Alexander also captured the throne tent with complete Persian imperial escortent, as well as the Persian king's mother, his wife and two unmarried daughters. He was very kind to them, and treated them with the honours due to royal guests. Twice Darius sent letters to Alexander, offering to pay a ransom of 10,000 talents for his family, cede all his lands west of the Ephrates to the Aegean Sea, and give him one of his daughters in marriage. The Macedonian king replied haughtily that he was expecting Darius to address him as lord of all Asia. In vain Philip's old and faithful commander Parmenion attempted to bring the victorious young king to reason, reminding him that a continuation of the campaign would surpass even his father's wildest dreams. The sources relate that when Parmenion said

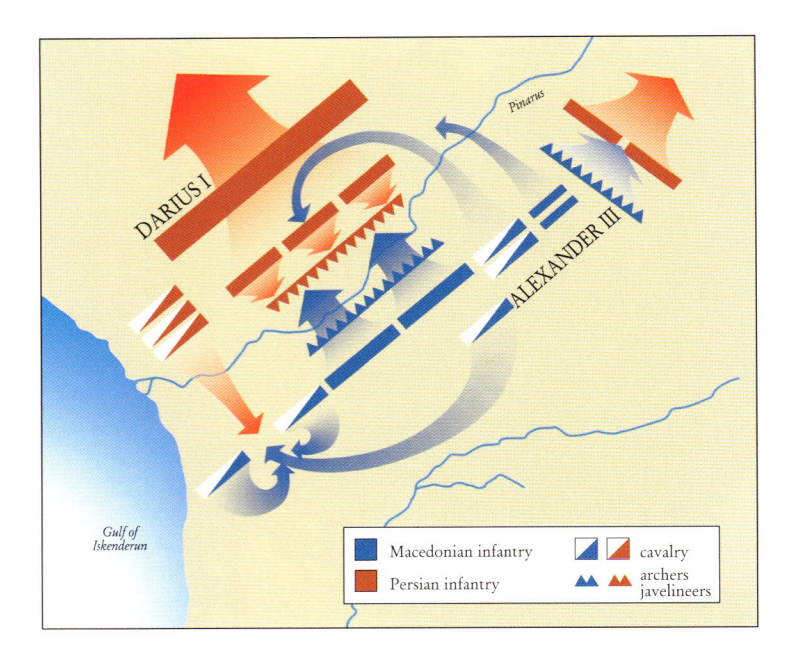

Plan of the battle at Issus, 333 B.C.

The battle at Issus. Mosaic, Pompeii; Reconstructed replica of the Roman copy of the original by Philoxenus of Eretria, 4th c. B.C. Illustration by Hristo Hadjitanev

he would accept the peace if he were Alexander, Alexander retorted that he, too, would, were he Parmenion, but as he was Alexander, he would fight to the end. Indeed, time showed that the road Alexander had chosen would lead him to unprecedented victories and world renown, but there was another aspect to it, too. Standing at the gates of Asia, Alexander gradually started changing his views and plans. He was much different from the Balkan king he had been two years earlier, as if he had gradually begun to burn the bridges for his return to Europe. By passing the Taurus Mountains and invading lands that had hardly ever seen Hellenes, Alexander became a historic figure with a new attitude toward space and time, as if he had no ancestors or past. His biogra-pher Plutarch wrote that when he saw the luxury in the captured throne tent, he exclaimed: "So this is what it means to be a king."

Alexander's victorious march continued along the Syrian and the Phoenician coast. After several months of siege, he took the famous city of Tyre, selling into slavery the few surviving men, women and children. He only spared the temple of the Phoenician Heracles. Alexander's way to the Egyptian land was now open. He was welcomed with high honours as a liberator, and the priests crowned him as a pharaoh. Numerous embassies from Hellas rushed to his court.

After a long journey through the desert, Alexander finally reached a famous sanctuary with an oracle of the god Ammon (Zeus) from whom he descended according to legend. He finally had the answer he wanted. Before leaving Egypt, the king founded at the delta of the Nile a town he named after himself, Alexandria, which would long remain the most flourishing and important centre in the Mediterranean.

In the early spring of 331 B.C. Alexander again led his army into Asia. The decisive battle was approaching. This time, Darius chose the plain by the village of Gaugamela, near the Tigris. The Persian army made an impressive sight. The Persian king had called to his colors allies from the northern and the eastern regions, and had brought war elephants and battle chariots with blades attached to their wheels. It was in October, at the time of a lunar eclipse. Although his army was smaller, Alexander again put the enemy to flight, and captured the chariot of King Darius. Again he refrained from chasing the humiliated king. He headed to Babylon, where he was welcomed by the priests with rich gifts. Soon the royal residence Susa surrendered with 50,000 talents in the treasury and the wealth of the royal palace. The Macedonian king sent back to Athens the statues that Xerxes had once taken. He then proceeded to the so-called Gates of Persia, and took the capital Persepolis while the royal treasury was still intact. He set fire to the palace of the Achemenidae and razed it to the ground – "to serve as an example".

Without delay, Alexander went on against the vast eastern satrapies: Moedia, Parthia, Hyrcania and Bactria. It was the last hope of Darius III to stop Alexander's army by luring it into the desert lands. The chase continued day and night while the horses were dying of exhaustion. When he finally caught up with Darius, Alexander only found his dead body: the fifty-year-old king had been killed by his own satraps after he had crossed his kingdom as a fugitive. Alexander, however, gave him a royal funeral, and was kind to his children.

From that moment, the burden of the Persian kings' political heritage fell entirely on his shoulders. To gain control over the eastern satrapies, he had to fight for years with unyielding and belligerent nomads in barren, waterless lands. Finally, he was attracted by the riches of North-Western India. Some of his soldiers were killed in battles, others had died of exhaustion and diseases. With time, Alexander grew ready to make compromises, he no longer concealed his taste for Persian luxury, he gave up his Macedonian attire for Persian brocades, and wore a Persian turban. He also introduced the practice of proskynesis – the hierarchical prostration of inferior to superior, following the local custom, and imposed it even on his closest hetairoi who had been beside him in dozens of battles. Many of his faithful companions disliked that. With an increasing frequency, Alexander fell into drunken rage. On one such occasion he killed Clitus who had saved his life at Granicus. On another occasion, he struck down his court historian Callisthenes, a relative of his tutor Aristotle. His rage took

RULERS OF ANCIENT EUROPE

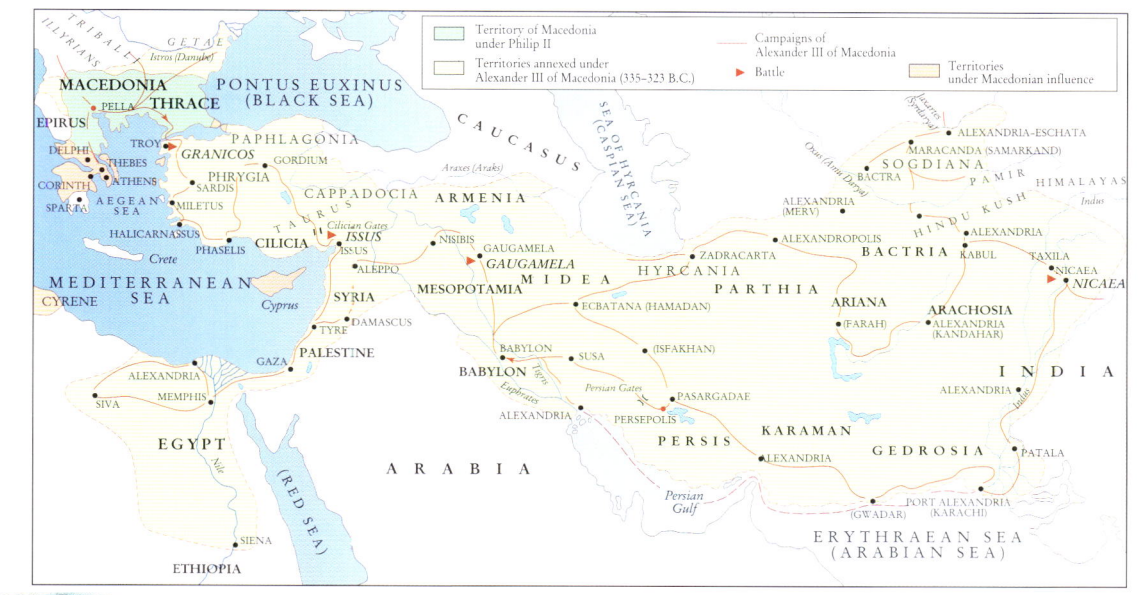

The campaigns of Alexander to the heart of central Asia were both a great military achievement and no small political and cultural feat. The toppling of the Achaimenides dynasty and the advance of the Greek army to India brougth about the creation of a universal Greek state. The map shows Alexander's progress, the chief battle sites and the new cities he founded.

the life of the proud Philotas, the son of his faithful general Parmenion; after killing him, Alexander sent his men to kill the father, too. In the last years of his life, he became painfully distrustful, and often fell into deep depressions. He not only demanded that his men acknowledge his divinity; he even stamped his image with the symbols of the god Ammon on the coins he minted.

Alexander set off on an expedition to India with part of his army through barren lands, while his faithful general Nearchus sailed with the rest of the army across the dangerous and little known Indian Sea. In 324, Alexander was in Babylon, making plans for a campaign in Arabia. Fate, however, did not give him time to organize his vast kingdom. He was considering a kingdom mixed with the peoples of Persia, Macedonia and Hellas. He was famous for the mass weddings of his soldiers and Persian women in Susa.

Alexander died a painful death of fever or poisoning after a feast in Babylon in the summer of 323 B.C., without leaving a heir to his kingdom. Soon after his death, the Bactrian princess Roxane gave birth to his son Alexander. A hostage of political intrigues and fighting between pretenders and the former hetairoi – the Diadochi – the boy did not live to maturity. Where Alexander the Great had stepped, nothing was as it had been before. A year later, Aristotle also died. He was probably the only man who was capable of evaluating the rise and the fall of his celebrated student. According to the biographer Plutarch, after the king's death the orator Demadus said: "There is now such a confusion in the Macedonian camp that they look like a Cyclops who has lost his eye." The new epoch boded trouble for Europe, Asia and, North Africa alike.

*The founding of Alexandria in Egypt.
A legend goes that according to the ancient Macedonian custom, Alexander ordered that the lines of the future city walls be drawn with barley. The birds, however, ate it all. Alexander took that as a bad omen but he brightened up when prophesiers interpreted the event as a sign that the city would flourish and provide subsistence to many people from different countries.
Illustration by Atanas Atanasov*

Lysimachus
305 – 281 B.C.

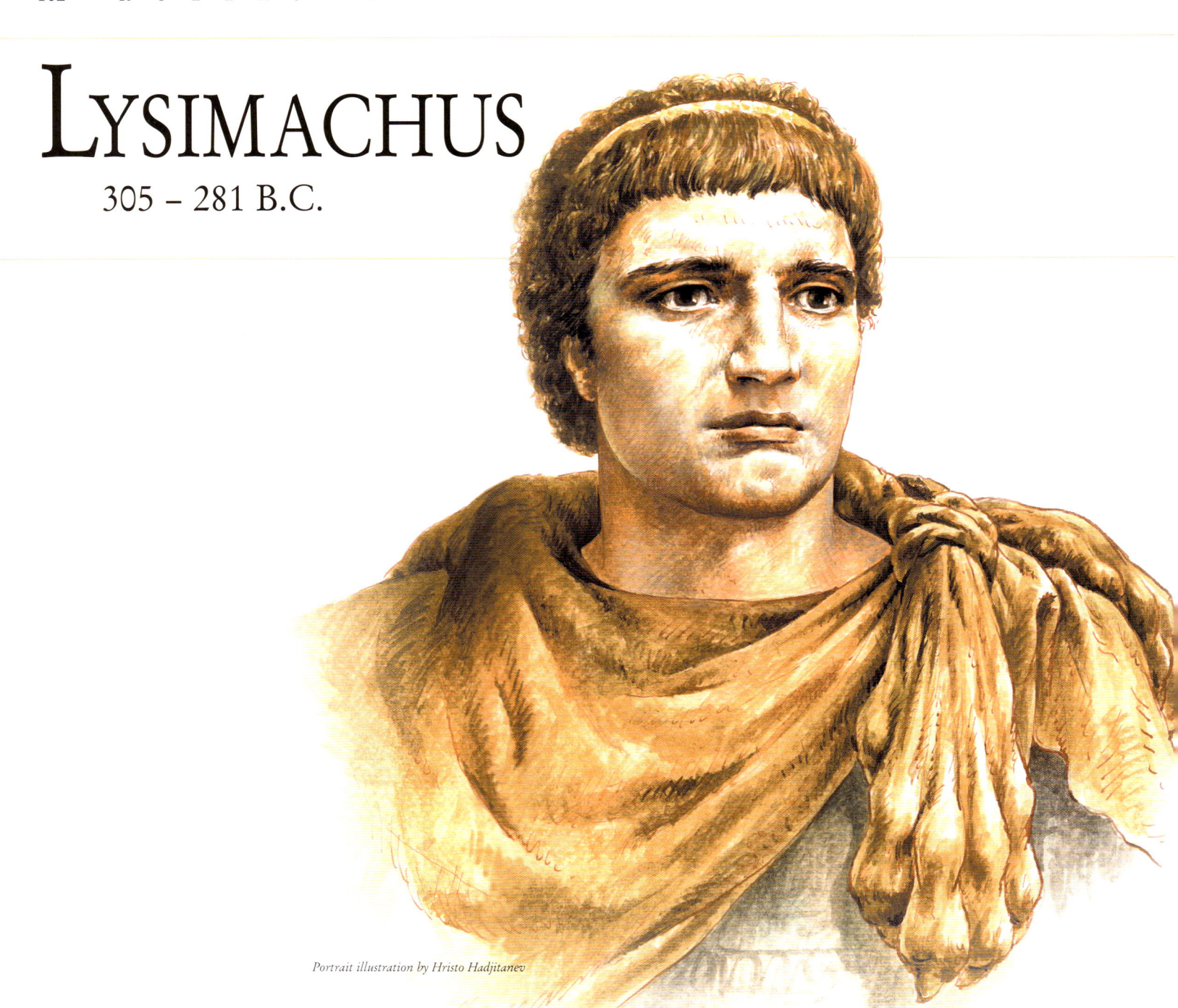

Portrait illustration by Hristo Hadjitanev

LYSIMACHUS, the son of Agathocles, was born in the 350s B.C. in the Macedonian capital Pella, a peer of Philip's son Alexander. He later became one of the most distinguished statesmen in the history of the Balkans, but his star went on the ascendant only after the death of Alexander III the Great, just as the stars become visible only after the sun sets. A similar fate was allotted to all great men in Alexander's entourage who outlived him and inherited sizable portions of his vast empire. We know little of the life of the Macedonian aristocrat Lysimachus from the time before the great king's death. Undoubtedly, as Alexander's peer, he was raised at the court of Philip II, and from an early age he lived with the king's bold strategic plans and with young Alexander's infectious ambition for heroic deeds. He ought to have witnessed the conflicts in the royal family that resulted in Philip's sudden death. Alexander found himself the heir to a heavy political burden that he could hardly handle without the support of his father's faithful commanders and his own companions or hetairoi. Indeed, the name of Lysimachus is not mentioned among Alexander's early favourites (like, for example, Hephaistion), but during those years he certainly matured and prepared himself for Alexander's historical undertaking with its unprecedented scale and anxieties about an obscure future.

From an early age, Lysimachus was distinguished for his physical strength and courage. The coins he later minted as a king, and the few preserved ancient portraits show massive, coarse features that suggest an impetuous, even violent nature, ready to accept any challenge. Ancient sources relate the story of his participation in a royal lion hunt during Alexander's expedition, at Sidon in Syria, in 333 B.C. Lysimachus killed the attacking lion although his shoulder was torn. That heroic achievement was not lost on Alexander the Great who since his early childhood imagined himself to be a descendent of Heracles the lion-fighter and performer of heroic deeds. According to some ancient sources, Alexander was angry with Lysimachus for killing the royal beast and had him locked in a lion's cage but Lysimachus survived. At any rate, one thing is certain: by the end of the campaign, Lysimachus was one of the king's few trusted personal guards. For his valour and loyalty, Alexander presented him with a gold wreath at the royal residence in Susa in 324 B.C.

Although the ancient sources say little of his life before Alexander's death, the scarce information shows a strong character. Lysimachus was one of the few who tried to stop Alexander's drunken outrage in which he killed Clitus, his Macedonian friend who had saved his life at the Granicus. After that tragic and senseless death, Lysimachus lamented the great king's moral degradation, and mourned the death of the court historian Callisthenes to whom he loved to listen and whom he respected for his great erudition. The sources relate the following story, which is indicative of the spiritual harmony of Lysimachus. Alexander had profound respect for the wisdom of the Indian philosopher Karan. Karan fell ill and was so feeble in his old age that he decided to put an end to his earthly suffering and offer his body to fire. Alexander organised for him a royal funeral. The procession was led by his other bodyguard, Ptolemy, the son of Lagus. Soldiers and horses carrying gold and silver vessels and royal garments followed him. A horse worthy of a king was prepared for Karan. The philosopher climbed the pyre to the sound of war trumpets and the roar of war elephants. He gave up all his material possessions, and before lighting the fire, presented his horse to Lysimachus, one of his favourites and a companion in wisdom.

Alexander's death in the hot summer of 323 B.C. caught his generals by surprise. His only heir was his half-witted brother Philip III Arrhidaeus whose ineptness to rule became evident in a matter of days, and resulted in bloody conflicts. One of Alexander's wives, Roxane of Bactria, was six months pregnant. Hoping for a male child, the king's loyal hetairoi assumed a hostile attitude to the supporters of Philip III. Alexander's direct political successors, with their newly acquired pride and self-confidence, called themselves Diadochi. Some of them wished to preserve Alexander's empire intact, while others demanded immediately its division into smaller kingdoms even while Alexander's relations were still alive. The Diadochi faced a difficult task; some of them cherished disastrous ambitions, but they all realized that no one was worthy of taking Alexander's place. He had achieved everything a man could dream of. His virtues, wrote the ancient author Quintus Curtius, were attributable to his nature, while his vices were due to his excessive luck and young age. This is why the struggles among the Diadochi were inevitable and relentless, and went on for over four decades. Their king had only just expired when they crossed swords over his body. Alexander stayed unburied for seven days, and wars would later be waged for his body as a symbol of legal power at the center of the contemporaries' political universe. Finally, Ptolemy prevailed and took Alexander's body to Alexandria in Egypt where it was buried in a magnificant sarcophagus. Lysimachus was one of those reasonable hetairoi who did not deny the rights of Alexander's successors Philip III and the newborn Alexander IV, but continued to represent Macedonian power and the Macedo-nian dynasty in those provinces of the empire he was in charge of. The same year, 323 B.C., Lysimachus was assigned the rebellious land of Thrace and the neighbouring regions all the way to the Pontus (the Black Sea).

Lysimachus headed to his European dominion, and arrived in Thrace with a relatively small but handpicked force of 4000 foot soldiers and 2000 cavalry. Naturally, his heritage included only those Thracian lands over which his predecessors Philip II and Alexander III had gained some control. Thrace was a cold and harsh land, the home of belligerent tribes and proud kings, fighting for their dynasties' political rights and making every effort to drive away the small Macedonian garrisons from their strongholds. The Thracians' belief that they were immortal, and the teaching of the kings' divinity even in their lifetime, were a major challenge to any invader. As early as in 339 B.C., the subjugated Thracians south of the Haemus had rebelled against Philip II, and Alexander also had had to spend the first year of his rule in reducing the Thracians on both sides of the mountain range to submission. There had been rebellions in Thrace in the year when Alexander reached the heart of Persia (330 B.C.) The blow had fallen on the local generals and Alexander's deputy in Macedonia and Europe, Antipater. The rebellious Thracians were seeking to restore their statehood and were mustering their forces for resistance.

Lysimachus had to conquer back his portion of the empire and to prove his right to rule over that land by force due to a decision made in faraway Babylon that did not even give him the title of basileus. More than the other Diadochi, he had to maintain good relations with his rivals. In Thrace, he did not even have a capital or a place to keep his treasury, nor even trusted local associates. As he advanced into inland Thrace, he faced the Odrysian king Seuthes III who had already erected a stronghold and – with a self-confidence that was not inferior to Philip's or Alexander's – had called it after his own name, Seuthopolis (near present-day Kazanluk). He minted coins with his own image on horseback stamped on them. His features on the coins bear a resemblance to a ruler of the magnitude of Cotys I. However, the strong ambitions of both Seuthes and Lysimachus faced the harsh laws of the new epoch. Seuthes had a force of 20,000 foot soldiers and 8,000 cavalry. The battle between the lawful local ruler Seuthes and Alexander's lawful successor Lysimachus was long and hard. Arguably unbiased ancient sources say that Lysimachus lost many of his men but inflicted much heavier losses on the enemy. They both left the battlefield with the feeling of having won a questionable victory, and started preparing for a decisive battle.

In the meantime, Lysimachus consolidated his position in Thrace by installing Macedonian garrisons in the one-time Odrysian strongholds in south-eastern Thrace, and in the large Hellenic trade centres such as Odessos (Varna), Calatis (Mangalia) and Istria (south of the Danubian delta), as well as in the Danubian fortresses of the Getae. With his actions, however, Lysimachus was only keeping an occupied zone under control instead of building a state, and that fuelled the native population's hopes that his power would be temporary. Further in the spirit of political compromises of his time, in 322 B.C. Lysimachus married the daughter of Antipater, Alexander's successor in Macedonia, but it so happened that Antipater left the throne not to his son Cassander but to Poliperchon, and Lysimachus suddenly found himself involved – by kinship and by interests – in the power struggles of the Diadochi. He sided with Cassander, Ptolemy of Egypt, Seleucus, and Antigonus Monophtalmus, governor of Asia Minor. These powerful allies backed Cassander but he proved so ambitious that he ordered that Olympias, the mother of the divine Alexander, be stoned to death. The same year (316 B.C.), he decided to get the young pretender for the throne Alexander IV and his mother Roxane out of the way, so he imprisoned them and five years later had them murdered. His ambitions and aspirations were no secret to anyone. He married Thessalonica, one of the daughters of Philip II,

Lysimachus and his son Agathocles at a feast given by the king of the Getae Dromichaetes at his residence.
Illustration by Marin Marinov

and named after her a city in Chalcidice. He also renamed the ancient city of Potidaea after himself, Cassandria. Cassander's increasing influence definitely raised the self-confidence of his ally Lysimachus, too.

The relations between the Diadochi were strained. Enmity flared at the moment when their interests and secret plans crossed. The recent ally Antigonus in Asia Minor was becoming a dangerous neighbour for Lysimachus who was far from the thought of limiting himself to the rebellious province of Thrace. Having accumulated much wealth from the eastern provinces, Antigonus now had a sizable treasury, and his readiness for a prolonged war was alarming. Besides, Antigonus had the support of his son Demetrius, also known as Poliorcetes (Besieger), an outstanding commander. Around 313 B.C., Antigonus instigated the city of Calatis on the Pontus to rebel against Lysimachus. The surrounding trade centres joined in, and so did the Scythians and the population of inland Thrace. Lysimachus besieged Calatis, and starved it. Many left the city to save their lives. Lysimachus was a step away from success when the news came that Antigonus had sent forces by land and by sea to help the rebels. Lysimachus gave up the siege and headed towards the eastern passes of the Haemus but there he met the army of Seuthes who had allied himself with Antigonus. It was a hard battle but despite great losses, Lysimachus eventually reached the Dardanelles and, taken by surprise, Antigonus' army was routed.

In 311 B.C., exhausted by war, the Diadochi reached an agreement, which proved neither friendly nor lasting as it solved none of the territorial claims. Lysimachus realized that he would have to fight on several fronts: against the rulers of the Odrysae and the Getae in Thrace, against Antigonus and Demetrius in Asia Minor, and for influence and a portion of power in Macedonia. This is why, in 309 B.C., he established his capital at Lysimachia in the Thracian Chersonese, the borderpoint between Europe and Asia. This new strategic position suited his ambitions but it also provoked more bloodshed.

In the years after 311 when the last living relatives of Alexander had been eliminated, bitterness set in between the Diadochi. In 306 B.C., Antigonus and Demetrius defeated Ptolemy of Egypt in a major naval battle at Cyprus, and took the title of basileis. The following year, the other Diadochi, including Lysimachus, followed suit. Indeed, the title gave them royal honours but they were yet to fight for their dominions. In 301 B.C., Lysimachus, Cassander, Seleucus, and Ptolemy defeated Antigonus in a fierce battle at Ipsus in Asia Minor, and Antigonus himself was killed. Thus, Lysimachus added to his European possessions the whole of Asia Minor to the Taurus Mountains, and gained control of the straits between Europe and Asia. He married Arsinoe, the daughter of his ally Ptolemy. Seleucus, the king of Syria and the eastern provinces of Alexander's empire, became jealous of his vast dominion. Lysimachus spent much effort and resources on seizing the rich Hellenic poleis in Asia Minor from Demetrius Poliorcetes. While he was away at war, the Getae in northern Thrace rebelled under the leadership of Dromichaetes. The war between Lysimachus and the Getae took place in 292 B.C. Chasing their enemy, the soldiers of Lysimachus found themselves in a difficult situation, without supplies or water. Lysimachus himself, his son Agathocles, and many nobles from his retinue were captured. The ancient sources say that the king of the Getae not only treated his noble prisoner with respect, but he even invited him to a feast and called him "father." He convinced Lysimachus to enter into an agreement with the Getae by ordering his servants to lay two tables: one of simple wood with wooden chairs, covered with straw, offering the simple food of the Getae, and the other with lavish couches and rich food in gold and silver vessels. Having thus demonstrated his people's poverty and virtuousness, Dromichaetes presented Lysimachus with generous gifts and restored him to liberty. Lysimachus in his turn gave him back the strongholds along the Danube.

For years, Lysimachus had difficulty keeping together his disunited kingdom from the Taurus Mountains to the mouth of the Danube. Only luck and frequent political turns helped him to attain glory. That happened in 286 B.C. when Lysimachus and Pyrrhus of Epirus divided Macedonia, and Lysimachus took the title king of Macedonia. As with Philip II, his downfall came shortly afterwards because of domestic conflicts. His third wife, Ptolemy's domineering daughter Arsinoe instigated him to put to death his son Agathocles for allegedly conspiring against him. Agathocles' wife and his political supporters, however, found refuge with Seleucus, and urged him to go to war against Lysimachus. The result was the unfortunate battle at Corupedion where the seventy-year-old Lysimachus was killed. His body lay in the battlefield for days, guarded by a dog. Later he was buried in his capital Lysimachia. They say a temple was erected to him as if he were a god. Soon, however, Lysimachia was seized and razed to the ground by the Thracians.

Lysimachus had his blaze of glory, he proved to be an excellent strategist but he failed to establish a tradition of state-hood and bring peace to the long-suffering numerous tribes in those lands between the East and the West. His kingdom dispersed with the news of his death. He was remembered in the temples of the larger settlements where he had been honoured as a benefactor in his lifetime.

Lysimachus strongly promoted the city of Ephesus in Asia Minor, which gradually displaced in significance the rebellious Miletus. He did not have time for more during his tumultuous rule; he probably also lacked the qualities of a statesman. Unlike the generous Alexander, Lysimachus was known for his thriftiness. The story goes that he once scared a companion by putting a wooden scorpion into his clothes. "Then I shall frighten you too," the companion responded. "Please lend me a talent [26.5 kg of silver]". Ironically, shortly before his death Lysimachus lost his sizable treasury that had been in charge of one Philetaerus in Asia Minor. Those 9,000 talents laid the foundations of the new kingdom of Pergamum whose rulers, the Attalids, had little to do with Lysimachus' fleeting aspirations for fame. It turned out to be easier for him to kill a lion than to turn the occupied foreign lands into an united kingdom.

Lysimachus' dominion in Thrace and the Odrysian state of Seuthes III.

Pyrrhus
306 – 302; 297 – 272 B.C.

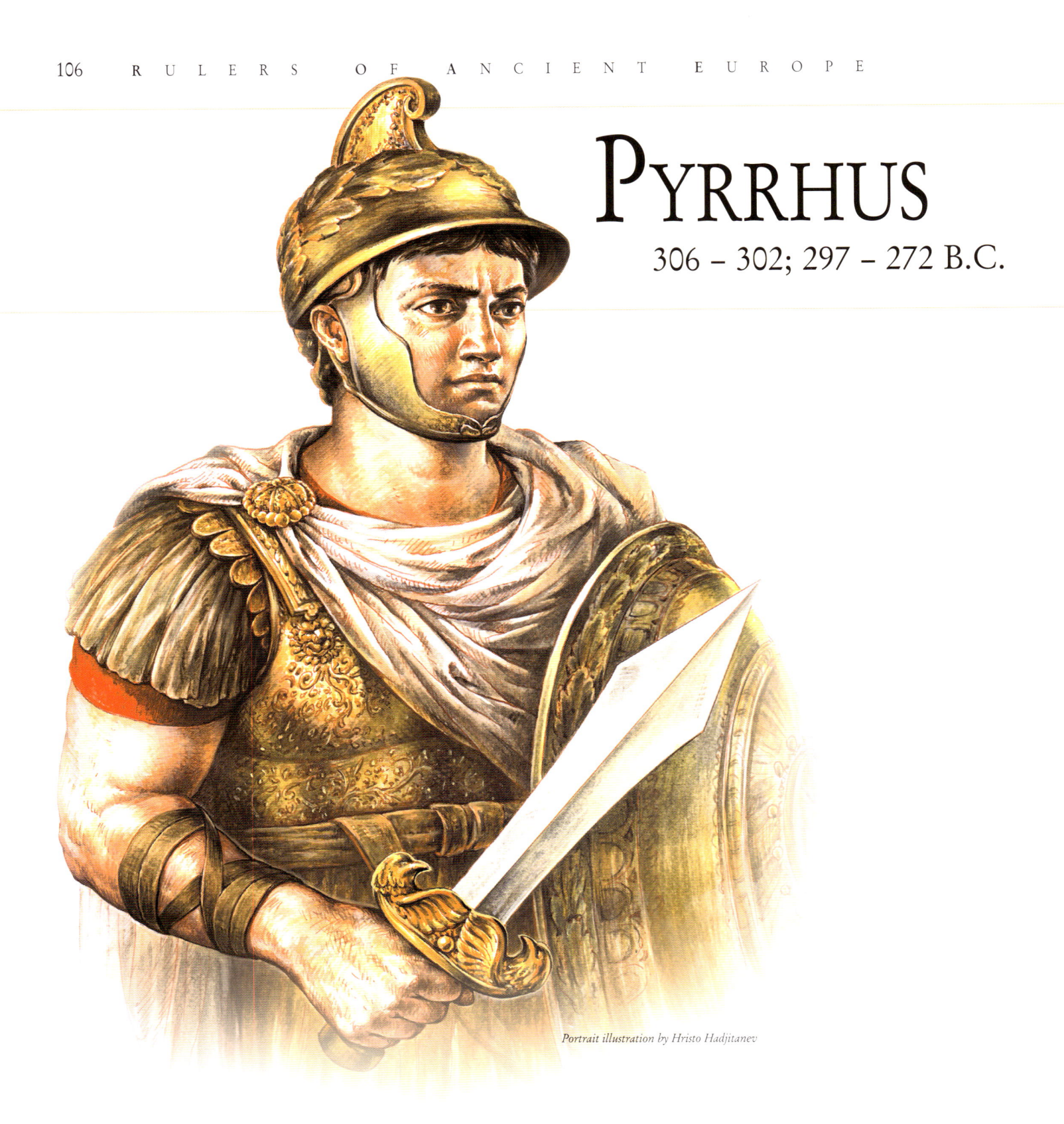

Portrait illustration by Hristo Hadjitanev

THE MOLOSSIANS were one of the largest, strongest, and best located tribes in the region of Epirus in northern Hellas. Since ancient times, two kings of the same dynasty shared the rule, and often headed the combined forces of all Epirots. In 319 B.C., a baby boy was born to king Aeacides and his Thessalian wife Phtia, who already had two daughters, Deidamia and Troas. The boy was named Pyrrhus – a name reminding of his descent from Neoptolemus, the son of Achilles and founder of the dynasty, who in his youth had also been called Pyrrhus. After Alexander the Great, the descent from Achilles attracted much attention at the time young Pyrrhus was born. On his father's side, he was related to Alexander's mother Olympias who not only outlived her celebrated son but also struggled hard to keep the Macedonian throne from the aspirations of the Diadochi. Pyrrhus was only two years old when his father lost his kingdom as a result of the ambitions of the unscrupulous Cassander who had set out to exterminate all relations of Alexander III of any significance. It took him only a few years to carry out his sinister plans. All neighbouring rulers were afraid of the merciless Cassander, and after overcoming many obstacles, Aeacides' loyal men took the young Pyrrhus to the Illyrian King Glaucias. Although with much apprehension, Glaucias agreed to raise the son of Aeacides. His life might well have passed in hopeless exile, had he not caught hold of an altar of the gods and spreading his hands about it, raised himself up, which Glaucias took as an omen.

When Pyrrhus was twelve years old, Glaucias brought him with an army into Epirus and made him king, but as he was too young, he had to have a regent. At the age of seventeen, he left for Illyria to ask for the hand of one of Glaucias' daughters, with whom he had been brought up. His enemies immediately staged a coup, and he lost his kingdom. Pyrrhus then went to the celebrated commander Demetrius Poliorcetes, the husband of his sister Deidamia, and found himself involved in the endless wars between Alexander's successors who had recently titled themselves basileis. Like Alexander, the eighteen-year-old Pyrrhus fought in the decisive battle at Ipsus in 201 B.C. where Demetrius' father Antigonus Monophtalmus was killed. Having happened to side with the defeated, Pyrrhus was sent as a hostage to the court of the Egyptian King Ptolemy I. There he won the sympathies of the royal family, and married Antigone, the daughter of Queen Berenice.

Several years later, the now mature Pyrrhus returned to Epirus and came to terms with Neoptolemus, agreeing that they should share the government according to the ancient Molossian tradition. As a result of a series of court conspiracies, however, Pyrrhus eventually killed Neoptolemus and, from 297 B.C., established a monocratic rule. He felt that the murder of Neoptolemus had appealed to his commanders, as they were still cherishing memories of Alexander's times and hopes for new exploits. Moreover, the king's worst enemy Cassander had died a year earlier. Over the years, Pyrrhus' hard and changeable life made him an ambitious and belligerent ruler. He no longer concealed his intentions to add Macedonia to his dominion. Thus, from a recent ally and benefactor, Demetrius Poliorcetes became his enemy. Meanwhile, Antigone died and Pyrrhus married Lanassa, the daughter of Agathocles the Syracusan from Sicily. Lanassa was to play an important role in her husband's career as in 290, offended by his favouring the Illyrian Bircenna, she fled to Demetrius, taking with her the large island of Corcyra to the enemies of Epirus. In those times of political instability and sudden vacillation nothing was lost permanently. Three years later, the Macedonian army deposed Demetrius and proclaimed Pyrrhus the king of Macedonia. To avoid war with Alexander's much older and experienced commander Lysimachus, Pyrrhus was compelled to partition his dominion. Lysimachus, however, was not satisfied with that arrangement, and in three years conquered the greater part of Macedonia. Feeling deep respect for Lysimachus, whose possessions spread from the Taurus Mountains in the east to the Danube in the north and the Adriatic in the west, Pyrrhus once again yielded and concluded a peace.

For the first time, he had an opportunity to rule his father's land in peace. He even started preparing the city of Ambrachia for his capital, spending lavishly on its embellishment. That kind of life, however, was alien to his impetuous nature: even his name meant "flaming blossom." Like his ancestor Achilles, he could not stay idle. His thoughts were forever set on battles and new conquests. Thus, before having settled the affairs of his own kingdom, oppressed by the feeling that he was an exile in his own country, he accepted the invitation of the Tarentines in southern Italy to help them in their war against Rome. The Italian lands were little known to Pyrrhus but the invitation opened new horizons to the west and raised hopes that he might finally find an opportunity to show his exceptional courage and expand his power. He went to the most ancient sanctuary in his land, the oracle of Zeus in Dodona, where he got a favourable answer about his expedition. Pyrrhus valued highly the oracles given by the centuries-old oak. He himself had the habit of wearing oaken boughs on his helmet. Ancient sources relate that he was much influenced by his dreams in which he often received omens. He also had the supernatural ability to heal by touch, for which he was much loved by his soldiers, and they were ready to follow their king in any undertaking. The greatest difficulties, however, were still ahead. Pyrrhus was boldly and confidently drawing a map of his future conquest which included not only Italy but also the rich island of Sicily and the famed Carthage.

Leaving behind the small scale of the Balkans, in 280 B.C. he sailed off to Tarentum with a great fleet and even greater hopes. Pyrrhus led 20,000 mercenary foot soldiers, 3,000 elite Thessalian cavalry, 2,000 archers, 500 slingers and 20 war elephants: animals that had never been seen in Italy. In his plans, Pyrrhus relied on the numerous tribes in Italy that had until recently been fighting fiercely for their land against the expansion of Rome. After all, the Romans were exhausted by the continual warring, particularly after the battle of Sentinum in 295 B.C. when most of their enemies had allied against them. Luckily for the Romans, Pyrrhus failed to reach the Italian coast with all his formidable army: a violent storm swept away most of the ships. Only the royal galley got ashore. It took Pyrrhus a long time to gather his scattered army after that disaster. Only his high courage and strength of mind helped him to focus on its target.
In Tarentum, Pyrrhus was welcomed as a benefactor and protector, and having been assigned the title of strategos, started preparations for the coming war, for until then, most Tarentines' heroic deeds were done only in words in gyms and feasts.

Pyrrhus fought the first battle with the Romans at Heraclea. There he faced the legions of the consul Laevinus. Pyrrhus never underestimated his enemy, and prepared his army for a prolonged fight. According to the ancient historian Plutarch, Pyrrhus' rich and beautiful armour made him conspicious, and he proved emphatically that his fame was indeed due to his dauntless courage. There were seven turns of fortune, Pyrrhus lost his horse and finally changed his scarf and arms with a friend and obscured himself. The friend was killed, and the spoils were carried about and shown among the ranks, and the Romans were filled with joy. At that moment, Pyrrhus led an assault and routed them. Both armies suffered crippling losses. The Romans lost 7000 men, and 4000 of Pyrrhus' soldiers were killed. It was probably after that battle that the king famously commented: "One more victory like this will be the end of me" which inspired the expression "Pyrrhic victory" for any victory that is too costly. The next victory was at Asculum (279 B.C.), in which Pyrrhus already had the support of local allies and more money for the local mercenaries. In his victorious march, he advanced so far

108 RULERS OF ANCIENT EUROPE

The landing of King Pyrrhus of Epirus in Italy was an unprecedented event, decades ahead of the campaign of Hannibal of Carthage in Italy during the Second Punic War. Particularly spectacular were the war elephants in the armies of a few adventurous rulers following the campaign of Alexander the Great in India.
Illustration by Emilian Stankev

that he was within 60 km of Rome itself, although he neither intended nor was ready to storm the strongly fortified city. The King of Epirus proposed peace but a Roman of the name of Appius Claudius convinced the Senate and the Roman people to keep the army ready for action.

Meanwhile, the new situation in southern Italy prompted Rome to conclude a peace with Carthage, the other major force in the region that controlled the western Mediterranean. That peace marked a turning point in Pyrrhus' victorious march. Hellenic envoys came from Sicily to beg for his help against the Carthaginian advance. At any rate, Carthage had long controlled the western islands. Pyrrhus had two alternatives: to finish his expedition in Italy and return to Epirus where the fearsome Celts from the north had killed the Macedonian king Ptolemy Ceranus in battle, or to pursue glory in Sicily. Again Pyrrhus chose the greater risk. He seemed to shun the places where his great-ness was not readily recognized. In Sicily, in rich Syracuse, was the kingdom of his father-in-law Agathocles. Pyrrhus regarded his dominion as his rightful heritage. Soon, he conquered almost the whole of Sicily, and pronounced himself king of the island. Only the town of Lilybaeum held by the Carthaginians refused to open its gates.

The power-loving Pyrrhus, however, had to suffer the consequences of his unfinished undertakings. The Romans took town after town in southern Italy. The Italian Greeks again called on him for help. In the late summer of 276 B.C., Pyrrhus had to leave Sicily, reportedly commenting: "How brave a field of war do we leave for the Romans and the Carthagians to fight in!" Whether actually said or not, these words soon proved prophetic, but Pyrrhus was to suffer two major defeats first. While sailing to Italy, his fleet was almost entirely destroyed by the Carthagians. In 275 B.C., he fought his last battle with the Romans at Beneventum where he faced the armies of two consuls. To quote Plutarch again, "Thus fell Pyrrhus from his Italian and Sicilian hopes, after he had consumed six years in these wars, and though unsuccessful in his affairs, yet preserved his courage unconquerable among all these misfortunes and was held, for military experience, and personal valour and enterprise, much the bravest of all the princes of his time, only what he got by great actions he lost again by vain hopes, and by new desires of what he had not, kept nothing of what he had."

After the defeat, Pyrrhus returned to Epirus. There he resumed the old conflict with Macedonia, ruled at that time by Antigonus, the son of Demetrius Poliorcetes. He was the founder of a new dynasty, the Antigonids. Only two years earlier he had proved his abilities as a warrior in a battle in which he routed the invading Celts. His power was strong, and he had much influence over the Hellenic cities. Pyrrhus changed the situation. He fought success-fully against the Macedonian king and even plundered the ancient capital Aegae. He then headed to the Peloponne-sus where he dared attack Sparta, as if seeking to crush its centuries-old fame and to outshine the success of Epami-nondas of Thebes. Having failed to take Sparta by storm, he went on to Argus where Antigonus had taken up good positions. A traitor let Pyrrhus through the gates, and the thousands of soldiers and the war elephants thronged in the narrow streets. It so happened that an old woman watching from her roof saw her son fighting with Pyrrhus, threw a tile down and broke his neck. It was a miserable death for a commander second only to Alexander the Great – at least according to one of the great ancients, Hannibal of Carthage. When they took the cut-off head of Pyrrhus to Antigonus, he cried bitterly. In his enemy's sorry lot he saw the frailty and senselessness of such fame.

Even today, King Pyrrhus of the Molossians remains an enigma. It is hard to evaluate such a remarkable personality whose life was continual fighting and ended so unexpected-ly. Pyrrhus often saw Alexander the Great in his dreams. His soldiers called him Eagle, the sacred animal of Zeus the Thunderer. In the eyes of his contemporaries, his countenance, his swiftness and his motions expressed those of the great Alexander, and they thought they beheld there an image and resemblance of his rapidity and strength in fight. According to Plutarch, other kings represented Alexander merely by their purple and their guards, by the formal bending of their necks and the lofty tone of their speech, while Pyrrhus only by arms and in action. Still, unlike Alexander, Pyrrhus was not the founder of a new epoch. It seems that he aspired to repeat in large-scale military campaigns in the West what Alexander had achieved in the East. What he did not realize, however, was that his enemies were Rome and Carthage, two new historical forces destined to determine the history of the Mediterra-nean over the following centuries. A talented commander, Pyrrhus won positions and titles but never came up with a realistic strategic plan. He lacked the strong motivation that had once sent Alexander against Persia. Pyrrhus not only abandoned his country in the difficult years of the Celtic invasion, but he also let his Celtic mercenaries plunder the royal tombs in Macedonia. He was the ruler of pieces of land rather than a statesman with a vision of the future. This is why the "Pyrrhic victories" were his lot. Only a few decades after his tumultuous rule, the Molossians drove the kings out of their lands forever.

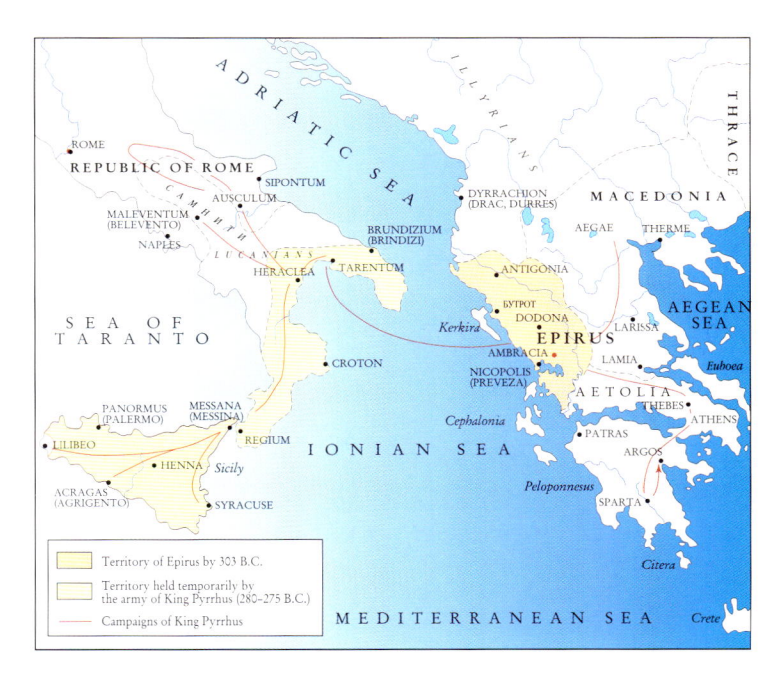

The kingdom of Pyrrhus was not large but had a strategic location in the Hellenic world.

Philip V of Macedonia
221 – 179 B.C.

Portrait illustration by Hristo Hadjitanev

THE YEAR WHEN PHILIP V ascended the Macedonian throne coincided with the beginning of the famous ancient author Polybius' *Universal History*. According to the historian, it was a remarkable time because, although there had been significant events before it, they had never been so interrelated. Around the year 221 B.C., however, history seemed to become integrated. For the first time the events in Italy, Africa, Asia, and the Balkans were so interwoven that they had a common result: the expansion and the establishment of indisputable Roman domination over the whole of the Mediterranean.

It is hard to relate the story of Philip V, and even harder to make an assessment of his rule. Philip was born and lived in times of unscrupulousness. He had a host of enemies in all neighbouring states, while political friendships and military alliances were as variable as the seasons. Very often, the events in Philip's time depended almost exclusively on his personal qualities, which in their turn were molded by his deeds. His contemporary Polybius, who had the deepest knowledge and understanding of the Macedonian king's character, wrote: "There is not a more formidable witness, a more cruel accuser than the conscience that dwells in the soul of each of us."

Philip was born in 238 B.C., the son of the Macedonian king Demetrius II and Phtia of Epirus. Ironically, the contemporary relations between the dynasties brought the grandchildren of two sworn enemies together in marriage, Antigonus Gonatas and Pyrrhus. However, that did not give Philip much power and happiness on the throne. When he was six, the Epirots put an end to monarchy in their lands. At the age of eight, he lost his father whose rule had been a sequence of hard and useless wars. Philip succeeded his father but until coming of age, he was to have a regent, his father's cousin Antigonus Doson. Antigonus was a wise ruler who won the support of the Achaean League and thus gained at least several years of security in Hellas. On his deathbed, he sent the young Philip on an important diplomatic mission: to negotiate with Aratus, the strategist of the Achaean League he appointed a council to help him in the government. Philip V was only sixteen. Very soon, the faults of his character became evident: the typical rashness of youth, greed, a desire for monocratic rule, and never heeding to his advisors' opinions.

In the meantime, the Aetolian League that controlled the sanctuary at Delphi, and had won an increasing number of supporters among the Hellenic poleis, was growing stronger. Very soon, without weighing the benefits of such a war, the young king was drawn by the Achaean Aratus into the conflict between the Hellenes. Philip used Corinth as his base, and fought successfully in the Peloponnesus. He displayed remarkable courage in battle, and won the admiration of his allies; even his enemies could not deny his merits. He was only twenty, and many hopefully compared him with his celebrated predecessors on the Macedonian throne. In the end, that war among the Hellenes brought much suffering. The sanctuary of Zeus in Dion was set on fire, and the statues of the Macedonian kings were overturned. The Aetolians desecrated the land of the Dodona sanctuary in Epirus. Philip V took revenge on his enemies by plundering and razing to the ground the temples at Thermus. Ancient authors comment that in his youth Philip did much injustice by both human and divine laws.

The troubles at his own court were aggravated, too. Philip's advisers were not unanimous on the relations with their Achaean ally Aratus. In order to put an end to the disputes, the king took a firm, perhaps even cruel position. He had an advisor who had once helped him to the throne executed; other associates he urged to suicide, and thus he managed to keep his alliance with Aratus, although the unanimity at his court had too high a cost.

When he heard of the decisive victory of Hannibal over the Romans at Lake Trasimeno in the summer of 217 B.C., Philip started making plans about Illyria and an expedition in Italy. The same autumn, he helped establish peace in Hellas, which he evidently regarded as temporary. Few would listen at that time to Agelaus the Aetolian who warned in a remarkable speech that the conflicts between Macedonians and Hellenes would sooner or later bring the Roman legions into their lands. At that time, no one could foresee the outcome of the war between Rome and the talented commander Hannibal. After the Carthagian's next victory at Cannae, Philip V sent an embassy to him offering a treaty. The Macedonian king still believed that his war with the Romans over Illyria, when was at his own doorstep, was of crucial significance. It so happened, however, that the Romans intercepted his envoys. This was sufficient reason for the Senate of Roman nobles and for the armed Roman people to start the First Macedonian War (215 – 205 B.C.) against Philip V.

While the Romans were still facing a long war with Hannibal, their war with Philip did not change much in the Balkans. There were no decisive battles or large-scale military operations by either land or sea. These years demonstrated the instability of the relations between the Hellenes and the Macedonians, for which the Macedonian king himself was much to blame. It was only out of political frivolity and unbridled temper that he committed a senseless massacre in Messenia. His old ally Aratus came to him with his son Aratus the Younger, who upbraided Philip sharply for the massacre, casting a shadow over their alliance. In his arrogance Philip went so far as to take Aratus the Younger's wife Polycratea to Macedonia, marry her and have by her a son, Perseus, his future successor to the Macedonian throne. With time, Philip repelled all his allies. Even those historians who took every opportunity to extol his merits as a soldier could not overlook his vices. Along with his cruelty, he forsook all self-restraint in regard to women. On one occasion in the ancient Argos, he took off his crown and regal attire, violated dozens of Greek women, and humiliated and tortured their husbands and sons. In 213 B.C., Aratus died and his son Aratus the Younger took over the command. Philip could no longer rely on his military alliance with the Achaeans. The same year the Aetolians made an alliance with Rome against their common enemy, the Macedonian king. Soon Athalus I, king of Pergamum, joined in. As a result of this treaty, Rome was in a position to act as an arbiter in the conflicts in the East, for the first time.

In 205 B.C., a peace was reached between Rome, Macedonia, and the Hellenes. It didn't change the political map of the Balkans much but did allow Rome to intervene in Balkan affairs in case of violation of the treaty – which was to take place soon. Philip V reached the age at which Alexander the Great had died and had not achieved anything comparable to his predecessor's success. A year later, the young Ptolemy V ascended the throne in Egypt. Antiochus III and Philip V, who had some 20 years on their thrones behind them, agreed to seize and divide the possessions of the young Egyptian king. Philip took the key towns at the Dardanelles and the Bosphorus on both the European and the Asian side, as well as the island of Thassos which was rich in gold and silver. As a result of this, he suddenly faced the opposition of his old enemies the Aetolians, the free merchants of Rhodes and Athalus I of Pergamum whose kingdom lay at the gate to Asia. Bloody naval battles off the western coast of Asia Minor followed.

Rome did not remain indifferent to these important developments. In 201 B.C., a peace was concluded with Carthage while the great Hannibal was still alive and looking for shelter at the royal courts in the East. Philip's increasing power filled Rome with apprehension. In July 200 B.C., the Roman legions voted for a new war against Macedonia: the Second Macedonian War (200 – 197 B.C.) The decisive battle was

Map of Macedonia under king Philip V.

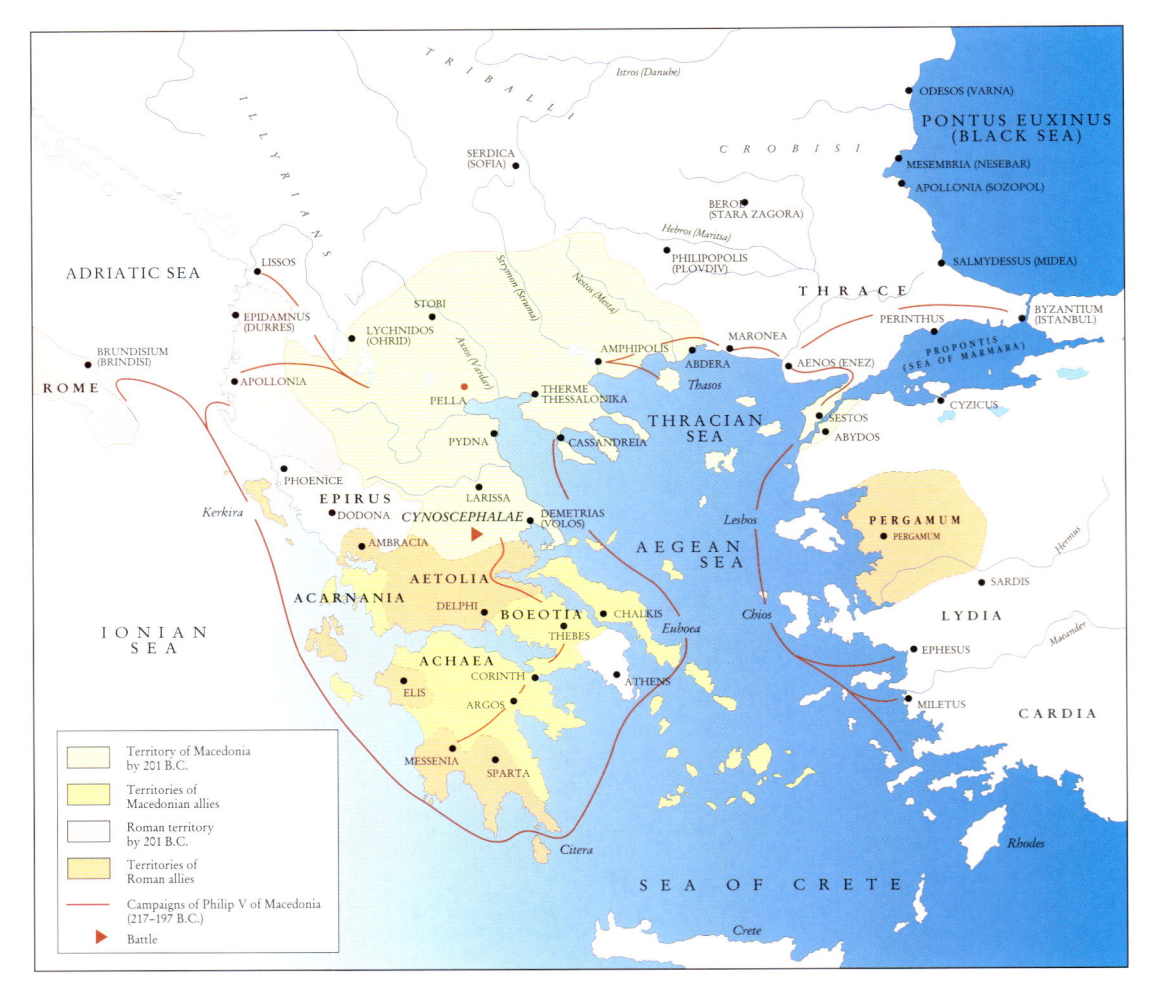

The triumph of the legions in Rome following their victory at Pydna over the last Macedonian king Perseus, the son of Philip V, who was imprisoned in a cage in this procession.
Illustration by Rossen Toshev

fought in Thessaly at Cynocephalae in the year of the consul Titus Flaminius (197 B.C.) As it could have been expected, both the Aetolians and the Achaeans sided with the Romans, not because of any friendship between them but because of their common hatred towards Philip V. Only Thracian mercenaries joined the Macedonian king in the hope of spoils. The rough terrain gave the advantage to the Roman commander, routing Philip despite the great courage he displayed in the battle. This battle was historical inasmuch as two major military formations crossed swords for the first time: the flexible and mobile Roman legions and the outdated clumsy Macedonian phalanx whose glory was by then a thing of the past. Put to flight, the Macedonians had 8,000 killed and more than 5,000 captured while the Romans lost only 700. Philip himself fled with a few associates. The same night he ordered that his royal archive with records of his secret alliances and military plans be destroyed.

The following year Flaminius returned to Hellas with 10 envoys of the Roman Senate to conclude a peace with Philip V. The Macedonian king had to withdraw his garrisons from all towns outside Macedonia and to surrender all his warships but five that he could use to deliver supplies to the Macedonian coast. He was also to pay 1,000 talents to Rome in the course of ten years. At the Isthmian games once founded by Heracles, Flaminius, who was a great admirer of the Hellenic culture, announced the liberation of all Greek cities in Europe and Asia. Previously subjected to the Macedonian king, they were now free to live by their own laws. The heralds spreading the words of Flaminius to the enthusiastic crowd at the Isthmus were a moving sight. The Hellenes could hardly believe that Rome could indeed be so generous. Only the Romans' faithful allies, the Aetolians, were unhappy with the peace arrangement and the survival of the Macedonian kingdom. In their joy, few realized the high price of that freedom – the kind of freedom so frequently – and hypocritically – granted by monarchs to the poleis and never really intended to last.

According to ancient sources, after defeat Philip behaved for a while with the prudence and humility characteristic of those who have suffered great vicissitudes of fortune. Indeed, the Macedonian king seemed to have become a loyal ally of Rome. He sent his son Demetrius as a hostage to Rome, and did all he could to help the Romans crush his recent ally, the Syrian king Antiochus III, in both Hellas and Asia. Philip provided supplies, guarded the Roman supply train from sudden attacks, and built roads for the Roman legions through lands that he had once dreamed of conquering. These years, however, were hard to tolerate by a man of such an impetuous nature as the Macedonian king. Rather, thus fostered his hypocrisy. Deprived of his army, he started accumulating sizable wealth. To populate inland Macedonia, he moved some of the coast dwellers there, and let belligerent and loot-thirsty Thracians settle in his lands. According to ancient sources, Philip became so rich that he could support an army of 30,000 foot and 5,000 cavalry – the size of the army that Alexander had led against Persia for ten years. In secret, the Macedonian king prepared weapons for a much greater force. They say that in 181 B.C. he went to Thrace and climbed one of the high Haemus peaks to take a good look of the vast plains where the future war with Rome was to be waged. Philip's grandiose strategic plans are still an enigma, as they never materialized because of a tragedy in the king's family.

Having spent some time as a hostage in Rome, the king's son Demetrius returned home, full of reverence for the Roman military might and social order. He was educated, prudent and straightforward, and he soon fell victim to his older brother Perseus' intrigues. Perseus used a forged letter from Titus Flaminius brought from Rome by Macedonian envoys to accuse his brother of conspiracy, and Demetrius was poisoned and strangled. Philip later found out the truth, and could no longer find peace of mind. He was about to deprive Perseus of succession when he died at the age of fifty-nine at the old Athenian colony Amphipolis. To help Perseus ascend the throne, the court physician did not announce the king's death. Thus, Perseus not only came to power but he also managed to eliminate all his rivals.

Under the new king, Philip's plans soon became obvious, giving the Romans cause for the Third Macedonian War (171 – 168 B.C.). The Roman consul Aemilius Paulus defeated Perseus at Pydna, and brought back to Rome for procession the captured Macedonian weapons, prisoners, Macedonian treasury money, gold and silver vessels, jewellery and fabrics, and the royal archive. Perseus and his family in chains walked before the chariot of the victor Aemilius Paulus, who was dressed in gold and purple. That was the pitiful end of the Antigonids, the heirs to Alexander's glory. Perseus was the twentieth and the last Macedonian king. It was an interest-ing coincidence that he surrendered to the Romans on the island of Samothrace, the place where the Macedonian aristocrats were usually initiated into the divine secrets, as if the great gods had also accepted the Roman victory. The his-torian Polybius, who was himself captured at Pydna and taken hostage to Rome, described imperturb-ably the end of the centuries-long history of Hellenic and Macedonian statehood, as he realized that after all the conflicts in those ancient lands a traitor was not the one who accepted the reality in the name of the common good but the one who sacrificed other's lives for his own glory and benefit amidst universal suffering.

DECEBALUS
c. 86 – 106 A.D.

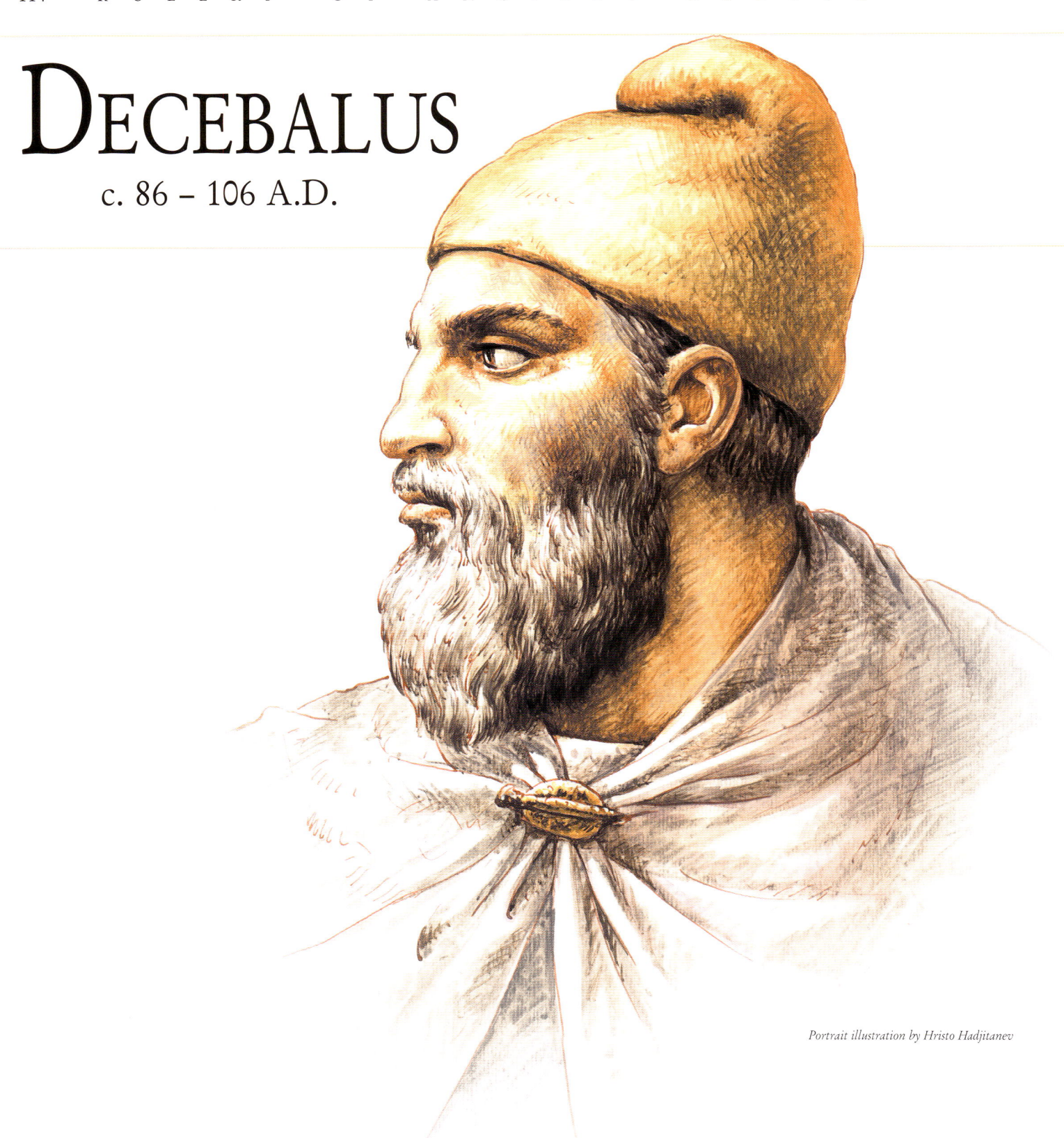

Portrait illustration by Hristo Hadjitanev

FOR CENTURIES, the population of the Balkans waged backbreaking wars with the Romans with no chance for success. The Hellenic poleis probably accepted most readily the consequences of the Roman conquest as they had been accustomed to the claims and the encroachments of the Hellenistic kings of Macedonia, Egypt, Syria, and Pergamum. Owing to their old greatness or to their reputation as centres of the Hellenic spirit, some of them were granted self-government rights, tax concessions, construction projects and new feasts by the vainglorious Romans. In fact, the consul Aemilius Paulus, who defeated the last Macedonian king Perseus, said that he who knew how to be victorious ought to know also how to make a feast and a spectacle. Rome had already established its strategic policy of "divide and rule," and the widely proclaimed universal freedom – more for some, less so for others – eventually proved illusionary, and inevitably led to the conquered lands' transformation into Roman provinces.

To the Balkan dynastic houses with centuries-long traditions, it was even harder to put up with the invader. Macedonia was the focal point of both discontent and great hopes for salvation in the profound changes occurring in the ancient Balkan lands. It was ruled by ambitious and power-loving kings whose strategic plans were often devised at feasts or in the course of the preparations for decisive battles. Unlike the Macedonians, the Roman public order won an increasing number of supporters because of its rule of law, military discipline, and charismatic statesmen. No wonder that in 146 B.C. Macedonia finally became a Roman province with Roman governors, paid an annual tribute to Rome, and gave half of its land and natural resources to the Roman state. The same year, Roman roads were built on the Aegean coast for the envoys, merchants, officials and armies travelling from Italy to Asia.

Macedonia was inevitably followed by the vast lands of Thrace – from the Carpathians in the north to the Straits and the Aegean in the south. For centuries, these lands had been inhabited by Thracian tribes, and each of them had had its period of flourishing. Many harboured old enmities which became aggravated with the Roman invasion of Macedonia.

That was exactly what the Romans needed: a discord between the Thracian tribes and inside the royal courts. Thrace's transformation into a Roman province was only a matter of time. It took almost two centuries – not only because Rome was still waging a difficult war in the Mediterranean, or because of the bloody civil wars inside the empire, but because the Romans were not yet prepared for the conquest of a land where there were not enough settlements and strongholds for their strategic plans.

Thrace was remarkable for its variety of terrain. The Danube with its many tributaries and the high mountains were a serious obstacle to the Roman legions. The lands of the freedom-loving highland Thracians were the most difficult to conquer. They were not used to submitting to foreign lords, or sometimes even to their own kings. Being remarkable soldiers, they had always been in demand as mercenaries in the Hellenistic kings' armies.

In 45 A.D., under the emperor Claudius, they became the province of Thrace. The Dacian kingdom soon followed.

The kingdom of Decebalus, king of the brave Dacians, was the last stronghold of resistance against the Roman invasion in the Balkans. Many other Thracian rulers before Decebalus had crossed their swords with Rome – and had failed. A famous figure among them was Burebistas, king of the Getae of the lower reaches of the Danube.

According to ancient authors, the Dacians were also a Thracian tribe whose language was similar to the language of the Getae. They inhabited the lands north of the lower reaches of the Danube, west of the delta all the way to the Carpathian Mountains. At the time of the Roman domination, they had mixed with other tribes. King Decebalus of the Dacians united his lands and subjects. He was a remarkable commander, and always knew the right time to attack and to retreat. He was skillful in laying ambush and undefeatable in battle. He always took advantage of his victories but he also knew how to take defeat. The Roman historian Dio Cassius described him as an estimable enemy. Domitian (81 – 96 A.D.) was the first Roman emperor to wage war with Decebalus, in 85 – 86 A.D. Domitian was notorious for his dissolute and

The column of Trajan featuring scenes of his battles with Decebalus and the Dacians. Rome, II c. Reconstruction.
Illustration by Hristo Hadjitanev

drunken outrages, even during war. They say he could not endure physical discomfort, and he left the war to his commanders. Twice Decebalus offered peace but Domitian sent his favourite Fuscus with a large army against him. Fuscus was defeated and, having to fight with the neighbouring Germanic tribes, the emperor sued for peace in 89 A.D. Under the humiliating treaty, Rome was to pay an annual tribute to the Dacians. The emperor covered all the expenses for the peace treaty, and he even sent military experts and builders of roads and bridges to Decebalus. Despite his failure, Domitian did all he could to present the situation in a favourable light. He distributed decorations and money among the soldiers, sent envoys on behalf of Decebalus with a faked letter to Rome, and gave a lavish feast with fine vessels which he said he had taken from the Dacians and which, in fact, came from his own imperial property.

Over the years, the Dacian king grew richer, stronger and more self-confident. Rome could not put up with the presence of such a powerful neighbour whose borders were protected by the largest river in Europe and who raided with indemnity the nearby Roman provinces. The Romans had only just begun organizing these provinces, building military camps and settlements there. The situation became intolerable when Decebalus went so far as to raise an army from the lands controlled by Rome.

In March 101 A.D., the ambitious Roman emperor and talented commander Trajan (98 – 117 A.D.) set about forcing the Dacians into submission. When the Roman legions approached the Tape pass (present-day Iron Gate by Orsova), where the Dacian army had made its camp, the emperor was brought a huge mushroom on which Decebalus had written his message to Trajan in Latin. Decebalus suggested that the Roman emperor go back to Rome in order to preserve the peace. Unlike Domitian, however, Trajan never retreated. Many Dacians were killed in the battle. Decebalus then sent to Trajan his noblest envoys. They threw their weapons on the ground and kneeled before Trajan, asking him to meet with Decebalus in person. The meeting did not take place, and Trajan took fortress after fortress. Only after he had suffered heavy losses, when he was told that his sister had been captured by the Romans, did Decebalus accept the humiliating conditions of the peace. He surrendered his weapons, and his battering rams, and destroyed the strongholds he had erected in the conquered lands. He was also forced to accept Roman occupation garrisons at his capital Sarmizegethusa and all other Dacian fortresses. Finally, he sent envoys to Rome to conclude the peace, and only then did Trajan return to Italy in 103 A.D. In celebration of his victory, the emperor became known as the Dacian, and gladiatorial fights were held.

Hardly two years had passed when Trajan started receiving messages that Decebalus was preparing for war, disregarding all provisions of the peace treaty. The Senate again pronounced Decebalus an enemy of Rome, and in 105 A.D. Trajan himself led the expedition against Dacia. Many of the Dacians fought on the Romans' side. In vain Decebalus

Noble Dacian envoys in their typical costumes and felt hats, appearing before the Roman Emperor Trajan.
Illustration by Marin Marinov

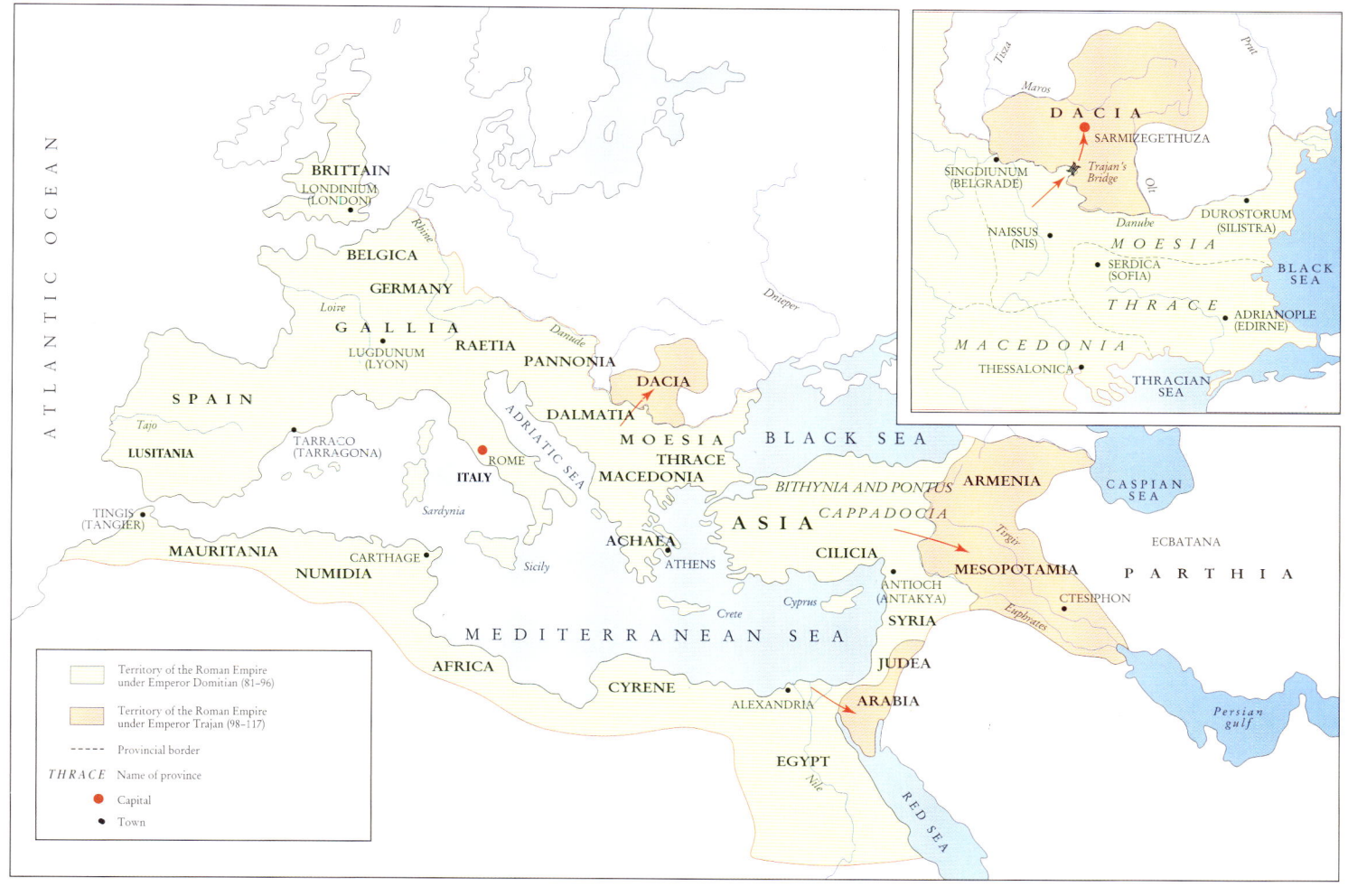

Map of the Roman Empire.

called on the neighbouring tribes for help. Suffering defeat after defeat, he decided to send mercenaries to kill the Roman emperor. While in war, Trajan was in the habit of receiving anyone who asked to talk with him. One of the assassins, however, raised suspicion – he was tortured and revealed the plot.

Decebalus also tried to discover Trajan's plans. He invited one of the bravest commanders in the Roman army, a man of the name of Longinus. Having failed to get anything out of him, he took him prisoner and started negotiating with Trajan for concessions against the liberation of Longinus. Longinus, however, committed suicide so as not to pose an obstacle to his emperor's victory. From that point on, the war became bitter as never before.

The Roman emperor built a stone bridge over the Danube, supported on twenty columns – a remarkable and admirable structure. With a strategy of caution and persistence, Trajan finally defeated the Dacians, and conquered all the lands of Decebalus, including his capital. The Dacian king committed suicide, and his head was taken to Rome. The treasures he had hidden in a riverbed close to his capital were also discovered. Decebalus had diverted the water of the river, had buried all his gold and silver, and had restored the river to its course. He had also hidden precious objects and fabrics in caves, and had killed all prisoners who had done the work so as not to leave a living witness. A close associate, however, betrayed the treasure's whereabouts to the Romans.

In the provinces of Dacia and Moesia, Trajan founded new towns to commemorate his victory. He was the last Roman emperor who made large-scale plans for Rome's expansion, and carried them out with a remarkable ability. His victory over the Dacians was a major success. Naturally, he marked it by erecting monuments in Dacia (a monumental trophy in today's Adamclisi) as well as in Rome where in the forum (city square) he built the tall Trajan's Column, encircled by a continuous spiral relief portraying scenes from the Dacian campaigns. A statue of Trajan himself was placed on top of the column.

The subjection of Dacia allowed the emperor to carry out a daring expedition against the old Roman enemy, Parthia. Trajan briefly believed he might conquer more lands than the great Alexander himself. After his death, however, his successor demolished the stone bridge over the Danube.

By extending Roman occupation beyond the widest European river, Trajan went beyond the sustainable borders of the empire and challenged the nomadic North. Instead of the Dacians, Rome now had to fight new, more distant, more belligerent, and more unyielding tribes. It is no coincidence that after Trajan's wars against Dacia and Parthia, the Roman Empire became known as far as China, and was mentioned in Chinese chronicles. The Romans inherited the centuries-old riches and troubles of the Balkans, whose population lost its political independence. For the first time it was united, but not in a community with traditions of statehood and spiritual pursuits: the inhabitants of the Balkans had become provincial Roman subjects.

Macedonian phalanx

Philip II of Macedonia

DACIA

Decebalus

Alexander III of Macedonia concludes a peace treaty with King Syrmus of the Triballi and the Celtic envoys from faraway lands.

Syrmus

Seuthes II

THRACE

Lysimachus

SEUTHOPOLIS

King Pyrrhus' fleet casts anchor in Italy

Pyrrhus

Alexander I the Philhellene

Sitalces

Cotys I

MACEDONIA

● PELLA

Archelaus

Agamemnon

EPIRUS

Philip V of Macedonia

TROY

GREECE

AEGEAN
SEA

Epaminondas

Miltiades the Elder

EUBOEA

The fortress of Mycenae

● THEBES

● ATHENS

SAMOS

DELOS

The battle at Leuctra

● SPARTA

Pausanias

Alcibiades

Pericles

Cleisthenes

Licurgus

Peisistratus

The Acropolis

Solon

ANCIENT SOUTH-EASTERN EUROPE AND ITS STATESMEN – THE FOUNDERS OF EUROPEAN CIVILIZATION

The age of antiquity was the matrix from which European civilization emerged. In the cities of the Balkans, Asia Minor, and the Aegean islands, philosophers, politicians, poets, playwrights, architects, and artists set the standards of thought that we use today. Having made masterful achievements in the sciences and arts, as well as in the political traditions of the Eastern peoples (the Egyptians, Phoenicians, and Assyrians), they established their own political structure and aesthetics. This volume's portraits of twenty-four eminent statesmen of the ancient European South-East embody the dynamics of fourteen centuries of political and cultural development. In years of friendship and peace, as well as in times of conflict, these statesmen were forever bound by their common roots. From the heroic battles of the Trojan War in the 13th c. B.C. to the rumble of the Roman Emperor Trajan's campaign against the Thracian King Decebalus in 106 A.D., the deeds and ambitions of the rulers of ancient Europe were the emblems of their age and transcended the time limits of their rule.

Glossary

A
Aditon – The innermost sanctuary of the temple at Delphi where visitors were not allowed and where the prophecies were made
Ageloi – "Flocks" in which Spartan children were raised after they turned seven
Agora – The Hellenic polis' central square where the public buildings stood and the market took place
Amphyctionies – A council with the sanctuary of Apollo at Delphi
Anarchy – A year of absence of government in which an archon was not elected
Archon – An elected official in the Hellenic polis, particularly in ancient Athens; representative of the executive (minister)
Areopagus – Council of the elders in ancient Athens, named after the location where its meetings were usually held – "the hill of Ares"

B
Barbarians – The non-Hellenes who spoke roughly and unintelligibly to the Greeks; "chatterers"
Basileus – The Hellenic word for "king"
Beotarch – Commander of the allied forces from the Hellenic region of Boeotia
Boule – Greek for "council," "Council of the 400" (until Cleisthenes), "Council of the 500" (after Cleisthenes); a permanent, representative, elected body of the Athenian democracy

C
Cavalry – In ancient Athens, citizens with an annual income between 300 and 500 medimnoi; wealth was also defined by the ability to keep a horse
Chiton – A Greek garment like a shirt, with or without sleeves
Consul – Supreme elected magistrate in ancient Rome

D
Demagogue – A self-seeking leader of the people in the democratic poleis of ancient Greece
Demes – Small administrative and territorial units in ancient Attica
Democracy – "Government of the people;" a political system characteristic of some Hellenic poleis
Demos – The Hellenic for "people"
Diadoch – "Heir," a direct political successor of Alexander III's rule
Diakrioi – The poor population of the hilly inland of Attica
Dionysia – Religious festivals in honor of Dionysus
Dynasty – A succession of rulers of the same family

E
Ecclesia – An assembly of Athenian citizens; soldiers' assembly
Emperor – Initially, a general term for an official with military prerogatives in ancient Rome; later, the title of the ruler of the Roman Empire (after 27 B.C.)
Ephor – An elected magistrate in ancient Sparta; representative of the executive
Eupatridae – A social class; the aristocracy in ancient Greece

F
Forum – The central square in a Roman town

G
Gerusia – Council of the elders in some Hellenic poleis
Great King – Title of the Persian rulers of the Achaemenid dynasty (mid-6th c. B.C. - 330 B.C.)
Gymnasium – A building with several halls used for exercises and education, often including a library

H
Helot – A slave in ancient Sparta
Hetairoi – "Companions;" the Macedonian king's closest associates
Hoplite – A heavily armed foot soldier in the polis army

I
Isonomy – Greek for "equality before the law"

K
Kurbeis – Human-size revolving wooden boards on which the laws of Solon of Athens were written

L
Laconic style – After the region of Laconia where Sparta lay; a brief, clear, and meaningful style of expression
Legion – Basic unit of the Roman army, with a varying number of soldiers
Lescha – An assembly where the Spartan elders assessed the newborn children's fitness

M
Magus – Supreme Persian priest
Medimnos – Unit of measurement for dry and liquid products, varying in different Hellenic poleis from 40.36 to 72.74 lt
Megaron – The main hall in a ruler's home or palace at the time of the Mycenaean heyday; it serves both as a sanctuary and as a reception room
Monarch – Greek for "absolute ruler"

O
Oligarchy – "Government of the few," a system characteristic of some Hellenic poleis
Oracle – A place in ancient temples where deities were consulted
Orator – see Rhetor
Ostracism – An extreme practice in democratic Athens designed to remove someone by sending him into exile. Initially with the tyrants' supporters, this later included any political opponents. From the Greek word "ostrakon" meaning "potsherds" on which the names of those proposed for banishment were written in the vote

P
Paideia – Greek for "education"
Panatheneae – Major religious festivals in honor of Athena in the polis of the same name
Paradynast – Greek for "co-ruler" in a monarchy
Paraleis – The coastal dwellers of Attica whose source of living was the sea
Pean – A hymn to the gods, most often to Apollo
Pediakoi – Large landowners in Attica, having estates in the fertile plain
Peltast – A lightly armed foot soldier of cavalryman, from the word "pelta" meaning a light circular or semi-circular shield made of wood and covered with leather
Pentakosiomedimnoi – In ancient Athens, citizens with an annual income over 500 medimnoi
Perioikoi – In ancient Sparta, a population that was free but did not have full rights
Phalanx – A battle rank
Phyle – One of the earliest territorial divisions of the population in the Hellenic polis by ethnic or territorial factor
Polis – A word of obscure origin, the Hellenic idea of a city-state; a state of a small territory, or a larger city-type community created by merging several communities
Politai – A polis citizen enjoying full rights
Province – An administrative and financial division of the Roman state
Prytan – In the Athenian Boule, a representative of a phyle on duty
Prytaneion – The building where the prytans (50 representatives of each phyle) stood guard – 35 or 36 days every year
Pythagorean – A follower of the religious and philosophical teaching of Pythagoras of Samos
Pythia – The high priestess at the temple to Apollo at Delphi; later, any fortuneteller

R
Rhetor – An educated person, trained specially for public speaking
Rhetra – A law distributed by word of mouth

S
Sarissa – A Macedonian lance, up to 6-7 m long
Satrap – Governor of a satrapy, subordinated directly to the Persian king but with broad prerogatives; most often a relative or a close associate of the Great King
Satrapy – A province in ancient Persia
Senate – Council of the elders in ancient Rome
Somatophylax – Greek for "bodyguard"
Sophist – Greek for "sage"
Spartiate – A citizen of ancient Sparta enjoying full rights
Strategos – Commander; in Hellenic poleis, this was an elected person
Strategos-Autocrator – "Supreme Commander," in Hellenic poleis, an elected official
Syntagma – A battle unit of 16 ranks of 16 soldiers each in the Macedonian phalanx
Syssitia – Common meals of the citizens of ancient Sparta

T
Themenos – A sacred plot of land given to an Achaean ruler or to a temple
Thetes – In ancient Athens, citizens with an annual income below 200 medimnoi; the poor majority of the population of Attica
Trireme – A highly maneuverable ship of average size, with sails and three tiers of oars, used both in warfare and for commercial purposes
Tritties – Small administrative and territorial units in ancient Attica
Trophy – A monument to a victory
Tyrant – An absolute ruler who has often usurped the power against the will of his subjects and the against the law

V
Vanax – Supreme ruler from the heyday of Achaean Mycenae
Vassal – A dependent ruler

Z
Zeira – A cloak, often hooded, ankle-length, and made of wool, which was typical of the ancient Thracians
Zeugitai – In ancient Athens, citizens with an income between 200 and 300 medimnoi; their wealth was also defined by the ownership of a pair of oxen